Contents

Part II

Acknowledgments

For telling me the first time we met that you and Judith Regan would be interested in seeing a Mancow book, for loving the book and getting Judith Regan to read it, and for your first edit, where story after story fell like soldiers on Flanders Field as you cut the book down to publishable size, thank you, Monica Crowley.

Thanks also to the devoted audiences of *Mancow's Morning Madhouse* and *Fox & Friends,* without whose potential readership this book would never have been published.

And finally and firstly, thank you, God, for giving me this trip through the carnival.

Mancow Muller
December 2002
Chicago, Illinois

Part 1
Outside the Lines

Mom, Dad, and a bouncing baby Mancow.

Fatherland

"Girls in Berlin no fuck!"

Odd words coming at 1 A.M. from a Ku'damm streetwalker who just told me 100 marks is her price and invited me over to her place. I'm two steps into going when six teenage boys bolt on the scene with their leader shouting, "You take one hundred marks from my friend and no fuck? For one hundred marks, you fuck!"

I suddenly realize I had asked her price but not what it included. The thin blond beauty, in lime-green fuck-me clothes and pump-me shoes, edges away from the gang of six who wanted to get their rocks off and found them stolen instead.

"I never say 'fuck.' Never. Girls in Berlin no fuck!"

"For one hundred marks, you fuck!"

The broken English shouting match carries on until the tourist kids cool down enough to get on with their night of partying after being reminded that if it looks too good to be true, it probably is.

My interest is tweaked.

"So what does a hundred marks buy me?" I ask.

"Blow job," she says, knowing I'm questioning even that now, and knowing another interested man will cruise past in no time with no clue at all to the truth.

Does she take off her clothes, I wonder?

Can I touch her?

Does she give the blow job to me? Or to a chicken or something?

"The guidebook says these Ku'damm women are hard, Mancow." It's my friend the dwarf.

"What can happen?" I ask. "You've got my passport, my credit card. You'll be standing outside. Dude, I'm in the longest dry patch I've experienced since I turned sixteen and started driving my 1972 yellow Ford Maverick in perfect working order down the dusty hormonal back roads of my Missouri youth. I haven't gotten laid in more than two weeks! This is my first night ever in Germany! I want to have some fun! I want to see the rest of the scam. I actually want to be stung. I want to get a load off my mind. Give me the money!"

The dwarf counts different colored bills from his pockets. "We've got eighty-five marks, Mancow."

"You said we had money!"

"We've got eighty-five marks. And plastic up the yin-yang."

"Dammit, dwarf! The slit in her lime-green polyester liederhosen won't read credit cards!"

"Sorry, Mancow."

"Eighty marks!" I call to blondie, twenty feet away from us now at the Kurfürstendamm curb.

"Hundred marks," she shouts back as a silver Mercedes taxi pulls up with its windows down.

"A hundred marks for a blow job?" I shout back. The taxi drives away as I realize every taxi I've seen in Berlin is a Mercedes—they're like Chevys in Chico, California. The dwarf points to a nasty-looking pimp moving toward us across the boulevard. We hustle away.

As we pass Tiffany's, I have an idea—to super-glue dimes onto straight-pin pinheads and give away dime-and-pins (sounds like "diamond pins") to *Mancow's Morning Madhouse* listeners as a stunt. I like it.

"P. T. Barnum made his first million charging people a nickel to see the Six-Foot Man Eating Chicken," I tell the dwarf. "Barnum gave the crowds exactly what he said he would, and let their own minds trick them. What they actually saw was a six-foot man eating a Popeye's chicken dinner. A banner hung by the exit; a painted finger rested on painted lips, the caption read, 'Shhh!' P.T. took your money, pulled your leg, and then made you a partner in his joke. Brilliant. I want to own something of Barnum's. I want his signature on something. P. T. Barnum belongs in my memorabilia collection!"

"Of all the stunts you've done, what's your favorite?" the dwarf asks.

"When I blew into Chicago a year ago, I wanted the burly city to see me coming. Billboards showing me pointing a gun at a cow's head over the slogan 'Listen or the Cow Gets It!' snagged some real attention—but not enough. I wanted the world to know that *Mancow's Morning Madhouse* was coming. We did that. Mancow's Chicago arrival became a story on every nighttime TV news show including Fox, because the day before the *Madhouse* hit Chicago's airwaves, I sent every talking hairdo anchorman their very own live cow."

"Barnum would be proud, Mancow!"

"It was my dad's idea. My idea was better, but when my radio boss asked, 'Who do we talk to for permits?' I knew live cows on commuter trains would never fly."

• • •

I've broken every rule ever imposed on me—until now. Now I've hit a rule I can't break, a wall I can't get around, an authority I can't buck. It's the first time in my life, and I hate it.

The professor who taught me promotions at Central Missouri State University told me every performer performs for his own personal audience. He's right. In 1991, when the first ever *Mancow Radio Show* shot KDON radio in Salinas, California, from a six to a nine share in seven weeks, my dad applauded from Missouri. Ten months later, when *Mancow's Morning Madhouse* pulled a twenty-one share for KDON, my dad said, "No one's ever done anything like this in the history of radio, son."

My dad knew what he was talking about. He knew radio. Together, we listened to *The Stan Freberg Show, The Shadow,* and hundreds of old radio shows he'd taped on reel-to-reel. We both knew that Salinas/Monterey, America's twenty-eighth largest radio market, was just a big hick town radio-wise but my dad applauded all the same. When I moved to San Francisco, America's fifth largest radio market, created Wild 107, and took it to number one, my dad was clapping and stomping.

But when *Mancow's Morning Madhouse* took Chicago by storm, catapulting Rock 103.5 from the bottom of Chicago's ratings heap to number five in less than a year, that thrilled my dad more than anything else I could have done. Sure, New York and L.A. have bigger radio markets, but *Chicago* is a Midwest traveling salesman's Mecca of success, and my dad was a traveling salesman from Missouri.

• • •

When the roller coaster attendant brought the bar down across my lap four years ago, he smiled. "I hope the track goes all the way this time," he said. "We've been having trouble." When he pulled that lever, my car shot forward to click its way up and hurtle me into the heart of the unknown. I love roller coasters—especially inside a fun house, where I can't see the turns or the drops in advance and hysterical, mechanical clowns jump out to laugh insanely as I fly by. Exhilarating. Terrifying. Ever since Mr. Cow's Wild Ride went live on KDON radio, I've been rocketing forward and picking up speed, slamming into the turns, whipping over the rises, falling far and fast in stomach-losing plummets. It's the biggest, most exciting, most dangerous ride I've ever even imagined. It never stops. It never slows down. Sometimes I feel like I'm on a runaway train and I have to build track in front of it as fast as I can or I'll shoot into airless nothingness around the next bend.

· · ·

My dad, John Muller, the old storyteller, told me stories all my life. He always wanted to visit Europe—Germany in particular. Even though he never saw the place until 1990, my dad told me stories he learned from his dad, who left Bavaria in 1912 and went back to Europe only twice—to fight two world wars against his fatherland—as an American.

"It feels so strange to see a man I've known all my life as strong and sharp become so weak and confused," I told the dwarf after my dad's heart attack in 1994, when he was saying "blankets, blankets" and pointing to the thermostat because he felt cold.

"You have to see Europe, Erich," my dad said after he'd recovered enough that his brain worked again.

"I want to see Berlin. I want to see Neuschwanstein. I want to see a concentration camp. I want to stay one night in a fine European hotel. I want to drive the autobahn. I want one day in Amsterdam," I told the dwarf, who lives half the year in Italy. I'd threatened a visit since we first became friends in California in 1990. "Figure out how we can do all that, and then make the reservations," I said. He did. I bought my plane ticket in March, just before the doctors told my dad his cancer was terminal.

This afternoon, outside in a Ku'damm biergarten, I ordered the first German beer I would ever drink in Germany. I was happy for my Revos; without my sunglasses all of Berlin would have seen how much I was crying. After a lifetime thinking I'd see Europe first with my dad, I won't.

Twelve hours ago I flew from Kansas City to O'Hare, where I caught my Chicago flight for Berlin. To make my connections, I had to leave my dad's funeral early.

Two full steins of German beer sat on our table a long time before I could drink. Finally, we lifted our glasses.

"There's only one possible toast," the dwarf said. "To John Muller."

The principal rail, the guiding rail, the power rail of my life—the brightest face in my audience, the one that has been there the longest, and clapping the loudest, laughing the hardest—isn't out there anymore. My universe defies control. And comprehension.

Life is a gift of tragedy. In tragedies, people die.

Yet life is always a gift.

At sixty-two, my dad was far too young to die. I guess every one of us is.

But every one of us does.

Really taking in that fact changes your life.

Suddenly, mortality has a human face.

$$\bullet \; \bullet \; \bullet$$

Stories about my dad poured out of me like the tears. Celebrating. Grieving. Each time I got embarrassed about my crying, the dwarf told me to let the tears out. Often I sat in silence with the only friend I have who knows what I'm feeling. Sometimes he told stories of his dad, who died in the summer of 1993. We cried and drank on the Ku'damm until my jet-lagged body finally cried for sleep. When I dropped into bed at 4 P.M., I was happy the sun was shining.

Now it's 3 A.M. in Berlin. I've been in Germany thirteen hours. Lime-green fuck-me blondie is two hours behind us. On our nighttime wander we pass through a dimly lit neighborhood of big expensive houses where the Jewish girl in *Cabaret* might have lived before Hitler took power. The tree-lined street, high walls, and iron gates dissolve so suddenly into three-story houses built right to the sidewalk that I have to look back to make sure the street didn't change width. Bright advertising marquees narrow the street even more. Hawkers line both sides and work hard to pull us in.

"Do you take American Express?"

"Of course! Come in. See live fucking onstage!"

"Let's see a show!" I say.

"The guidebook says they're shams designed to rip off suckers, Mancow. I wouldn't give them my credit card."

"Have you been rear-ended by the sugar truck, dwarf?! Anything that ends with naked women begins with a rip-off!"

I hustle to a Live Show doorway and sweep open the ratty red curtain before the beefy hawker can get in my way.

"Fifty deutsche marks," Hawker shouts as he whips the curtain closed. Huh? Two hundred ratty seats in a theater the Allies didn't bomb to dust and not a soul in sight. Maybe the guidebook's right.

When I worked at Wild 107 in San Francisco, I went to the Mitchell Brothers O'Farrell Theater once, just before Jim shot his brother Artie dead in the grand finale of a warped Stepford Wives Do Porno kind of story line. Alone in the Mitchell Brothers shower room I hear one of the cuddling lesbians say, "You're Mancow Muller, aren't you? You can touch if you want." Okay! All those Mancow posters on the SF Muni buses are paying off. But, as I dive for touchie-feelie I cross the beams of laser sensors I don't even know are there. Wham! Three ex-49er linebacker types burst through the doors with faces that say I'm dead meat. "Wait! It's okay!" the talking lesbian shouts. "It's Mancow!" The guys ease off.

"Hey man, love you, love your show!" one linebacker says. "What the fuck are you doing?"

"I told him he could touch but he misunderstood," the talking lesbian says. "I meant you could touch yourself, Mancow."

Whoa! Why would I want to do that with them here?

As the linebackers left, so did I.

"Mancow, what happened to your Chinese girlfriend?" It's the dwarf again.

"That's over. I mean . . . I move her from San Francisco to Chicago with me, she's looking for a job but not having any luck, so I say, 'You know about computers, why don't you set up my new one for me? I'll pay you.' A week later she hands me a bill for eleven hundred bucks! I mean, I'm paying the rent, I'm buying the food, and she's bitching about cleaning the bathroom floor! I fought to get rid of Suck Wee all the months my dad fought cancer, but I won my fight. Oh, man! Single again after months of live-in hell. I celebrated my balls off! I gave my number to every woman who was interested. Any time I wanted, I had a woman in my bed—a different woman every morning, afternoon, and night for over a month.

"Then a time came when the phone would not stop ringing. Twenty-four hours a day women called. Women I'd never met. Women I'd never seen. Women I'd never heard of!

" 'Hi, this is Nancy, you don't know me but I'm a friend of Dianna's. Would you like me to come over?'

"Well, yeah! But not at 10:30 Tuesday night when I have to get up to prep my show in four hours! I couldn't believe what was happening. I suddenly understood what Jagger and Tommy Lee and Magic and the others have felt. I mean, there was more pussy coming on to me than I had time to shake my stick at. I couldn't get any rest. I actually tired of my independence. I had my phone disconnected. The silence felt like bliss. Holy-moley!"

· · ·

She is a vision in white. Brown hair pulls across her shoulder as she moves her head, then falls into her soft linen blouse to brush against the flesh of her breast. Underneath she wears only a tan.

The dwarf and I sit down at a biergarten table as White Linen walks in beauty from outside table to outside table. She sits down two tables away. Huh. Wish I'd learned German. But what would I say? Nobody knows who Mancow is in Berlin. I'm powerless. My tongue and my reputation are the only two weapons I've got, and they don't count for shit here in Deutschland.

"We'd like two beers." Must be the dwarf, my tongue has forgotten language.

"You are drinking the Farts tonight?" the waiter asks.

"Uh . . . just two beers, please."

"Drink the Farts," Waiter says. "House beer here at Windmill."

"Oh? Yeah, okay. Bring us two Farts then," the dwarf tells him. "Do you take credit cards?"

"Yah, but not for eleven marks. You have maybe the marks?"

"Yeah. We do. We're fine."

As Waiter leaves, White Linen laughs.

"How . . . much . . . cash?"

"We have eighty-five marks, Mancow. Same as before."

"Wish we had more."

"If we had more, you'd have spent it on a lime-green blow job. Send her over a drink."

"Do you think those two guys she sat down with are her friends? I think they must be friends."

White Linen speaks. Her voice makes German, the international language of obedience, actually sound sweet.

"If they're not friends she's a hooker. You want me to try to buy her?"

"For eighty-five marks? A woman like that . . ."

"Your Farts," Waiter says, setting down the bottles. The dwarf depletes our cash stash further by handing the waiter a tip. My dad always told me that tips were included in the bill in Germany.

"People are dancing inside, ask her to dance."

"Dude! She's sitting with two other guys!"

"So was Bibi when I asked her to dance in Greece."

"How is your giant girlfriend? Shit! Dwarf! She's leaving."

"No, she's not."

Twelve steps into the Windmill, White Linen sits at the bar.

"She's sitting alone. Ask her to dance, Mancow."

"I . . ."

"Well, I'm dancing."

On the dance floor a blond woman (more robot than flesh) dances from the waist up. Her eyes are dead. Goebbels trained her to dance. Maybe to kill on command. In the little booth, a DJ jockeys discs like my buddy Larry-Larry did at the college club in Warrensburg, Missouri, and like I did at weddings and high school reunions. God, I'm glad I don't have to do *that* anymore. The dwarf, not knowing a word of German, begs frauleins to dance with gestures until he gets a taker. The dwarf has a nice view of women; for him slow dancing is almost oral sex. The DJ does a seamless shift into driving disco before Roy Orbison finishes singing "Only the Lonely." The lyrics make it obvious that the title of this disco tune is "Be My Lover" I look at White Linen—her right elbow on the bar, her right foot on the rung, her left leg swinging free. I've never envied a stool before in my life.

● ● ●

The first time my dad came out to Monterey he brought me Max, the bulldog puppy he gave me when I turned twenty-one. As he toured my tiny house, Dad noticed my mobile DJ setup sitting in the garage.

"You use this equipment anymore, Erich?"

"No, I don't, Dad. Thank God, I don't have to."

"One-year contract at KDON, figure you don't need it anymore? How much was all this stuff? Forty-two hundred and eighty-three dollars, if I remember. Of course, it's used now."

"You won't find better for less, Dad."

"Of course I could! Quality's gone up, prices have come down across the board on electronics. You been too busy to notice?"

My dad loved to argue. He'd go ten rounds and only stop for exhaustion. Whenever he won an argument (and he always won in the beginning) I'd go away, sharpen my verbal machete, and flail back into the thicket of things. While I fought ideas, my dad fought to sharpen my wits. He forced me to define my ideas, to see that someone who wasn't stupid could hold a radically different view, to see that I could never convince some people, to see connections I'd never considered. He also taught me not to agree when I didn't. Ever. Dad never changed the rules when we argued. He didn't get angry at me as a person, didn't tell me I was stupid, didn't smack me in the face, or storm out of the room. Until I was big enough to defend myself, he never pulled a power play to win. I was blessed to be his third son. Dad had learned some things during the ten years he raised my older brothers, Johnny and Mark, before I arrived. He bruised my spirit sometimes, but I knew he wasn't trying to hurt me.

I like conflict. I like pushing as hard as I can against the resistance of a good antagonist. I have never encountered one as good as Dad. No one else can ever know me as well.

For sheer pleasure I sparred with Dad for six rounds that day. That was enough.

"What do you want to do with the equipment, Dad?"

"Well, I was thinking, son, you know those parties that your mother and I always go to . . ." I waited. "The DJs who play those things are schlockmeisters! So, I was thinking . . ."

"The equipment's yours, Dad. Take it back to Kansas City with you."

"No! The equipment's yours, Erich! You bought it, dammit!"

"So, I'll loan it to you. If you don't take it back I'll just have to ship it to you. You'd be great up there spinning your polkas and Big Band stuff." My dad's record collection was huge. Wearing white cotton gloves, he'd take old 78s out of their paper sleeves and play them once to record them onto tape. Growing up I heard more music from different eras than anyone else I know. He opened my ears to music no radio station has played for fifty years, and I loved it.

He had three Kansas City bookings before he could turn around. When he called to tell me the good news, I could feel his jangling nerves through the phone, so after my KDON show Friday morning, I flew from Monterey to Kansas City to be with him for his first DJ gig. Saturday night, as I set up the equipment, he put into order all the old-folks 33s he was going to play. One minute before it was time to start, he caught my eye with that look that always said he wanted something.

"Would you just . . . would you start things off for me, Erich?"

"Dad, you can do this."

"I know. Just . . . get me started. Okay? Besides, I want to dance the first dance with your mom."

The look in his eyes made him seem about seventeen years old. How could I say no? I put on the headphones, set his first LP on the turntable, and cued it up to the tune he wanted played. Dad switched on the mike, welcomed the crowd, and then told them all that his boy, his kid, his son, Mancow Muller—the next great radio personality in America—would start things off with the Glenn Miller Orchestra. As people applauded, the sneaky bastard nodded to me. The finger I'd been using to hold Glenn still while the turntable spun beneath him flicked the disc to 33 rpms. The diamond needle sent "In the Mood" into the room. My dad went down to dance and didn't come back all night! "You're doing fine, son!" he called each time he swirled past me.

So much for Dad the DJ!

• • •

In Berlin, as I pick up my bottle for a drink, I say a silent toast to my dad. I swear to God, I hear him toast me back. As I drink a long slug I wonder if there's German beer in heaven and if my dad has a body to pour it into. I pull the bottle away from my lips and laugh out loud when I see the blue letters F-A-R-T arcing across the label top and fatty ass cheeks connected to nothing blowing out a puff of blue wind.

With head gestures a waitress says the two new bottles of Farts she's brought are from the dancing idiot dwarf. When the DJ shifts to another disc, the dwarf runs up, gulps down his Fart, and heads back out to dance.

I suck on my Fart slowly.

I watch White Linen.

I am full of Farts. I have to leave White Linen. At a Windmill urinal I watch my pee hit both porcelain walls at once. I am a two-streamer. When I hear the Windmill DJ start to talk in German, I remember my buddy Larry-Larry's announcement to the Central Missouri State University crowd from his booth at Warrensburg's best party club.

"Hey, everybody! In the men's room toilet! See the turd of the century!" I'd sent a buddy up to tell him what I'd discovered.

"A tremendous turd, a hellacious hawker, a staggering piece of crap! Something only a fool could flush!" I shout from my guardpost at the men's room door, knowing universities hold maybe more fools per square foot than anywhere else in the world.

"The length of this thing is stunning! Only twenty-five cents to see it! Less than a penny an inch! The longest turd you'll ever see in your life!"

There was a mad, shit-viewing rush.

When the men's room was packed, I shimmied under the door of the dank and stinky center stall, and opened the door. One at a time I let in the crowd to see a hawker that curled once around in the bottom of the bowl, snaked up until it broke the water's surface, laid against the porcelain up to the seat, crossed over the worn white wood, and hung three inches down toward the floor. Spectacular! Twenty-nine inches of Guinness world's record brown without the foam.

"Everybody! Listen up! About halfway down the bowl there's a perfectly formed corn smiley face in that world's record piece of shit," Larry-Larry announced from his DJ booth. "That's worth the price of admission on its own!"

We took in $26.85. For shit.

P. T. Barnum said, "Behind every crowd is a silver lining." He didn't say there's a sucker born every minute. Everybody gets played for a sucker sometime. Hell, we all fall in love! P. T. Barnum sucked you in to make you laugh, to make you wonder, to blow open the doors to your imagination.

Two Germans splash out Farts in the urinals beside me.

I'm in Berlin!

True fact: for Adolf Hitler to orgasm he had to be shitting in someone's face. Yuck! But it kind of explains Poland.

I haven't written a joke since I left Chicago. The only thing I've come up with is Mancow dime-and-pins. I'm overflowing with tears, not ideas. Time with my dad in Missouri has already kept me off the air five days longer than I've been away from any *Mancow's Morning Madhouse* audience anywhere—ever. I should be on the air tomorrow, not spending a week in Europe. There are no guarantees. The fastest-rising show in Chicago radio history could plummet even faster. My audience could leave me as quickly as my dad did. But what could I say if they did tune in? My sense of humor is gone. I don't know if it's ever coming back.

Back in the Windmill, my White Linen brunette still sits on her stool.

"I'm buying a pitcher of Farts," says the dwarf, dripping from dancing. "Ask her to dance, Mancow. Buy her a drink."

"I can't do it. I don't know why." Or maybe I do. I've just lost my dad. I can't lose anything else. Not tonight.

Jesus, he's not . . . he is! The dwarf points at me while he talks to White Linen. She looks straight at me. She's smiling. I can't read her eyes from here. Is that a fuck-you smile? White Linen shakes her head. What does that mean in German?

"Dammit! What did you say?"

"I told her you've fallen madly in love. I told her you want to take her to the Hotel Savoy for a night of unbridled sex. I told her about your 1972 yellow Ford Maverick in perfect working order." The dwarf shoves an empty glass in my clenching fist and Farts in it from the pitcher. "To the future!"

I grab his arm.

"I told her you wanted to buy her a drink. She speaks some English. Talk to her." The dwarf goes back to begging every fraulein who's breathing to dance until one accepts. I look at White Linen. She smiles. Dammit! I wish my show broadcast in Berlin.

Two hours, four pitchers of Farts, and five toilet visits later, a trio of fancy Berlin party people arrive to take over the dance floor. Black-haired man strips off his tuxedo coat while his two blond Aryan escorts press against him front and back. DJ says something German. Black-haired man strips off his ruffled shirt. Both women grope his naked chest and fuck while pretending to dance. You couldn't fit a toothpick between those bodies, but Mr. Black-hair puts a hand on each fraulein's ass and pulls them in even tighter. I want a tourist sandwich! I haven't gotten laid in weeks! The Teutonic mating dance ends when DJ says good night. Maybe it's good morning. White Linen has left without me.

On our long stumble back to the Hotel Savoy, leaning on each other, the dwarf and I fall down many times. As I struggle up from the hard Berlin pavement after fall number—I don't know—six, I'm staring into a store so full of wonderful cow things that I stand amazed and drooling. Holstein salt and pepper shakers stare at me from the window. A Black Angus bull with a James Dean face lies on his back asking smokers to stub their butts on his belly. The udder of the five-foot standing cow tells me it's 6:03.

"Remember how to get back to this store!" I command the dwarf.

"Look! A park!"

We monkey through the jungle gym, cross the rope bridge like Incas, and swing on the swings like five-year-olds. With our arms outstretched, looking up to a rosy sky, we spin around until we fall down. My Fart-filled head spins together with the earth.

Like Wile E. Coyote, I chase the bluebird of happiness—always just out of reach—forever worth pursuing.

But maybe not in Berlin. Girls in Berlin no fuck.

As I doze on the playground grass, White Linen kisses my face and caresses my crotch in my dreams. Why is she growling?

"Danger, Will Robinson!"

I slowly open my eyes to the big white teeth that ate Red Riding Hood's grandma. The wet snout of a German shepherd noses my chin with a growl. I close my eyes. I lay as still as a board. I may be a crazy rule-breaking son of a bitch, but I'm not stupid! I remember the local cops showing off their German shepherds at my school. Those bitches (always bitches—males are too cocky to train) threw themselves over eight-foot walls, scaled a twenty-foot ladder, pulled a baby doll gently out of a burning stroller, and mutilated a full-sized human dummy. As two dogs poke my body with their snouts, my mind races.

—Germans are insane. If they weren't, how could David Hasselhoff be their favorite singer? Did these two German shepherds hear me ask David on the radio if he waxed his crack hair or plucked it?

—If Starsky and Hutch's Ford Torino raced against the General Lee from *The Dukes of Hazzard,* which would win?

And if *The Dukes of Hazzard* car were up against Kitt, the car from *Knight Rider,* which would win?

And if the *Knight Rider* car were up against the Coyote car from *Hardcastle and McCormick,* which would win?

And if they all went against *My Mother the Car—*

who would care?

—Why did Eddie Van Halen name his son Wolfgang? Why didn't he just hang a sign around the poor kid's neck telling the boys at school to beat him up every day of his life?

—I asked Peter Graves, "Are you named for the place where all the male baby foreskins get buried?" He laughed. He'd never been asked that before.

Finally, I start to pray. Then I realize it's my dad I'm praying to. Is that right? I don't know. Parents must be every kid's first image of omnipotence. Huge. Strong. Lightning fast. And without their love we die. Help me out here, Dad!

As both dogs nose my cock I see John Wayne Bobbitt's flaccid penis in the Wild 107 studio as female listeners work to get that recently reattached manhood hard before it's time for 1,000 bucks. Could doctors reattach my penis if one of these bitches bites it off?

Please, Dad. Please, God. Please, somebody. Help me here!

A man's voice says something curt in German.

—Why do I suddenly think of Courtney Love?

The muzzle in my face pulls away.

The muzzle in my crotch pulls away.

Maybe I don't have to die today.

I slowly open my eyes to see a man in a blue-gray military-cut suit. Bone buttons (maybe human) close the coat tight to the neck. The upright collar circles a starched white shirt. The clot of a tie is bloodred. He starts to move away slowly, two leather leashes in his hand. I close my eyes. My mind races.

—My dad used to garden in a suit. I don't know why. I never asked him. He always wore suits. Maybe the only old clothes Dad had (because he wasn't a yuppie jag-off) were the salesman's suits he'd worn too long to sell in.

Kids always know who the neighborhood villain is. They're never right but they always know. Scary Old Widow Withers down the block was our unanimous verdict. Widow sounds like "witch" to kids. Old women on their own scare us.

When the fish in the newspaper arrived on the porch, I knew it was from Old Widow Withers and her ape friends from Oz. My parents thought the same because they took that fish around to the garbage like it was poisoned. Each time a new fish arrived it went straight around the house to the garbage can. We had cats for miles.

One day Mom goes out for mail. Her screams are loud. They last at least a minute. Dad and I run out. Dad holds her. Mom breaks into tears, and points to the mailbox. Inside I see a dead rabbit, sliced down the belly, bleeding on the bills. In my head I see the rabbit cages in Old Widow Withers' backyard, the ones we opened sometimes to give her rabbits their freedom. This was one of her rabbits.

We got dead rabbits and bloody mail for weeks.

Widow Withers was clever. She got so hysterical over her dead rabbits that she convinced my parents she hadn't sent the fish.

But I knew.

She was tormenting us!

The truth, though, was even more terrifying.

Sick at home one day, with Mom and Dad both out at work, I got up during *Lost in Space* commercial breaks to stretch my poor body. I walked to the window to look at the only true friend I had, the best thing in my life, Happy, the family cocker spaniel. He trotted, trudged really, around the backyard grunting.

Blam!!!

Happy's head splattered to meat loaf on the lawn.

Old Widow Withers was not the culprit.

I cowered in terror until my parents got home.

My fear, my shaking body, convinced them I'd seen our nice Italian neighbor blow Happy into headcheese.

They called Aunt Kathy in New Jersey who called someone who knew someone who called someone who knew something. Uncle Frank called back to talk to Dad.

"The mob is huge in Kansas City, John. Your next-door neighbor is a KC Mafia kingpin whose old man clawed up high in the mob by killing people and stuffing their bodies down sewers. It's why they called him 'the Rat.' They're sending a message, John."

A message straight out of *The Godfather.* No horse's heads in suburbia!

"Dammit, what's the message?!"

"Stop doing whatever you're doing to them, John!"

"But I'm not doing anything. Really!"

"Well, I'll check it out some more."

My dad, John Muller, had the exact opposite of a green thumb. At best, when my dad gardened, he looked like he was pretending. Tie this in with his constant buying, selling, and trying out huge new electronic equipment in our yard, and the call from Jersey makes sense.

"John, are you FBI?"

"What? No!"

"They think you are. Take down the satellite dishes, John. They think they're bugging cones. And don't wear a fucking suit anymore when you garden! Okay?!"

Dad took down the satellite dishes. When he wanted to garden, he sat inside. He couldn't go out naked.

Poor Dad. A broken-down Willy Loman cast unfairly as Eliot Ness.

Through someone who knew someone who knew someone who knew Uncle Frank, the Kansas City mob got the word that—no matter what it looked like—John Muller was not a government agent who blew his cover big time every time he gardened in his suit. He was just a broken-down salesman running on very hard times.

No more rabbits.

No more fish.

No more Happy.

When he was murdered, Happy was seventeen years old. He was so arthritic he could barely move, but I still miss him grunting under the table for my lima beans.

Ten days later our gangster neighbor came over with new Lee jeans, a blue denim work shirt, and work boots for Dad to garden in. He knew Dad's sizes and everything.

"Will you kill our next dog too?" I asked innocently.

My parents wished I hadn't.

"He was getting old anyway, son," the Rat Bastard said as he tousled my hair. "Saved you the trouble of putting him to sleep."

Thanks.

As Erich von Stroheim finally closes the gate to my Berlin park behind his two German shepherds, I wake the dwarf. We skedaddle.

• • •

After my dad died, I looked through old family photos: John and Dawn before they were married when they were kids themselves, fourteen and seventeen, eighteen and twenty-one. She looks at him like he excites her down to her toes. He looks at her like nothing else matters on earth.

Weird, to think of your parents as sexual beings. (Or, Jesus, going to the bathroom.) But since no wise men showed up in the stable when I was born, I'm pretty sure Mommy and Poppy had hot monkey sex.

Yuck!

When we get back to Berlin's Hotel Savoy, we hand our passports to the cute new blonde behind the 200-year-old, thirty-foot-long wooden counter. She gives us our keys. On her forest-green uniform jacket, over her left breast, I notice her silver name tag.

Mrs. Muller.

Big brother Johnny
with Pop and me.

Life Is a Cabaret, Old Friend

When I wake up the sun is shining. Hell,
it was shining when I went to bed. And when I fell asleep in the park. My
bed's a mess like always. I roll out of the pool of sweat I created in this
hellishly un-air-conditioned room. I wear my sheet to the bathroom.
After a shit and a shower, I punch the dwarf awake. Berlin awaits.

As we eat our Big Mac breakfasts, I watch Berliners dipping fries in
mayonnaise. Huh? Anyone who likes that swallows.

Along the Kurfürstendamm we see the eerie half-destroyed tower of the old church that's been left as a reminder of WWII.

"I guess that church tower's been a landmark here for a long time," says the dwarf. "Whole, unbombed, it's what you see through Greta Garbo's window in *Grand Hotel,* which is what . . . ?"

"MGM, 1932, classic," I say. As I look at the bombed-out skeleton of the tower, I feel like Joseph Cotten arriving in postwar Vienna to find Orson Wells—Harry Lime—*The Third Man.* "Look at that poster! They call *Die Hard 2, Der Skyscraper 2* here."

"Germans are strange."

"And violent. How many posters have we seen for *Die Buddy Holly* in the last four blocks? Why does Berlin want to kill Buddy Holly? Isn't he already dead?"

"Maybe it's a vampire flick, Mancow."

"I read that George Lucas, Steven Spielberg, and Francis Ford Coppola would give millions of their dollars to see their ten favorite films again—for the first time."

"What a concept!"

"I'd pay for it. Imagine! To be able to go back and do something you loved, something that changed your life, over again for the first time! The excitement, the mystery, the terror, the enchantment. There's nothing like that first time!"

"What films would you pick, Mancow?"

"For me it's *RoboCop, Predator, Die Hard*—you know that moment in *Die Hard* when Bruce Willis turns and says . . ." As I say it, I realize someone is saying it with me. I spin around to find this guy almost beside me who is moving like me and talking like me. A crowd of 200 people laughs. "Did you see—he just—we gotta watch this."

We sit down at the only sidewalk table left in a Ku'damm restaurant-biergarten to watch the copycat work. A woman walks her dog. She's eighty, moves oddly, and talks to her dog. A quarter-step behind her, the imitator duplicates her perfectly. People laugh. The old lady keeps walking, talking to her dog, unaware that anything's happening. Hell, I wouldn't have known either if Copycat hadn't imitated Bruce Willis with me. The imitator turns on his heel, leaves the old lady, and instantly becomes a flouncy tourist girl in Daisy Duke shorts walking the other way cattering to a girlfriend. The walk, the arms, the bobbing head—everything is perfect. Laughter. One girl sees him. Now the other. He shrugs. They smile, and walk on. Instantly Copycat becomes a dour Berliner planning WWIII who's walking the other way. Copycat gets him exactly. With the laugh, Dour Man turns, not because he thinks anything's happening but to glare at people who dare to laugh in his world. Copycat walks right through his dour scowl, still doing his imitation. This guy is good. I start the applause. Dour Man glares at me, at Copycat, at the audience, and continues off in his huff.

"Bitter?"

"Uh . . ."

"What would you like to order?" Waitress asks, changing to English.

"What have you got?" It's the dwarf.

"The menu is on the table."

"We don't want to eat."

An excited woman yammers to her weary husband. Copycat does them each in turn.

"Cocktail? Beer?"

"Do you have Farts?"

"This is not Windmill. I will bring two lagers. Did you see the ice cream?"

She's got my interest now. She's not bad looking. Brunette. In a sleeveless blouse, nice body, good tits.

"Ice cream is over there." Waitress lifts her arm and points.

"Dude! Did you see it? She had hair under her arms!" I say to the dwarf on our way to the ice cream cart.

"Lots of European women have hair under their arms, Mancow. My girl has more than I do. I kind of like it."

"That's disgusting, dwarf! What hair though? Pubic hair?"

"Under her arms! The taste of the pit tells you if the cat's worth cleaning."

"When I worked as a waiter at Emile's in Kansas City, I dated a girl who had hair under her arms. If my little French maiden was just out of the shower, that hair could taste fine, but once the sun hit her she turned into Pepe Le Pew. If she'd sweat just a little when I licked that pit, it was the next best thing to licking farther down. And whenever it was 'her time' that underarm hair was all she would give me, period."

Wait. I feel that old familiar surge as things inside me shoot toward my head like Independence Day fireworks. Yes! Finally! Here they come. Brainflashes!

—Parody ad: Whisker Biscuits. "They're Good Eatin'!"

—Phone scam a hair wax guy: Call up wanting a full-body pluck. Be hairy as a yeti. Want him to pluck me hard.

—Phone scam a furniture store: Call wanting a hutch. Already have a Starsky.

Yes! Not many. But reassuring. My first spurt of creative seeds since I went to Missouri three weeks ago to be with Dad.

"My God, they have checkerboard! Right there! Vanilla ice cream and orange sherbet in little squares. Checkerboard was my dad's favorite . . ."

"What?"

"I'm six years old. My dad's showing me how to eat a chili dog. Take a bite, inch down the paper. Take another bite, inch down the paper. That's still how I eat chili dogs. Give me some marks to drop in Copycat's hat."

"You have your own."

"Oh, yeah." I peel off a five-mark note. I hand the rest of my cash and my Amex card to the dwarf. "Put them in your other pocket and don't get them confused. I bought breakfast. You buy the beers."

Copycat spins and points at white socks and sandals while everything except his pointing hand moves exactly like the Englishman's wife.

"Mancow, if you could go back and *do* something over again for the first time what would it be?"

"I'd do the squirmies again in a second!"

"Define!"

"That first time you touch a girl's skin—when you feel her whole body tighten and ripple and squirm—and yours is doing the same as she touches you. Those are the squirmies! When every part of your body finds a life. When every cell kicks off a chain reaction that affects every other cell in her body—and yours. When you explode with new sensations. When nothing gets old. When everything feels like the first time. I'd go back there. I'd relive the squirmies."

"That's one."

"I've got more?"

"You've got ten," says the dwarf.

"I'd be seventeen again. When I turned seventeen, my dick up and said, 'Hey, I'm in charge around here and there's nothing you can do about it!' Man! It was hard all the time. Jerk-off? Have sex? Didn't matter! It was hard before I cleaned up. That thing was indestructible. I walked around with a hard-on for a solid year. I'd relive that for the first time in a heartbeat. I loved that time. I was the human stickpin."

"That's two."

"Huh. 'Do Gramps and Grandma like sucking face?' Do you know where that's from?"

"Twelve-year-old Billy's famous question from *On Golden Pond,* Mancow."

"I asked that question twice a day every day except Monday for, like, 814 professional performances of *On Golden Pond.* The theater company was breaking like ten different child labor laws every day, and if I knew it, I didn't care. I loved doing that show. I'd relive that again. Oh, my God! Look at that camel toe!"

"What? Where?"

Is the dwarf blind? "The girl in the shorts! Between her legs, buddy! What does that pubie patch look like?"

"Damn! You're right. It could be a Deerpan or a Monkey Fist."

Put a woman in really tight clothes, and the camel toe appears. This camel toe stares at me from jeans cut so short and pulled so high that, well, I ain't deaf but I can read her lips. Braless tits bounce free inside her T-shirt. Fewer women wear bras in Europe. I love braless tits! As she passes, her ass cheeks sun themselves out the bottom of her shorts.

"Whoa, dude!"

"That was sweet."

"I'd relive those drives to and from *On Golden Pond* with my dad. Six days a week he drove me into Kansas City to perform. Two hours in, two hours back. My dad was in the audience smiling, laughing, and clapping for every performance. It was amazing. Henry Fonda came once, before he decided to do the film. Sometimes I still hear the loons. I didn't realize the burden it must have been on my dad until years later. Never did he let me feel that burden. He always made me feel like helping me do this thing I loved so much was total pleasure for him. When I ask myself if I could do the same for my kid it worries me—I still can't answer yes."

"Not many can. That was an amazing thing he did."

"My dad was fantastic. I've never heard anyone else express his philosophy. Let me share it with you. Kids are always looking for something that excites them, and my dad was always helping in the one real way dads can. When baseball was the thrill of the moment, man, I had the mitt, the shoes, and the uniform, and Dad was out there rooting. But if two weeks later it wasn't baseball that excited me anymore, that was okay too. Everyone tells me that's a rare trait in fathers. Most dads look at the money that's just flown out the door for the baseball stuff, and when their kid feels an itch to play the violin, most dads don't let them scratch it. You wanted to play baseball, so they want you out there playing second base instead of moving to second fiddle. It's like families have this built-in depreciation schedule on each of the things their kids do, like mom and dad are looking to get their money's worth out of that glove and uniform before they can willingly let their kid move on to something else. There's a real problem there. Enthusiasm gets squashed. What you thought was going to be fun turns into prison. Next time, you're a lot more careful about getting enthusiastic: I'd *like* to tell them I like this, but they'll make me do it forever!

"My dad wasn't like that. If I were into baseball for two weeks and astronomy suddenly snagged my soul, well, the mitt went in the closet and the local pawnshop sold my dad a telescope, which in its own time moved to the closet as well. But he always supported my searching. When enthusiasms changed we were never criticized. Dad never forced our searches into some plan of his own that we knew nothing about and which had nothing to do with us. Dad's hidden agenda was to let his kids keep searching until they stumbled on to something they were good at!"

Crying on the Ku'damm, I'm happy for my Revos again.

"Unluckily for children, most parents' single parenting thrust is making junior toe the line. For assembly-line kids with preassembled parents, childhood is a molding instead of a growing experience. 'Let's make sure our boy gets the basics so later he can use them to live a basic life.' My folks noticed I wasn't a drone; they saw I was a smart-ass. Hell, they could hardly miss it the way I came out for school most days, but Dad didn't make me change my shoes, my clothes, my hair, my hat. Unfortunately, public schools didn't follow my dad's philosophy."

"The guys who designed America's schools are the same guys who designed our prisons," says the dwarf. I'm not surprised.

"My dad tried to tutor me in math, but much more importantly he drove me into Kansas City to audition for commercials. Dad and I talked about everything. When Mom drove me around she'd say, 'It's all right, Erich, but someday you have to buy me a house, like Elvis did for his mom.' The driving paid off. I got print work. I got commercials. I got cast in *On Golden Pond.* Dad's work as a traveling salesman suffered a lot, but I didn't know that. Damn! There's enough muff there to knit a sweater."

Ding!

"Man, I love that fuzz. Miss the panty line though."

"Mancow, she's sixty."

"Whoa! You're right. But stop at the tits, she's looking fine."

I think about getting laid all the time. It's like the hard-wired basic program that let's the rest of me run. Computers have that bell that goes off whenever a question box appears: Would you like to save before closing? Are you sure you want to erase this disk? Straight through wonderful thoughts of my dad, the hard drive Mancow question flashes. Ding! Wouldn't you like to get laid?

YES

It's sick.

Sometimes sex is a distraction I don't welcome. I've lost jobs because of it. I've lost friends because of it. But whenever my hard drive engages, it pumps out the Mancow Question. Ding! Wouldn't you like to get laid?

Sex is hard-wired in us all. It's sensory and immediate. It's biological. In the cells of *all* living things, little cellular voices scream, "Preserve the species!! Drop a load there!" Lots of people spend their lives fighting that inner voice. I can't. I don't want to. Sex is natural. Healthy. And fun in most cases.

"My God! Look at that bush!"

Ding!

Wouldn't you like to get laid?

I could never be a nun.

A weird-looking army armored truck races up the other side of the Ku'damm with its German siren blaring. Bee-aaawp! Bee-aaawp! It spins around the next little park and races back to a screeching halt at the curb ten feet away. Even before it stops, a man in fatigues jumps out the passenger door. The door across the back flies open. A German shepherd and four more cops hurl out. They surround a dreadlock blond kid and his buddy walking a bike on the sidewalk. They don't touch. They don't fucking need to! Those are Lugers in their belts and two Uzis point at the sky.

"Are those cops?"

"Berlin police," Waitress says, setting down two more beers.

"What did those guys do?"

"They think one of them stole . . ."

All the money in a bank? A nuclear missile? What?

"They think one of them stole the bicycle."

"What?! Holy God!"

Did I just duck in here? Onto this planet? Into this life? Am I a convict from some different solar system sentenced to doing time here on Penal Colony Earth?

They've got the dreadlock blond kid in the back of the truck. But the doors are open. I'd like to see what's going on, but I also don't want to get shot.

One cop is a woman! Wow! Look at that duck's ass haircut, look at how her khaki greens pull so tight around her butt. Never seen a uniform look so good. Look at that pistol, that nightstick! Ding! Maybe she'd come to the hotel later and cuff me? I'll be Hogan if she'll be a Colonel Klink Bombshell.

In twenty minutes it's over. No arrests. No executions. The dreadlock guy and his buddy continue up the sidewalk with their bike. The dwarf refuses to hand my uniformed honey the napkin I wrote our address on.

* * *

"That looks great!"

The dwarf's right. Every item of food outside the Ku'damm restaurant we're passing looks fabulous. Inside, there are twenty restaurants under one roof to tempt our senses. We collect the food. We pay, find a table, and sit down to eat. Five bites in we realize Hitler conquered France to get a decent meal. We leave four plates piled high with fabulous-looking but shit-tasting food.

The guidebook says Berlin porn is hot, so we check out a porno shop. Nothing impressive. Would my dad have sprung for those mail-order penile weights if I'd told him I wanted to be a porno star like John Holmes? Prob'ly not.

A huge, portable bratwurst wagon sits at the next corner. Yes! They have knockwurst. "You have to have one," I tell the dwarf. "Knockwurst was my dad's favorite food."

When I was a teenager my dad had a friend named Geoff—a good friend, close to the whole family. Dad had some money then and threw huge barbecues. Once, after everybody else had already eaten, Dad stood at the grill, cigarette hanging out of his mouth, belly hanging out from under his shirt, turning the only thing on the grill, *his* knockwurst. He turned that sucker over the coals until it was perfect. When Dad turned for his plate, Geoff speared the sausage.

"Gimme back my knockwurst!" Dad yelled, but Geoff danced away displaying the sausage on his fork like a treasure. "Gimme my knockwurst, goddammit!"

"Listen, you old cocksucker, this knockwurst is perfect and I'm eating it," Geoff said as he bit off a third. A bomb went off in my dad. Had my dad been a faster man, Geoff would have died from a fatal barbeque forking that day. But Geoff, younger and quicker, jumped in his Camaro with the knockwurst in his teeth, and the best my dad could do was fork the paint job as Geoff burned rubber.

"Dad, it's only a knockwurst," Johnny said.

"That son of a bitch called me a cocksucker!"

I knew—we all knew—Dad missed Geoff a lot. But he could not forgive.

"Is Geoff coming back ever?"

"No! He called me a cocksucker!"

I saw Geoff . . . God . . . was it only the day before yesterday? My dad never saw him again.

These Berlin sidewalk knockwurst are grilled to John Muller perfection. After we gobble seconds, the dwarf and I cross the Ku'damm to a record store. I buy the single of "Be My Lover" and two Kinks CDs with songs that were never released in the United States.

"Did I tell you I got to see them?"

"Who?"

"Buddy, I first heard the Kinks pounding through the walls of the womb whenever my mom would go into my brothers' room. I have always loved the Kinks. But by the time I was old enough to go to concerts the Kinks were no longer performing. Hell, they weren't even a group anymore. I figured I'd never see them. Then I heard they were reuniting for a weekend at the L.A. House of Blues. I called everybody and finally scored tickets to all three shows. The Kinks! Live! Amazing!"

I wanted to party with the Kinks! But I couldn't even meet them. The timing was impossible. Being a whiny little shit I told the guy who got me the tickets how disappointed I was. 'I think we can work it out,' he says, 'I think I can get them on the *Madhouse* in Chicago.'

" 'You have got to be shitting me!' I scream, 'The Kinks! On my show?' "

"How was it?"

"Ray Davies comes on the second week I'm back. Every cell I have is looking forward to it. I have Kinks records I played so many times you can read the newspaper through them. I read an advance copy of Ray Davies' autobiography, *X-Ray*. We were born on the same day. Different years, of course, but . . . could that be why I have always felt this kinship with the Kinks? Ray Davies—my favorite songwriter *ever*. Songs of the nonconformist, unconventional little guy—with a twist. 'Tired of Waiting for You,' 'Apeman,' 'Do It Again,' 'Lola,' 'Deadend Street,' 'Set Me Free,' 'I'm Not Like Everybody Else.' I have always felt the Kinks were speaking for me."

"June twenty-first. Summer solstice. Midsummer's night. Dead on the Gemini-Cancer cusp. Caught between air and water, head and heart, mind and soul."

"But I know how to feel them both! I am a two-streamer."

"What?"

"I pee in two streams. From the time I grew tall enough to pee in a toilet instead of into Donald Duck's head on my kiddie pooper, one stream hits the bowl while another chases the wall. My mom thought I was just really bad with my aim so she bought me toilet targets. Five points for the little floating rabbit. Ten points on the deer. Fifteen for the cow. I hosed the twenty-five-point bear until he went down. I think my mom made a mistake. I mean, hell, I couldn't control it anyway, but I totally forgot about the piss stream splashing the floor. Every woman I've lived with has bitched about cleaning my pee off the bathroom floor. 'It's dirty!' 'Disgusting!' 'It smells like ammonia!' One girlfriend told me to sit down to pee. What? Pee like a woman? Tuck that farm animal down between my legs? No way! I'm a male animal! I'm marking my territory! Hell, I'm better than most! I'm marking it times two! Whoa! You did it!"

Entering the cow store I know I'm in big trouble. No way will everything I want in here fit in my suitcase. Cow stuff up the wazoo! Hope they ship to the America!

Choice is hard. Confusing. But making choices is like exercise—the more you do it the easier it gets. Too many people agonize over which soap to use. Irish Spring! Move on! You get so much more done if you just choose.

Quickly.

But in the cow store in Berlin I can't choose; it's packed with amazing creative stuff. A dragonfly buzzes straight through my brain. Crystal body parts, weird metal legs, iridescent paper-thin wings of shell or mica. When objects call like this, I pay attention. Maybe it's a roach clip. I must have this bug. I open the glass display-case door and liberate my dragonfly buddy.

A hand grabs my upper arm and squeezes hard. Fingernails cut my flesh. I see blue Nazi eyes under blond Aryan hair above a firm German chin. Her lips look sewn together like the lips of the real shrunken head my dad gave me. All communication is through the SS chin, which never stops moving, through the SS grip, which never loosens, through the Nazi eyes narrow with hatred. The message is clear: put that dragonfly back inside its little glass prison now! Swinehunt!

But I've got American money!

The SS clerk pulls my precious prize away. The prison gate swings shut on my dragonfly pal and all his friends in their concentrated encampment. As blood trickles down my arm, I look at the Nazi cow and think, God! What could I do if my whole country were run by people like this?

As soon as she loosens her grip, I vote with my feet. No Brownshirts wait at the door to take me away like they would have in 1939.

Is it okay to hit a woman if she's much bigger than you are?

As we walk through Bauhaus architecture toward the Hotel Savoy, I see an intricately carved stone archway, hundreds of years old. It's all that's left of the synagogue Nazi-led Berliners destroyed in a single night—the night of broken glass, the night of broken dreams, the night every Jew in Germany knew what Hitler was and felt the hatred I just did in the cow store.

"My God! Do you think the whole temple was this amazing?"

"Through the door is a museum, Mancow. Let's find out."

The old Jewish ticket seller apologizes for having to charge us. Photographs show the old temple was awe inspiring. As we leave the depressing tiny museum through the magnificent portal arch, I see the policeman in his car in the courtyard, the policeman in the booth at the gate, the anti-car-bomb blocks of cement in the driveway, the two policemen pacing the sidewalk outside carrying Uzis. Jesus! This much protection for rubble? The hate must still live here.

We race up the steps to a movie theater that shows Jerry Lewis films all day, every day, and has for fifteen years! Today *The Nutty Professor* shows for fourteen hours. Tomorrow it's *The Bellboy,* then *The Patsy,* then who fucking cares? How can you respect a culture that finds Jerry Lewis funny?

At the Hotel Savoy the dwarf hands over our passports. Mrs. Muller hands us the key to room 3030. As she turns her head, for just an instant, she reminds me of Phone Girl. My Lolita. The sweet teenage virgin who answers phones on *Mancow's Morning Madhouse.* But being a Missus, Mrs. Muller prob'ly ain't a virgin, and Phone Girl would not be caught dead in a uniform. As I try to wash off the hatred, I realize I'm wrong. I've seen pictures of Phone Girl in her short skirt and letter sweater cheerleader uniform. I fall into bed wishing I were falling into Phone Girl.

"Do all Germans dip their fries in mayo?" I ask during a Big Mac dinner. The dwarf looks up and spits Coke all over the floor. *Beavis and Butt-head Do Berlin.* I've shoved a ketchup-dipped french fry up my nose. It's not *that* funny! But the gag always works.

We taxi to Metropol. The guidebook says Metropol swings like Studio 54 in New York used to. Our cab pulls up in front of a gigantic spot-lit 1920s Art Deco movie palace. Marlene Dietrich could arrive at any moment in a cut-front Mercedes limo for the premiere of *Blue Angel.* Berliner families in Hitler's time could have watched Leni Riefenstahl's amazing propaganda films here after seeing Nazi cartoons in which ravenous ugly rats take on exaggerated Jewish features, turn into ugly people, and turn back into ugly rats. Hungry ugly rats. Hungry ugly Jews. Exterminate the rats. Exterminate the Jews. Jesus!

Inside Metropol the music pounds. The dwarf dances. From the balcony I watch laser pinpoints cut through smoke into 2,500 dancers. La Bouche sings "Be My Lover." Songs used to let you create images. MTV has destroyed that.

Radio is now the final frontier of free imagination.

· · ·

The TV in the Times Bar at the Hotel Savoy shows *Cabaret.*

Joel Grey dances with his lover, a gorilla in a frilly dress, and sings:

If you could see her through my eyes
she wouldn't look Jewish at all.

I shiver as the camera pans through the audience of Nazi Brownshirts with swastika armbands. Fuck! I'm where all of that happened! As I rub my scabbed-up arm I swear I see the Eva Braun wannabe from the cow store in the cabaret. I feel darkness in Berlin. I had hoped that spirit was dead. It isn't.

I loved the Germany in my dad's stories.

I don't love the reality.

3

The brothers Muller (middle brother Mark with pet raccoon "Rascal").

Empires of Evil

The guidebook says it's one of the best museums in the world and the dwarf wants to see it, but as our bus takes us toward East Berlin the lush trees and green grass of the Tiergarten tell me I'd rather spend my day in nature than in the Pergamon.

The Berlin Wall is down, but man, I can still feel the dividing line. Hell, I can see it! As we walk through Brandenburg Gate into old East Berlin, there are tank tread scars and potholes everywhere in the huge plaza. Down Unter den Linden I see only dusty trees with amputated arms and dying leaves—no huge lindens stretching branches to meet across the broad avenue.

Wait a second! Nowhere on this vast plaza, nowhere down any street, nowhere for as far as my eye can see is there another human being. We're it! Like the Bradys in that ghost town. For twenty minutes we walk past decaying Communist office blocks and bullet-ridden Nazi ones. We see no cars. We see two people. The People's Apartment Complexes are each a block long and ten stories high—an infinite stack of ten-by-ten-foot gray concrete squares, each with a black window center. They look like massive hives for drones and workers. In Chicago they give these buildings names like Cabrini Green. The only interesting building—a sixty-story brick, brass, and glass tower that looks like a Tampax dispenser standing on the small tube—is a spy tower! The antennae and parabolic dishes hanging on its outside tell me it could listen to every word I whispered to a lover in Paris. Or Moscow. Or Kansas City. In East Berlin it can probably hear my thoughts!

Ronald Reagan was right! This was an Evil Empire. Dark. Empty. Lifeless. Soulless.

When the doors opened, everybody split.

We approach the Pergamon. It's filthy, bullet-scarred, and (thank you, Jesus!) closed.

We walk through the yellow trees of a dusty park, grassless and bordered by a trash-filled canal. We enter Martin Luther's church, where the leader of maybe the greatest protest movement the world has ever seen used to preach. I'm shocked by the ceiling frescoes, the full-sized statues of saints and angels, the confessionals.

"It looks like a Catholic church," I whisper.

"It was a Catholic church. Martin Luther was the priest here until the pope excommunicated him for protesting."

· · ·

I grew up a practicing believer. Hell, I was more than that—I had the calling. I would probably be a minister today if I hadn't run into the Question. At fifteen I went to our family minister, Roger Burnham.

"Roger," I said, "if some African woman in the middle of nowhere, or some Indian woman who worships a cow, is a really good, loving, generous, wonderful person who never heard of Jesus, is she going to burn in hell?"

"Yes," my minister told me.

"She's going to suffer for eternity?"

"Yes!"

"Even though she's living a good life she's going to suffer neverending pain in a pit of fire because, by happenstance, she never heard the name of Jesus?"

"Yes. Yes. Yes."

"But how can that be?"

"If you don't know Christ, you burn in hell," Roger said.

As my minster said those words I lost my calling. That idea of justice disgraces every concept of Love I have ever known. At that instant I realized my Church and I had different Gods. My God is loving; their God was not. I couldn't preach about a God like that. I couldn't even believe in a God like that. That isn't Jesus' God. It's not what Jesus taught! Jesus calls a Samaritan more God-filled than two churchgoing members of the faith who don't show love to the man in the ditch. But Jews hated Samaritans—worse than Christians hate Muslims, or even Muslims and Jews. So, was Jesus saying those we hate (Nazis, slackers, gangsta rappers, even Amway salespeople)—*if they love*—embody more of God than card-carrying churchies who just keep walking?

Ask the Schindler Juden.

I served fifth grade in a Christian school. What a bunch of bitchy-boy, uptight, terrified students they had there. I didn't understand why—

until the day I got stuck with a sharpened pencil. The lead went into my hand and broke off under my skin. It hurt like a son of a bitch. I blurted out, "Oh, God!"

I had taken the name of the Lord in vain, breaking one of the Ten Commandments. Punishment was imperative.

In the principal's office, I was purged of my heinous crime with "swats," Orwellian doublespeak for taking a two-by-four to the ass of a terrified little boy.

They called it the "Wisdom Stick"!

Those corrective "swats" bruised the bones of my pelvis through my ass cheeks and bruised the end of my spine. I was out of school for weeks. It was two weeks before my buttocks were no longer black-and-blue. It was three weeks until I could sit in a chair. It was four weeks before I could shit without wincing in pain. (I still do that wincing-in-pain face today when I make stinky—but just for fun.)

When the principal finished his swats he looked at me and said, "Jesus loves you."

I looked up from my bent-over crippled position and muttered to myself, "Bull . . . shit!"

What is this thing with Jesus and violence? How do they come together?

Didn't Jesus tell us to treat everyone else in the world the way we wish they'd treat us? Did the people running this Christian school want me to wale their ass with a two-by-four?

What is this thing with Jesus and rules? Jesus worked to break them!

Didn't Jesus say, "Judge not lest ye be judged?"

When priests brought Jesus a woman caught with her pants down enjoying adulterous sex, didn't he countermand the punishment of Moses? Didn't he force the accusers to realize they were sinners too? Didn't he then release the woman without killing her or hitting her with a two-by-four?

Am I reading a different Bible?

Jesus said God is Love.

When the temple sent a guy to ask him which was the greatest of Moses' commandments, Jesus skipped over Moses entirely to give the world a new commandment.

"Love God [and God is Love]," Jesus said, "with all your heart."

"And [he slipped in a second one], love your neighbor exactly the same way you love yourself."

> I did not put you here to suffer,
> I did not put you here to whine,
> I put you here to love one another
> And to get out and have a good time.

That's how the Rainmakers, my favorite Missouri rock band, put the message in their song "Let My People Go-Go."

People in church look miserable most of the time, but if religion doesn't seem a very inviting club to join, don't miss the message. God is Love—and that's a powerful thing.

Rules and punishment are meant to control you. Jesus was a longhair who was all about freedom! He took on Big Government and the Suits killed him. Jesus went out to the wilderness to get closer to God. I understand. I feel that Love the most when I'm away from people, away from all of man's trappings, sitting in a forest, canoeing on a lake, diving into my honey.

God is Love! Not a punishing parent. The Gospels don't tell us to beat children. They say we have to be like them! They even say that if we don't succeed in being like a child we don't get a pass to heaven! So—

Find your innocence!

Keep it!

It may just put you in paradise.

Not just after this life, but during this life too.

"Yes, Jesus loves me." But the rulemakers at Beat the Children Christian School didn't love me at all. They treated me with violence and hatred, and if what Jesus said is true, then BURN IN HELL!

"Our family minister, Roger Burnham, spoke at my dad's funeral," I tell the dwarf as we leave Martin Luther's church. "Coming together to say how great people were is a waste of time. We should get together to tell stories about them and remember how they made us laugh. That's the part of them I want to carry around all the time. That's the spirit I want with me. At my dad's funeral, when Roger got up to speak, he said, 'Well! One thing you can say about John Muller—he was a character.' I burst out laughing. I feel bad about it. Do you think it was sacrilegious?"

"Only one sin is unforgivable," says the dwarf. "Knowing the truth and teaching against it."

The toilet I go to pee in turns out to be co-ed. No urinals or toilets—just a porcelain square on the floor with foot pads and a hole. Glad I don't have to take a dump! We were once afraid their ideas would destroy America. I don't think so, komrad! We have toilets!

I'm ready to leave East Berlin.

We catch an S-Bahn elevated train, which, fifty years old and falling apart, is clearly East German. In the West Berlin Bahnhof, we pull up next to a modern train.

I'm ready to leave Berlin.

We reserve seats on the Eurostar. Yes! Tonight in Munich I'll get drunk in the beer hall my granddad got drunk in after he beat the Nazis single-handed. We say good-bye to Mrs. Muller and the Hotel Savoy. On the Bahnhof platform, the dwarf hands me a postcard he bought yesterday on the Ku'damm.

"Nelson Mandela. So?"

"Turn it over."

On the other side, I read what Nelson Mandela said when he was inaugurated President of South Africa after thirty years in prison:

Our deepest fear is not that we are inadequate. Our deepest fear is that we are powerful beyond measure. It is our light, not our darkness, that most frightens us. We ask ourselves, who am I to be brilliant, gorgeous, talented, fabulous? Actually, who are you "not" to be? You are a child of God.

After I quit, I broke back into Beat the Children Christian School and stole the fucking Wisdom Stick. And then burned it.

Free Nelson Mandela?

I'll take two!

So quietly I don't even hear it arrive, a sleek, white, immaculate piece of modern engineering pulls in to the Bahnhof. The front of the engine slopes steeply, aerodynamically, toward the rails. This sucker is built for speed; it's the Concorde on rails.

The doors slide open. At 3:18—exactly—the train pulls out of the station so noiselessly I don't realize we're moving until Berlin starts passing by the window of our air-conditioned private compartment for four. The dwarf sits in the luggage rack high above the seats like my guardian angel. His little legs swing above me messing up my hair. As the clean, thriving buildings of West Berlin end, the bombed, dilapidated, and unused factories of old East Germany begin.

In his book *X-Ray,* Ray Davies tells the story of his life from a point in the future when a faceless corporation controls everything. Society wants us to be only so creative, and whenever we exceed the limits, society crushes us back. Wear the hottest new tie and you're hip in Corporate America; wear the wrong pattern and you are suddenly out of the boys' club. Cut your hair in a mohawk and see how long Microsoft keeps you around. Faceless corporations don't want human beings—unique and spectacular in our creation, a sparkle of God's eyes—they want cogs. Fritz Lang knew it as far back as his 1927 film masterpiece, *Metropolis.*

I look out the window of our bullet train at the machine-gun towers and razor wire fences the Soviets used to prevent liberty-seekers from using this corridor to freedom.

"I've worked with people, talented people, who could not buck their fear of the machine enough to take a chance," I tell the dwarf. "And if you don't take chances you never make advances. John Mellencamp says he fights authority but authority always wins. So fight harder! I love to cross that line between the safe and dangerous, between the familiar and new. Let others sit in beehive rooms. I'm digging out! I've left people behind who I know had more talent than I do, but they didn't do the work. They spent an hour a day creating; I spent six. It mounts up fast. At the end of the week they had six hours of stuff; I had forty-five. Whose show is going to be fuller? Society just can't survive without all the creativity we can muster. I want to go out fighting like a lion, not led like a sheep."

The dwarf thinks nineteen divisions of the Soviet military might dissuade me. I don't think so.

We race through countryside as flat as America's heartland. I see another machine-gun tower. Evil exists in the world—and rises again and again. Somewhere out there is a spear point some people say a Roman soldier used to pierce the side of Jesus on the cross 2,000 years ago. The wooden shaft is long gone, but the point is still around—and it has a nasty history. The Roman caesars had it, and from Charlemagne to the Hapsburg kaisers the (un) Holy Roman Empire was built on it. In 1938, when Hitler annexed Austria, he went straight to the Hapsburg museum in Vienna, took the spear point from its display case, and carried it back to Berlin. People who knew the history, like General George Patton, said Hitler wanted Austria to get his hands on that spear with Christ's blood on it. Once Hitler had the spear that ended Jesus' revolution of love, he was ready for war.

Patton knew all about the Spear of Destiny. It's why he pushed so hard for Berlin when everyone knew the war was over. Patton wouldn't let the Ruskies have the run of Berlin alone; he wanted the spear found for America.

Some research I've done says a rich European family holds the bloody spear today. If they do, I say, "Beware!" If Patton found the spear, then it's somewhere in America today—maybe in the Pentagon, maybe at CIA headquarters. Maybe, like the Terminator's leg, the spear sits enshrined in some company's headquarters driving Corporate America to empire. With or without the spear, Corporations own more of the world today than Hitler ever dreamed of. To look in the face of Corporate America is to see into the eyes of Satan's best whore.

Damn the Suits!

● ● ●

At 10 P.M. we arrive in Munich, find a hotel, and split to the beer hall my grandpappy drank in and my parents rediscovered five years ago. The place is empty. I can't see it empty. I can only see it the way you described it to me, Dad, full of 2,600 drunken uproarious people singing and swallowing suds. Two old waitresses shuffle by breaking the vision. I see my mom, not here in Munich enjoying herself with my dad but hauling a tray full of dirty plates and glasses in Missouri, where she still works as a waitress. She's too proud to accept help from her little boy. "A hand up, not a handout," my dad used to say. Yeah, well, Dad, what about Mom? She's getting older and she's alone. Is it welfare to help her? A Turkish guy in a cheap toupee swirls his smelly mop over my shoes.

"Let's get out of here!"

The wall frescoes flash past my eyes as the dwarf spins me around. I feel dizzy like my drunken dad did when he fell down here heading for the toilet.

Outside, the fresh night air feels good.

Finally, the thirty-seventh taxi to pass stops to pick us up—not because Cabbie wants to, but because if he didn't stop, he'd be filling out a mountain of forms for killing a dwarf in the street.

"Take us to a biergarten," the dwarf says as he opens the door and pushes me in.

"There is only one biergarten still open," Cabbie says, looking at his watch, "and not for long."

"Well, take us there!"

The cabbie drops us at a massive old aristocratic house that's been a biergarten for 200 years. High walls surround it. We walk through the wrought-iron gates. The house is quiet and empty. Five acres of outside picnic tables sit filled with exactly four customers. The body of a waitress bobs in the sea of tables. We sit down hopefully in front of where the waitress is heading.

"We have finished serving food," she says, passing without stopping.

"Can I have a beer?" I yell after her. I've gotta have something my dad experienced here.

"You must leave now; we are closed," the biermeister yells from the opposite direction.

I hate Germany.

"Munich dances with life like a toad on a tractor tailpipe," my dad once told me. Dad made Munich live in his stories. But for me, there is no life here. It's dead. So is he. I want out.

It's a twenty-minute ride to a restaurant that's open.

"There is Olympic Stadium," Cabbie says, pointing into darkness.

Summer 1972. I'm a fetus basically, but the Olympic Games in Munich are big, big stuff for me. I want to be an athlete. I want to race and win. I want to be the best. I want that quest for gold. Johnny and Mark give me the chance. "These are the rules of the Muller Summer Games," they say. Yes! Our own Olympic Games! Re-created in the backyard by my older brothers. I'm excited.

BANG!

The imaginary gun goes off. I race against my brothers from here to the tree and back. I am determined to win. I do. I beat both of my older brothers. I'm proud. My brother Johnny creates my medal with some rope and a log from the woodpile.

"The gold medal goes to Erich Muller," Mark says as he places the log around my neck in the fake awards ceremony. I'm so excited and happy (and young) that I don't see my teenage brothers draping a piece of rope around my neck. I see ribbon. I don't see a log. I see Gold.

"Ready for another race?" Johnny asks. I nod, too winded to speak after winning five more Golds. "You're not too tired?" I shake my head.

"Then it's time for the Muller marathon," Mark announces. "First we have to get the route and the rules."

I don't want more rules!

But I'm happy for the time Mark takes to draw the marathon route in the dirt. While he draws the map, I stay on my hands and knees so the six gold medal logs I've already won can rest on the ground and still hang around my neck. Wearing your medals throughout competition is rule number one of the Muller Olympics.

"Any medals you take off before competition finishes, you forfeit," Johnny said when the Games began. I don't know what "forfeit" means, but it sounds like giving them back, and I'm not giving up the Gold!

When Mark finishes drawing the map, Johnny helps me to my feet. The three of us go to the line. Mark lifts the finger starting gun. BANG!

I'm racing for the most gold medals won by anyone—ever—anywhere.

I'm not disheartened when my brothers race around the corner in front of me; I've beaten them both in every race so far. I am surprised when I round the corner and find they have disappeared—run off without their annoying little brother. I sit down under the cord of wood around my neck and cry. Then, I remember my Radio Flyer. With my medals in my wagon (and still around my neck) I win the Muller marathon. All week long, I win every event my older brothers design.

"You're supposed to be watching him, not chasing pussy! Do you really think that's fair?" my dad screamed at my brothers over dinner that night. I didn't care if they chased cats. I had Happy, my big cocker spaniel and a huge stack of fool's gold from my victories in the Muller Summer Games.

Eventually, I let my parents use the stack of Olympic gold medals that lined my bedroom wall as firewood. As my medals started burning, I learned an important lesson some people never learn: life isn't fair.

Get used to it.

• • •

The dwarf is surprised. "You don't want to see the Glockenspiel?"

"Buddy, I don't care how great the guidebook says it is, I'm not staying in Munich to see a clock!"

I'm buying our hotels, the dwarf's buying our travel. I'm not surprised he reserved a cheapo compact rental car at Budget. A Fiesta's fine for him, but I've got legs!

In the garage I start grinning.

"Thanks, buddy!" I love the sleek black lines of our BMW 528i.

"Don't thank me. It's the only car Budget had. I'm paying compact rate." Vroom! "I live in Italy! I know what I'm doing!" Right. Still, Mario Andretti the dwarf driving through Munich traffic is terrifying. He can't see past the horn! Glad I put on my seat belt.

"There it is!" He points to a high stone chimney towering over everything like the spy tower in East Berlin.

"That's the . . . that's the chimney for the burned bodies?"

"Yep! They had to get that smell up high." Five minutes later, we're there. "Dachau?" the dwarf asks the man in the drive-up guard booth. The man looks confused. The dwarf points to the chimney. Then the man chuckles and points away as he speaks German. As we drive out I see the sign. "Gaswerks-Dachau."

"Real men don't ask for directions!" I say as the dwarf pulls up to a tubby old German woman with bleached blond hair.

"Probably why we're lost most of the time!" The dwarf rolls down my window from the Beamer buttons on the driver's side. "Dachau?" he shouts across me. As the woman gives directions she smiles like she's sending us to a party.

"The concentration camp?" I ask as she finishes.

"Yes. Yes." Her English is perfect. So are her directions.

The stone walls of Dachau, about eight feet high and topped with spirals of barbed wire, are low enough that anyone standing on the back of a flatbed truck driving down the road could have seen over the walls. Everyone could see the chimney. They couldn't know what it was for, of course. Except by the smell. Over the wrought-iron entry gate is the camp slogan: *Arbeit Macht Frei.* "Work Makes You Free."

"Dante's phrase is better: 'Abandon all hope, ye who enter here,' " spouts the dwarf. "I know a guy whose uncle died here . . . fell out of the tower."

We hit the showers. Two twenty-by-twenty-foot tiled rooms have shower handles on the wall, drains in the floor, and little Muzak-speaker showerheads in the ceiling. I can see bodies falling as the gas poured out.

In the crematorium every cell in my body tastes sadness, every fiber of my spirit feels oppression, every pore of my soul senses death.

I don't want to be here.

But I have to be.

I have to remember.

• • •

"My God! Look at this! Do you think . . ."

"No," the dwarf says as he hands back the tiny Star of David I found in the gravel. "That's recent." I lay it back where I found it.

In the Dachau museum we look at the lists of prisoners' names, the death orders, the pictures.

Outside, I really see the sculpture for the first time. "That is the most horrendous piece of modern crap I have ever looked at," I tell the dwarf. "Someone should kill the artist. Do the world a favor." Like a nice set of tits on a monster. It's still a monster! Nice statue, but it's still a death camp.

• • •

I like the car. No, I love the car! Until we're on the autobahn and I discover to my horror that the seemingly timid dwarf can only drive as fast as a car will go.

"220!" he screams. "225!" He's gone lunatic. A possessed speed demon. The G-force pushes my face back into the fine leather seat.

"How fast is that in miles?" Damn! It's hard to talk.

"230!" The dwarf screams.

"Watch the road! Not the speedometer!"

"235!"

I'm going to die.

What am I willing to die for? Not money. Not power. If I can only pick one thing, it's not even pussy. It's freedom.

"240!"

As colorful kamikaze bug guts swirl on the windshield, I see a twelve-year-old me serving time in a state school. "You're being too creative!" teachers scream at me.

Too creative? This is more impossible than every restaurant in Chicago serving "Chicago's Best Pizza." How can anyone be too creative in Creative Writing?

Why didn't the teachers just say what they meant and call their class Programming Minds by the Numbers!

"Put a paragraph here!"

"Put a comma there!"

"Induce a coma here!"

"Put more periods everywhere!"

"245!"

My teachers pounded me for too much creativity. How is that possible? I was on a slave ship with a wooden oar for a pencil.

"Put a line here!"

"Put a line there!"

"Put a paragraph here!"

"Not there, stupid!"

"Follow the structure!"

"Follow the pattern!"

"Follow us. Follow us! Follow!"

"Good! Now, write creatively."

"250!"

I wrote what I wanted. Hell! It was Creative Writing class!

"Creative? Yes. But he doesn't follow structure!"

The kids all liked my stories. When laughter drowned out the teachers, they banned me from reading my stories aloud, not just in class but anywhere in the school! "Too disruptive!"

"255!"

Right along with *Catcher in the Rye,* my school banned *The Tale of the Two-Ton Testicle That Destroyed Tokyo,* which I wrote.

When the whole class started imitating my writing, the rule makers realized things were straying dangerously outside the lines of their authority. I was free-and-easy West Berlin. Oppressed kids were flocking to me. The teachers saw no choice. If they couldn't control my creativity, they had to control *me.* So they built a wall around me! They built a wooden isolation cubicle around my desk to protect my classmates from the perilous freedoms I embodied, from the dangerous creativity leaking from my head. I yelled, "Attica! Attica! Attica!"

"260!"

Can people can drive too fast?

Can they drink too much?

Can they be too creative?

Some magazines published my childhood poems.

> Herman the slug was a delightful bug.
> The kind of bug you would have given a hug.
> You can take him out for a burger and malt,
> but go easy on the salt.

Some people still think I'm too creative: the SF county prosecutor, Bill Clinton, the American Red Cross, the Chicago police, Howard Stern;

but I feel good about me. You have to be willing to be proud enough, to believe in yourself enough, to fight conformity. You have to do that in this world. I will never color inside their lines again. Nor should you. It's your head on that pillow at night. If you're all right with it, it's all right!

"266!" the dwarf screams.

We barrel down the two-lane road to Neuschwanstein, crazy King Ludwig's fairy-tale hunting lodge castle in Bavaria. Wagner premiered operas there. Disney copied it and gave it to Cinderella. The Bavarian Alps rise higher as we rocket toward them. I can see elves building cuckoo clocks.

The dwarf pulls out, downshifts, and accelerates to pass a truck on the river-valley road.

"Shit! This truck is pulling two trailers," screams the dwarf with a madman's gaze.

Down the road, the car coming toward us starts flashing its lights. At the instant we pull in front of the truck, the Volvo coming toward us whizzes past.

Terrifying. Exhilarating.

Free! The only time I've felt free in this oppressive country. Maybe that's why BMWs sell so well to these Krauts.

Jut-chinned and hard-assed, my dad's dad was born and raised near here. In America he chased money. Then pussy. When my dad turned six, his daddy ran off with a twenty-year-old. Whenever he came back to visit, Grandma gave him her promise list. As she'd written each item down, she'd promised my dad, "When your father gets home he'll beat you for this!" And Grandpa did—for every item on Grandma's always long list.

Daddy's home!

WHACK!

The dwarf swerves out. A truck cannonballs toward us. He pulls back.

My dad hit my brother Johnny as he grew up, often enough that Johnny swore he would never raise his hand to his kids, and he never has. He has treated his kids with love and respect since they were born. Johnny never tries to control his kids with either threats or violence. Seeing my brother raise his kids this way drove our dad insane.

"You ought to take those kids outside and give 'em a smack to make 'em mind," Dad would say when Johnny would visit and his kids would act like kids.

"Sorry, Dad," Johnny would say in as calm a voice as he could muster while his hands shook with inner tension.

"I'm sad Dad will never see my children," I told Johnny.

He smiled, shook his head, and said, "Don't be too sure."

"What have you done with your life?!" my brother said imitating our dad. "You see that wall?!! You want me to push you through it?!!!"

"Do what I say or I'll beat you" isn't a family value. The Chinese call family the cradle of society. Well, we haven't got society right yet. Maybe it's time to crawl away from the cradle. But to what? I don't want Aldous Huxley's Brave New World, where fetuses gestate in huge glass tubes to be raised by the state when they're born. I want a world where everybody lives in love and peace and freedom. And if you don't agree, I'll dirty nuke your house.

At Neuschwanstein we park our Bavarian Motor Werks car under trees at the foot of the Bavarian Alps across from the Muller Hotel. We hoof it up the hill. As we stand in line for the last English-speaking tour of the day, a gorgeous brunette in a sunflower-yellow dress stands in line for the last French-speaking tour. She flirts with three male companions. I wish I were with her. This woman outshines White Linen.

Ding! Oh, yes! Yes! YES! I want to get laid!

The dwarf is drooling too. He's so short he can smell her musky scent from the source. "She's from Lyon. I know the smell." He licks his lips and smiles up at me. "I dated a trapeze artist from Lyon."

Our tour starts first. Through the magnificent rooms and the round towers we sometimes catch a glimpse of her behind. Neuschwanstein is almost as amazing—with secret compartments, secret doors, a secret passage beside a stream, the little stage where Wagner premiered *Götterdämmerung.*

"Do you think King Ludwig was gay?" asks the dwarf.

"Buddy, if he wasn't, his decorator sure as hell was."

• • •

Up the road from Neuschwanstein, at a roadside restaurant that's part of a farm, I eat a dinner of hunter-beef and spaetzle that's so good I order and eat another. Wow! My dad's first visit to San Francisco was on a warm fall night, the kind of November night the Midwest never knows. His Missouri winter's-comin' coat hung in the closet at my place while we walked down Green Street to Fillmore and turned the corner to the Oyster Bar. Shep shucked slimies while we sipped sake. Twelve oysters down each hatch, Dad ordered and ate another twelve.

Out on Fillmore, a glint in my eye, I say, "We just ate twenty-four oysters, Dad. What's twenty-four times three?" I cock my arm, he slides his through. Behind an invisible Harold Hill from *The Music Man,* we dance down Fillmore drunkenly singing "76 Trombones."

"Let's go see Luv Cheez dance!"

"Dad, I don't really think—"

"Don't be a stick, Erich!"

When I worked at Wild 107, I needed someone to get my stuff on tape. The man I call DJ Luv Cheez begged to help me. Sometimes people surprise you. Cheez turned out to be a wizard with a recorder and an edit machine. Dad had met Luv Cheez in the studio one morning as he watched me do my show. Before Luv Cheez started at Wild 107 he had made his living dancing. When I told Dad, I could tell he had no idea what a male exotic dancer did.

"Cheeze! Congratulations! You were great!" Dad says on the street after Luv Cheez won the competition. "But dammit—that bar was the most disgusting display of human flesh I have ever witnessed in my life. I think the nearest woman was back in Kansas City. No, there are two now. Oh, hell! Are they with each other? Dammit, Cheez, when I watch somebody strip I want to see tassels, and I'm sorry but it takes a woman's titties to get those tassels twirling! What does your girlfriend say about you dancing for men?"

My dad cocks his arm. He wants to walk arm-in-arm with his boy. He doesn't understand the Castro District! My Mancow picture decorates the ass end of every bus in San Francisco. I can't be photographed arm-in-arm with another man in San Fran's gayest area.

I will always regret that decision.

• • •

"I'm ready to leave Germany," I say as I finish another beer and toss the bottle on the floor of a car going faster than Speed Racer's Mach 5, driven by a dwarf who can't even see the horizon. "There's nothing else I need to see or do here."

"Get the map," the dwarf commands. "We're scheduled to turn the car in tomorrow in Stuttgart . . . I don't know . . . 400 kilometers away. We can make Amsterdam by dawn."

If we live.

• • •

In Stuttgart the dwarf convinces two young policewomen to frisk me for fun. Whenever I can pull my focus away from the Uzi on their shoulders with the safety off, these female cops do seem amazingly sexy. Ding! I want to spank them.

As my train to Amsterdam freedom pulls in, I dance down the Stuttgart platform. All my demon teachers are off my back. Truly and completely, the life I live is my own.

I don't have to answer to anyone.

4

Mancow goes Gonzo.

The Amstel Light

"Take us to the Red Light," *I tell our*
Amsterdam cabbie.

"It is 9:17 in the morning," Cabbie says. "No girls in the windows."

"Can you take us?"

"No. I cannot drive through. I take you close for a look."

"Okay!" I'm ready.

"Red Light comes on after dark. There it is."

Across a canal and another street, a seemingly endless line of three- and four-story houses sit on a dead, flat street, six feet above the water. Nothing sleazy. The place looks tidy. Cabbie's right—not a whore in sight.

"I would not come here. Well, for the experience, to see, yes. But not for girls."

"No?"

"No, no. All foreign. And not safe."

"Steal your money?"

"And disease."

SHIT! This is not the way I want my time in Amsterdam to start! Other people may come for van Gogh, Rembrandt, and Rubens, but I want to smoke pot, see porn, have sex, and visit Anne Frank's place.

"For good Dutch girls, very clean, very safe place . . ." He looks out his window and waves to another cabbie, creating an interest-building pause. "Yab Yum," he says. "Private club." Pause. "I can take you."

I just bet he can. I'm not a son of a salesman for nothing. "How much?" I ask.

"Here," Cabbie says as he hands something across the seat. It's brochure time! *Yab Yum* arcs across the cover of a well-thumbed magazine as a dark-haired woman, wearing feathers in her hair, splays across the cover in the best misty *Penthouse* style. Inside, gauzy women with gorgeous snatch ripple off page after page. Female pincushions! Take my money, I think to myself. P. T. Barnum didn't say it, but still, there is a sucker born every minute. "They don't really look this good, do they?"

"I swear." Cabbie holds up his hand like we're in court and his steering wheel is a Bible.

"Are they open now?" I want to ask.

"How much?" It's the dwarf.

"Not expensive."

Great!

"How much?"

"Hundred-fifty guilders for a clean Dutch woman who looks like that."

He can feel we're not in yet.

"And drinks." He's working. "All drinks included. Hundred-fifty guilders."

"How long do you get?"

"Seven inches." Cabbie actually chuckles. "Be with them all night if you want."

"Wow. How much is a hundred and fifty guilders?"

"About a bill," the dwarf says, but Cabbie gets more precise. "Ninety-one dollars forty cents this morning."

I've paid more for girls in Vegas who look like dogs compared to this, I think to myself. Maybe Cabbie hears me.

"Real Dutch girls. Beautiful bodies."

"Are they open?"

"Now? No. Later. I can take you. Yab Yum. Absolutely the best."

Mancow's getting laid! The longest dry patch I've experienced since I turned sixteen and lost my virginity in my 1972 yellow Ford Maverick in perfect working order will soon be over. But Cabbie let something slip.

"So, there are other clubs?" I ask. I know there are. I want to see the brochures! I want to find out all I can. I have three days here before I go back to *Mancow's Morning Madhouse.* Which private club will I visit before I leave?

Where to eat and where to get laid are the two universal tourist questions posed to cabbies. In Amsterdam there's another. I ask it. "Where can I buy grass?"

"Coffee shop every corner," Cabbie responds.

The roller coaster attendant brings the bar down across my lap and smiles. "I think you're going to like this ride."

Under four stories of marble lobby, our Amstel Hotel welcome woman says our room's not ready. Probably other people still humping in it at 9:30 A.M.

"Could you direct us to the nearest coffee shop?" Jesus Christ, dwarf! You don't ask that kind of question in a place like—

"With pleasure," says Marta, explaining our route while walking us to the door. "Would you prefer the cab?" she asks. The doorman opens the cab door at the foot of the stairs. The dwarf looks to me. He takes four steps for every one of mine.

"We've been cooped up all night. I think I'd rather walk."

"It's a lovely morning. Enjoy yourselves. Nice to have you with us, Mr. Muller."

I have never experienced this before. Wearing the rumpled shorts and T-shirt I tried to sleep in, unshaven, unshowered, looking like hell—everyone, from the bellboy who helped us out of the cab in his 1930s Western Union pillbox hat, to the doorman who greeted us in his full-length coat and top hat, to the elegantly suited counterman who welcomed us like his brothers, to this stunning Dutch woman in front of us now—everyone at the Amstel has treated us with class, taste, and panache—like we can really afford to stay here.

Marta's coffee shop isn't open yet. The guy packing his pipe with weed and lighting up at the bus stop (in broad daylight!) directs us to a coffee shop we never find. After a long, mapless walk, the Thursday flea market covering Waterlooplien stumbles into sight: antiques, new clothes, used clothes, crafts, and two girls selling T-shirts who could model for the Yab Yum brochure. A lace bra over a net T-shirt never looked so good—and those shorts!

The blond T-shirt salesgirl's gorgeous brunette friend has a German shepherd. He's a well-trained dog. He's helping unload their truck!

The girls know I'm staring. They enjoy it!

When T-shirt girl's shepherd delivers the final bundle of shirts, he jams his nose at her crotch, into that sweetest of creases, and only gets a smile and sweet words in Dutch. You lucky son of a bitch!

Berlin to Amsterdam—the differences are stark.

Every time I saw a German shepherd in Berlin my mind saw their sharp teeth shredding human flesh. In Amsterdam I wonder which old dogs are getting sex more often than I am. I'm in the longest dry patch I've encountered since I turned sixteen and lost my—

"There!" the dwarf says.

Across the street the pungent odor of burning marijuana greets us. Finally! A coffee shop! The menu lists fourteen different marijuanas. Ten kinds of hash. Prices range from fifteen to forty guilders. How much is that in real money?

"What's the Orange Roughy like?"

As the bearded barman pulls a Tupperware tub from under the counter, Red-eye Rick, the long-haired stoner at the bar with us, starts comparing the Orange Roughy stone to a summer's day or something. Barman pulls off the Tupperware lid to reveal a single orange-hair bud the size of my fist. It's the most beautiful thing I've ever seen. I lift it. I smell it. My God! But from Red-eye Rick's description, it's not the high I want.

"What kind of high do you want?"

People are reading my mind!

"I want something to make me relax, tingle all over, and let me know I've arrived in Amsterdam."

"Well, that's a blend of grass and hash." Red-eye Rick narrows the choices to three.

"And we want to be awake tonight for the Red Light," says the dwarf, startling our red-eyed host who hadn't seen him yet! Barman smiles and pulls up two Tupperware tubs. He opens them and sets them before us.

"Afghan hazel hash and van Gogh red hair—that's what you want. Is that all right?"

"That's great," I say. "We'll take half a gram of each."

"We have a one-gram minimum on the first purchase," Barman says as he hands me a white plastic card with little squares all around the edges. "When you fill this up, the next gram is free."

There's a marijuana/hash stash minimum you have to purchase?

I like this place.

Sure is different than back home in Missouri when I walked into a liquor store for the first time in my life.

"I'd like to buy a pint of Jack Daniel's," I said in my oldest voice.

"Don't I know you, boy? Aren't you John Muller's kid? You want me to tell your dad?"

Wow.

"Buy a fifth and start drinking it here. We have a minimum."

Missouri to Amsterdam—the differences are stark. Ten years of American prison sit openly in front of me on the Greenhouse counter.

"Give us a gram of each," I say as I slide the Greenhouse barman Amex gold for the fifty guilder total. How much is that in real money? It doesn't matter. Guilders are fairy-tale money. Don't leave home without them.

Wanna get high? Well at the Greenhouse in Amsterdam they don't take Visa but they do take American Express!!

Red-eye Rick lights the firecracker twist at the big end of his tight-cone, paper-filter, museum-quality joint. He lets the fuse burn, then hands the bomber to me.

"To your first Amsterdam stone!" says Red-eye Rick.

I pull the smoke deep into my virgin lungs.

"Don't take too much!"

But I'm a greedy American kid smoking legal pot in a legal place for the first time in my life. I cough for five minutes. My mind races. My vision blurs.

—George Washington wrote that he grew enough hemp to make good rope in summer and have good smoke all year. His face should be on the guilder!

—In seventh grade I dried grass clippings in the microwave and sold the result as, well, grass. I wasn't lying. Great idea! No one's going to admit they didn't get stoned. Soon, I bought that pair of Nikes the family couldn't afford.

I really can't catch my breath. I'm gasping for air like my dad did at the end.

—Fifty percent of America's prisoners are doing time for drug offenses. Thank God for all of America's "sheep people." Nancy Reagan's "Just Say No" campaign never mentioned Valium and Prozac!

Rick is a professional. He keeps the Greenhouse customers happy in their joints. He gives lessons in slowing down and rolling firecracker spliffs, just for the right to share your smoke. I'm not complaining. He's good at his job. Just another working stiff, rolling another spliff. I take a smaller hit this time. It tastes fabulous.

"We just got in from Germany," says the dwarf.

"Double bummer! You gotta get laid!"

Amsterdam—the premiere Fuckland attraction in this worldwide carnival we live in. Everybody gets laid in Amsterdam.

"Where do you go to get laid, Rick?" I ask.

"Red Light."

"Is it good?"

"It's great, man! Fifty guilders."

"We heard the Red Light's dangerous." It's the dwarf.

"No! It's not dangerous. It's wonderful. Pick your girl. Pay your fifty. Go inside. Easy."

"Are private clubs better?" I ask.

"More expensive. The Red Light is good."

"What private club would you recommend?"

"Yab Yum is best," Red-eye says so convincingly it's forty minutes before we learn he's never been there.

It's noon. I'm stoned. Time to find the Amstel while my legs still work.

• • •

Our smiling bellboy gives us a comic salute. Our doorman tips his top hat and opens the door with a flourish. Brunette Marta tells us our room is ready but instead of handing over the keys, she takes us to the elevator and up. "Did you find a coffee shop?"

"The Greenhouse."

"Oh! You are lucky! Last year the Greenhouse was voted top coffee shop in all of Amsterdam." She knows we're stoned. I'm hanging cool, but the dwarf grins like an Oz flying monkey, and his eyes are redder than a baboon's ass. When the elevator door opens, Marta leads us down the wide hall. She puts a key card in the door and opens it. "Please," she says. Why is this woman so totally alluring? "Here is your telephone and a list of numbers for all departments of the hotel, but if you just push 5, we can connect you. You have direct overseas dialing. Shall I demonstrate any special features on your fax?"

"We won't be using it. Thanks," I say.

"You are in Amsterdam for pleasure only, then?" That's what it is! She doesn't look away. When our eyes meet, she doesn't hang back. "Coming in Amsterdam for pleasure is always the best way," Marta says.

Does she . . . ? Of course she does. She knows exactly what she's saying. She's playing with me. I like this game.

"In the bathing suite . . ." (she's showing us the bathroom?) ". . . is your Jacuzzi tub. If you have any questions on how . . . no? . . . very good." It *is* a bathing suite! "The tub is designed for two. It can fit three," Marta says as her eyes flick from my candy store to the dwarf's. Jesus! You could fit fifty people in this room. The tub could float a U-boat! The shower room has its own window! My entire Chicago apartment would fit in the toilet stall!

In the living room Marta opens an armoire. "Here is your stereo system, both CDs and tapes. If you don't have any with you, our library is extensive." She has such a great accent. It turns up like the tip of her nose. She opens another armoire. "Here is your video system. We have a large library of tapes also."

Marta's eyes twinkle into mine. She knows I find her attractive. Hell, she finds herself attractive! "Your refrigerator is stocked with champagne, white wine, Dutch beer, soft drinks, and of course . . . Dutch chocolate." The excitement in the dwarf is clear. "Droste invented chocolate," Marta says as she opens a tube of Droste pastilles from the fridge. "They put the butter and sugar together with the cocoa and invented heaven. Or at least one form of it." She offers the Droste to the dwarf. He ain't shy. "Through here is—"

"The biggest bed I have ever seen in my life!" I exclaim.

"I'm glad," Marta smiles. "The spa is on canal level; weight room, Olympic pool, hot tub, sauna, steam room, cold plunge, and loungers by the canal. Press B in the elevator. Robes are here. Feel free to wear them down."

"Marta."

"Yes, Mr. Muller." Damn, I love her accent.

"We need two beds."

"We do?" Marta plays the sexual tension in the room like Metallica's James Hetfield plays guitar. "I'll send someone to take care of it." The instant I think she's making an offer, Marta changes the rhythm. She opens the door to leave. I'm sorry to see her go. Best sex my mind has ever had.

I spin the thermostat as low as it can go.

"Planning to freeze us out?" the dwarf asks from the open living-room window he's framed in, standing on the ledge.

"I like any room I'm in as cold as it gets. Prob'ly a reaction to Missouri summers when all we had was a fan and my dad didn't even want that running. I grew up hot and hated it." As I head to the other open window the dwarf passes the red-eye special joint to me. "And I love long baths," I say. "When I was a kid, four other people always beat on the bathroom door for something. When I'm doing my show, I take a two-hour bath every afternoon. It's my favorite place to write." I take a second hit and pass Red-eye Rick's tight-cone spliff to the dwarf. "Do we all fall in love with the stuff we're kept from doing when we're kids?" I wouldn't mind a bath, but I'm too dirty for one, the tub could take a long time to fill, and stoned as I am, I could drown. I stand a long time under a showerhead the size of a turkey platter. I love how marijuana makes me remember that every cell of my skin is alive. I lather up feeling like I'm taking a shower outside in the tropical rains of Dutch Singapore.

Wearing my ten-pound Amstel robe, I watch the 7,000-cm Phillips TV as I eat Dutch chocolate, drink Dutch beer, and suck on Amsterdam red-eye. After I surf CNN, MTV, two Dutch broadcasts, three German bands, and the English channel, I hit hard-as-it-gets, balls-to-the-wall pornography.

"Come in!" I yell down the hall to the knock on the door.

"You need me for your bed?" As I snap the TV to the next channel I turn to a bubbly blond whose white pantsuit makes her look more like a nurse than a maid. Her eyes twinkle into mine.

"We need the bed divided," I say.

Her eyes flick to the TV. Giggle. I turn back to see a Dutch girl filling up more holes than the woman on the previous channel. I punch the channel forward. One guy, five women—all attached somehow. She giggles. I switch the TV off.

"Amstel beds do not divide. They are very proud of that fact. With no crack, no one can fall through." Giggle. "Did you see the wallpaper?" she asks heading into the bedroom.

Am I just really stoned? Or am I dreaming? On an ivory background, red-etched eighteenth-century couples are in different parts of a scarlet forest. One couple walks down a lane. Another couple kisses in a gazebo. Another couple seems to be undressing each other behind some bush. A woman carves initials inside the heart on a tree trunk. From a bench nearby, her dog watches attentively hoping to see his initials.

Heidi's eyes dance into mine.

Ding! When the Mancow Question finally flashes, Heidi laughs, turns, and leaves. Dammit! No! Does every woman in Amsterdam play with sex this way? As the door closes down the hall, I flip the TV on. Porno is all I have. Then, I hear a giggle. She's still here!

As she strips off her blouse, she giggles. Everything makes her giggle except the things that make her laugh. Her trousers fall to the snowy carpet to reveal a snowy carpet of her own. Heidi pushes me onto the indivisible bed. She giggles as she squirms on top. When I throw her onto the bottom, we fight about what goes where until both of us are laughing. Which is hard with your mouth so full. But she does it! Someone with no idea who I am welcomes me to Amsterdam in a way I will never forget.

Heidi Hoe!

I must be dreaming.

I'm doing *Mancow's Morning Madhouse* twenty years ago. I can't.

The microphone technology won't allow it. And the FCC is setting fire to the studio door.

My dream channel shifts again.

"It's Governor Clinton," I whisper to brother Johnny who's in SF from KC. I'm finally getting it on with Governor Bill. I've been talking to his people for weeks to get this interview. Today, it suddenly looks like Clinton's going to be the Democratic candidate for president. My tape recorder is running. This is a coup for *Mancow's Morning Madhouse.* I can use this tape tomorrow. My time on hold finally ends. I hear the Southern drawl as Bill Clinton comes on the line from his campaign bus.

"Hello. Mancow?"

"Governor Clinton" is all I get to say before Johnny grabs the phone. "All I want to know about is the marijuana and the women."

Click.

"They hung up." Johnny laughs.

"Dammit! That really was Bill Clinton!"

"Yeah. Sure. You can't bullshit me, I'm your brother!"

Channel change.

It's three years later. I'm turning down a President Clinton interview because his staff wants to see all my questions in advance.

This is a strange mental mosaic—and all of it really happened.

My dream shifts channels again, to a picture of Air Force One. A news announcer starts to speak; he sounds like Walter Cronkite.

"Air Force One sat on the tarmac of runway six-niner at Los Angeles International Airport today while a Hollywood celebrity hairdresser . . ."

On my dream TV, I see the hairdresser race to Air Force One like Marilyn rushing to JFK.

Faux Walter speaks again: "Whether the hairdresser visited President Clinton for good old American hanky-panky or just for a British blow job, LAX was snarled for hours as air traffic controllers held all landings and takeoffs until Air Force One left the tarmac ninety minutes later."

I see all the traffic stopped. No planes landing. No planes taking off. While my president gets a blow job? What an abuse of power!

The channel shifts to the *Jerry Springer Show*. The dwarf and I are fighting.

"I think every guy should be allowed their blow jobs, Mancow. Having the blower come to the blowee is a presidential perk."

"No way!" I scream. "President Bill's blow job creamed LAX for hours!"

Finally. A commercial. What's my dad selling this time?

"Packed with *Morning Madhouse* madness—the best Mancow phone scams, priceless parody songs, the weirdest interviews, and the cream of the Mancow parody commercials. Call 1-8NOW-MANCOW or go to www. mancow.com for your very own Mancow CD (not available in stores)."

I want one of those! When did I make a CD? We're back to regular programming before I can figure it out.

It's me on my dream TV. I'm talking to a listener who is pissed as hell. Yesterday, when he heard his dad had been rushed to the hospital, my listener went straight to LAX to hop a plane back to Frisco. But his plane couldn't fly! For five hours it sat on the ground. Five hours Listener could have had with his dad. Instead, he got to the hospital ten minutes after his dad died.

I'm rushing to Kansas City to see my dad after his heart attack, but he isn't pointing at the thermostat and saying "blankets, blankets." He's dead! I missed seeing my dad because a presidential blow job delayed me? I'm furious! Listener's right. No one's mad enough at President Bill!

On my dream TV, White House underlings deny the delay ever happened. The public doesn't buy it, so they blame confused LAX traffic controllers. Just make it up! These spin doctors work to fool all the people this time. I need a hairdresser now! I want a British blow job in my cockpit. I want someone to race out to cut and blow *me*.

Luv Cheez finds me Antoine, the gayest, lispiest hairdresser San Francisco has to offer—a man who's taking hormones to plump his tits but wants Lorena Bobbitt to give him the chop. My God! That would be amazing radio! Instead of clicking his watch and saying he's late, San Francisco's White Rabbit Antoine clicks his scissors and says, "Chop! Chop!"

But where could a regular guy get a public access blow job and fuck things up as much as President Clinton did at LAX?

On my dream TV the Walter Cronkite wannabe speaks again.

"At the height of San Francisco's rush hour commute, with thousands of people on the Bay Bridge trying to get to work from Oakland and the East Bay, San Francisco shock jock Mancow Muller tied up traffic for hours by stopping in midspan for a parody haircut of the one President Clinton received three days ago at Los Angeles International Airport."

This Walter Cronkite is good. All the relevant footage is spliced into his show. There's Chewy my van guy out on the Bay Bridge in Mancow Mobile One. I'm in the studio broadcasting live with Chewy patched through on the portable phone. As Mancow Mobile One pulls to a stop, Chewy opens the side door and Antoine starts the cut.

"Go to the side of the road!" I scream at Chewy.

"There is no side of the road on the Bay Bridge," Chewy deadpans. He's right. Don't know if it's true of every bridge in the world, but on the San Francisco-Oakland Bay Bridge there are only lanes. On the upper deck, all of them head to SF.

Faux Walter's talking again. "It would have been nothing more than a stalled van on a bridge if Mancow Muller hadn't hawked the haircut to hell and gone on *Mancow's Morning Madhouse.*" I didn't count on the popularity of the show, Walter! Or the craziness of the fans. How did Walter get this footage? People slowing down to look at P. T. Barnum's latest on the freeway! The driver of a semi swerves across three lanes of traffic to get a better view! Things plummet downhill from there.

"Chewy! Get the hell out of there!" And Chewy does.

"In ninety seconds, it was over," says the talking hairdo on TV. "But as Mancow Mobile One rolled on, the Bay Bridge was left in chaos." The liberal media blew it way out of proportion. But I had just cluster-pumped the busiest bridge in the world! Chaos!

There's my Wild 107 station manager; he suddenly looks like John Wayne. "Get out of Dodge, pilgrim."

Outside I push through 100 reporters to my 1972 yellow Ford Maverick in perfect working order. I shoot home to hide out. Fat chance.

There's an Eye in the Sky following me. Seven—count them, seven—TV news vans block all access to Green Street. Thirty reporters mill outside my door. This story is hot! I'm hot!

I hang a U-ie. At SFO I hop a plane to LAX, scene of the original crime. I hide out in a cheap motel. Different faux Walters appear on the tiny black-and-white TV channels. "Not since the time Delilah sheared Samson has there been a more famous haircut than the one performed today on *Mancow's Morning Madhouse* when Mancow Muller shut down the San Francisco-Oakland Bay Bridge."

"You have to be joking, Walter! Mancow Mobile One stopped for ninety seconds! President Bill blocked traffic for ninety minutes!" God! I'm shouting at a TV! If I had a gun I'd pull an Elvis and shoot the screen. Letterman and Leno have a heyday over "this Mancow kid."

After my Wild 107 boss disclaims all knowledge of the Mancow Bay Bridge mission, Walter interviews an LAX traffic controller. "We held all landings to protect the president from any possible repeat of the runway accident here several months ago," the controller says.

Walter shows the accident. As a landing plane touches down, its wing slams into a 747 parked on an LAX runway. The parked plane bursts into flames to cremate every one of the 218 people on board! Thank you, Walter. LAX traffic controllers were protecting President Clinton from getting burned for a blow job! How did *that* story disappear?

Walter signs off: "And that's the way it is, May 26, 1993."

Next on my dream TV, I watch my brother Johnny close me up in the sofa bed in our Raytown, Missouri, family room like he used to. He farts at me through the cushions.

It's the next morning. I'm walking to breakfast. I pass an L.A. news-stand with 1,000 different papers. The headline "Wacky DJ Stunt" jumps from the *Chicago Tribune.* "Bay Bridge Closed by DJ Stunt" screams the just arrived Providence, Rhode Island, paper. The *Kansas City Star,* the *Des Moines Dispatch Courier,* the *Virginia Beach Sentinel*—on *every* paper the Bay Bridge thing is the top story! I am stunned. A Japanese paper has a six-column picture of Bay Bridge traffic under last night's incomprehensible Tokyo headline. No doubt about it! Mancow "closing down" the Bay Bridge was a worldwide media firestorm. My God! Does everything in the news get this badly misreported? They're sensational-izing everything! Just make it up! Sensational shit sells papers! The so-called reputable papers are further out there than the *Star.* People got madder at me than they did at President Clintler. They didn't charge Bubba with a felony. Our oversexed president wasn't fined, put on pro-bation, and required to perform 100 hours of community service. I was, though. The L.A. county prosecutor didn't go after President Bill for five million bucks. The IRS didn't suddenly decide he needed an audit. Bill got the blow job and his hair looked good. The rebel Mancow got his ass whipped hard by the politicos and the liberal media in bed with the gov-ernment. Ah hell! It's all water under the Bay Bridge.

My dream channels flip to more recent history.

"Thank you," Johnny says. "Really that means a lot." Everybody's call-ing expressing sympathy and solidarity. They've heard about our dad. "It's for you," Johnny says as he hands me the phone. "It's Roger Clinton."

"Wow. My bud! Nice of you to call," I like Roger Clinton. He's been on the show a bunch. We've done things together he's never done with his brother. We've inhaled. After we talk awhile, Roger hands the phone to someone else. "This is Bill Clinton, Mancow. I'm sorry to hear about your dad. It's a terrible loss even when sons don't like their fathers, and I know you loved yours a lot. I'm sorry he's gone."

"President Clinton sends all of us his condolences," I tell the family. This time Johnny believes me.

Wake up!

My dream channel shifts.

I'm having lunch with Robert Feder, radio writer for the *Chicago Sun-Times.* He's calling Mancow a Falstaff Everyman for a new generation. What does he mean?

"Robert, I can't structure every minute of my show before I do it, I don't have the time! Every day I go into the studio excited about what's coming and worrying about what won't work. Then I just move like hell. My job is to wake people up. Keep them awake. Snoozing through life is not where it's at. This is not a dress rehearsal!"

Wake up!

Wake up, America!

Wake up, Mancow!

"Dammit, I'm awake!" The beating on my arm stops.

"Time for some poooosie," says the dwarf in a faux Mexican accent. Outside the sky has darkened to a deep party blue. I get out of a bed big enough for six with the sail-sized sheet wrapped around me. The wallpaper vaguely reminds me of a laughing milkmaid who came before my dreams went sour.

As we head out to party, I pull the door shut behind us. I turn the little DO NOT DISTURB sign over so now it reads (in four different languages) MAID SERVICE, PLEASE.

As I remember the best maid service I have ever had in any language, I laugh.

"I have brought the extra bed for your room, Mr. Muller," says a middle-aged woman pushing a roll-away bed down the corridor. She wears a starched white skirt and blouse with green-and-gold Amstel piping. "Where's our other maid?" I ask.

"You have no other maid," she replies.

Heidi come back!

• • •

"Do you dream when you sleep?" I ask the dwarf.

"Doesn't everybody?"

"My dad dreamed once in his whole life. Like five years ago. It freaked him out. I sat on the end of the bed while he talked about it. He thought something supernatural had just gone on. Weird. I dream a lot. Always very fluid. Jimmy Buffett says he often wakes up needing a rest from all that went on in his dreams. That happens to me. Sometimes, I dream I'm a dream, that there's this alien that lives for a billion years, and a night's sleep for this being is like eighty earth years, and my whole life is just part of that alien's really elaborate dream."

"*Dallas*—last show of the eighth season," says the dwarf, "J. R. Ewing gets shot. All summer long America tries to figure out who shot J.R."

"Man, that's lifetimes ago. Every molecule in my body is different now. But I remember. For the whole next season of *Dallas*, every character in the show, and everybody in America, tried to figure out who shot J.R."

"You remember who did it?"

"Nobody does."

"That's right," the dwarf agrees. "Everything, from the beginning of the show where J.R. got shot, was just a Bobby Ewing dream!"

"America was mad. Everybody felt cheated. 'You mean this whole year of *Dallas* was just a dream?' Wake up, America! Everything on television is just somebody's dream!"

"Sometimes I'm convinced I'm just a character in somebody else's giant show," says the dwarf, "one I know nothing about."

"Yeah? Well, I played lots of parts as a kid. In college I was cast in CMSU's production of *The Diary of Anne Frank*. The night before we opened, someone torched the theater. Burned a million-dollar building to the ground. A lot of us believed it was neo-Nazi jag-offs. Huh. Anne Frank wasn't safe here in Amsterdam and wasn't safe fifty years later in Warrensburg, Missouri. I guess man still fears people and ideas that look different—even a play."

"Or a radio show."

"I've never bought into that fear. I want to see the attic where Anne Frank hid until the Nazis found her and concentrated her teenage body into part of their final solution."

"The Anne Frank house is closed this time of night," Cabbie to the Red Light says. "But Yab Yum is open."

I miss the connection.

Are all the rooms at Yab Yum tiny and secret?

Are all the girls fourteen?

"If Anne Frank were alive she'd be pushing seventy-five, along with

Marilyn, James Dean, Martin Luther King Jr., and Jackie O." It's the dwarf.

"From here you must walk to the Red Light," Cabbie says. "Five blocks."

The square and the streets ahead shimmer with moving humanity.

"That's a lot of people!"

"There will be more," Cabbie says. "Now is only 10:15."

Germany to Amsterdam—the differences are stark.

Only exhausted waitresses are still awake in Munich.

How some describe listening to *Mancow's Morning Madhouse.*

Red Light Means GO!

From behind plateglass windows, women in sleazy underwear beckon you into their boudoirs like sirens. The first Red Light woman I see is a beautiful Asian in burgundy panties and bra standing in a picture window. There's a sparkle in her eyes as they meet mine. I'm ready! But another man goes inside. I can see three other windows. A Nordic blonde with jumbo puppies smiles into my eyes, then down at my crotch. One window has its curtains closed. A petite blond in lacy salmon panties and bra stands in the next window over. A man goes to her door, she moves from her window to open it.

"How much?" he asks.

"Fifty guilders," she says. The man goes inside.

I look to the dwarf. "About thirty bucks, Mancow," he says.

We walk the street. The other Asian women wear white lingerie that glows bright in the UV lights of their rooms. Most of the blondes wear black. All the women wave, purse their lips, and touch their bellies and thighs. Dammit, I'm ready. All these women look better than lime-green blondie and they're less than half the price. But the dwarf wants to see the whole fucking district first, so we walk the ten square blocks of the Red Light. For five blocks along one side of the canal, five blocks along the other, a block deep on the side streets, every race and kind of woman shows her wares in the windows like smiling cuts of beef. Some of it prime. I'm hungry.

Prices range from fifty guilders for pretty and interested women down to thirty-five guilders for dogtown bitches with attitude. Jammed between the "woman windows" along the canal are half a dozen coffee shops, nine porno stores, and twelve different live-show theaters for people who want to get their rocks off watching other people screw instead of doing it themselves.

"Sleaze and filth, gentlemen. Sleaze and filth, all day, everyday."

"Come on in and watch the action. Two, three, and four people at it at once. What do you think about snakes?"

"You look like an educated man, professor . . ."

Each in their own way, twelve different hawkers pitch Dr. Amsterdam's feel-good snake-oil remedy for all that ails you. They give their spiels in English, German, or French, depending on who they think you are. I don't like the one who starts speaking to me in German—dammit, I'm an American! Some hawkers speak Japanese. I don't want a show. I want a woman. But first, I want to feel my body tingle.

As we settle into a Red Light coffee shop couch, Bob Marley sings "No Woman, No Cry." We order brewskies and puff on a not-too-spiffy spliff the dwarf rolls with his fingers that resemble my toes.

Brainflash!

—Phone scam idea: Call a window installer wanting Windows for my computer.

We head across the canal back to the first side street we saw. Burgundy Thai girl pulls me with come-hither looks and drop-your-load-here lips. I dew. She's hot. She smiles. I go to her door. She opens up. I go inside. She pulls the curtains across her door and window. I pull out fifty fairy-tale guilders. She takes my money. She takes my dick. She pushes up my T-shirt and kisses my nipples with soft Thai lips and a softer tongue. She pushes my fairy-tale bill into the slit of a box. I kick off my sandals and drop my shorts. She crosses to the wide single bed against the wall. I'm right behind her. I could come just watching that Burgundy Thai ass move. But I don't have to. She pats the bed. I lie down. Soft skin of her breasts and nipples slides along my face, into my mouth. Long black hair tickles my chest and belly, her mouth follows. "Mmm," she says, finding my fleshy Dr. Evil doll at stiff attention. She licks the head. She licks the shaft. She takes me into her mouth. Wait a minute, what about—she rips a packet open, sets the condom on her lips, and slides the raincoat over me with her mouth!

"Blow job? Or pussy?" she asks.

"I thought this was a package deal!"

"Both? Fine," she purrs.

Whoa! No hard sell here. I get whatever I want.

"We fucky," I say as I ease off her lacy panties. She lies on her back on the bed and pulls me in. I feel soft breasts under mine, I feel warm breath in my ear. She closes the door to Aladdin's cave and squeezes. Man, can she milk the Cow!

I'm doing a Thai girl in Amsterdam!

Happy, panting, and satisfied, I roll off my soft-skinned whore. She gets up, goes to a basin, invites me over. While she washes she points to a little trash can. I drop my raincoat in on top of fifty others. She washes me off and towels me dry. As she puts on her burgundy panties and bra, I put my clothes on. I walk into the Amsterdam street, one hole closer to feeling whole. She opens her curtains, stands in her window, looks at me, and smiles. Then she looks at other men.

"You oughta try this Thai girl out," I tell the dwarf. "Wow! But bring a stepladder." While the dwarf considers, another man succumbs to soft Thai charms and walks through the door to Bangkok.

All right! The dwarf bought a pipe.

After a bowl of smoke canal-side, I'm ready for number two! I drop trou' and fifty guilders for a big Nordic blonde to wrap her lips around me. The dwarf buys my leftover Thai food.

I feel great!

Then the handcuffs, black masks, and ball gags in a Red Light porno store pull my hazy mind back to thoughts of Mrs. Guttman—the most evil, damaging, and despicable person to ever enter my life. She claimed to be a teacher but really she was a gangster, a humiliating destroyer, a terrorist in pearls—Hitler in a dress. Her Auschwitz, Dachau, Buchenwald was in small-town Missouri. Most people called it an elementary school when asked but disclaimed all knowledge of the horrors that went on there. Is there anything more frightening than an evil teacher with tenure?

I entered fourth grade as a normal kid named Matthew Erich Muller. Before fourth grade was over, that person was dead and some other person entirely had totally taken his place. With the casual brutal power of an omnipotent prison guard, Mrs. Guttman crushed me, purposely destroyed me, shamed me every single day in front of all my peers.

I was bad with numbers, which became clear to Mrs. Guttman and to everyone in class on the very first "math race" day. I have no idea who she called to the front of the class first, but I know I was dreading the moment she'd call on me. In a Mrs. Guttman math race, students were called in front of the class to solve a mathematical problem. You had just so long to solve it. If you solved it, you got to sit down. If you didn't get the answer, then someone else came up in front of the class as well, and then the race was on because only the person who solved it first could go back to his desk and sit down. If neither could solve the problem in time, both had to stay in front of the class and keep trying until someone got it right—in the given amount of time and faster than everyone else. Mrs. Guttman put me on a competition treadmill I've been on ever since.

As fourth grade started, one thing frightened me even more than math: being in front of people. "What is four billion six hundred and sixty-nine divided by minus four?" was how each of the problems sounded—even before you added the whole class staring bullets through my back as I stood at the chalkboard. On that very first math race day, Erich Muller was the last child to take his seat, and not because he had gotten one right but because he never could. The next day, Mrs. Guttman ran another math race. I didn't have time to be too afraid. I was the first one called—and again, the last to sit down. The next day, Mrs. Guttman called on me first again. Every other child successfully solved a problem. But I could not. Crippled in my fear, I was the last to sit again.

I went to Mrs. Guttman and asked her, through my tears, to please let me not participate. The next day, Mrs. Guttman gave me a huge cheeky grin and called on me first again. I was last to sit down. I went to her again. I begged her to call on me later. She smiled like she liked my begging. The next day my name was the first on her lips. Again I utterly failed.

Mercifully, the next day was Saturday. I had lived through my first week in hell.

On Monday Mrs. Guttman called on me first again, and on Tuesday and Wednesday. A last tearful begging brought no relief. On Thursday she called on me first again. And Friday. And then on Monday. Always, I was the last to sit down. I worked hard to solve the problems, ashamed of being stupid, crushed by this constant ridicule in front of all my friends. It didn't make any difference. Every single day this devil-teacher ran another math race and called on me first. Nothing I could ever do kept me from being the very last kid in the class to sit down. Every single day the whole class beat me. Masses are asses. The Erich Muller that was, laid dying.

• • •

There should be Nuremburg trials for teachers like Mrs. Guttman, for crimes against children, for crimes against the world, for torturing human spirits and damaging mankind. They'll slaughter whatever spirits they want, to prove they have the power, to demonstrate control.

"I have the power, you wormy sack of shit. Squirm when I say squirm."

Standing in a porno store in Amsterdam, tears roll down my cheeks.

After months of constant humiliation in Mrs. Guttman's fourth-grade class, something inside snapped. What could I possibly lose? I was completely destroyed already. I accepted the fact I'd be called up first and accepted as well that I wouldn't sit down until after the math race was over. Since I knew I was going to lose, I stopped even trying to compete. I showed up at the starting blocks and when the gun went off, I started doing dances while the others ran the race. She could humiliate me if she wanted to, but she couldn't make me run. I stopped even thinking of math and wrote down fantastical answers that were just as wrong as the ones I'd worked so hard to get right all those months.

I remember the very first time I heard someone giggle behind me while I was up at the chalkboard. Every molecule in me responded. I'd just been reborn. The happy face I had drawn brought the laugh—and what is a happy face but an expressive zero? I gained courage. I started outlining my hand. I made a turkey out of it. The next day I outlined my hand giving Mrs. Guttman the finger. Breasts, a penis, an anarchy symbol, and lots more followed. Up in front of the class, I was finally winning.

I had the jokes erased before she could see them, but even so, Mrs. Guttman decided I needed punishment. She sent me up for a spanking. I got spanked most days after that until school ended. It made me more courageous. The pain became a rush. Spanking started to sound like clapping. Humiliating math race time slowly became my one-man show behind Mrs. Guttman's back. (My show still goes on behind her back.) I didn't want to sit down anymore. I wanted to get up. My ass still hurt from yesterday's punishments. A vicious cycle. But I had stolen her captive audience for up to twenty minutes every single day. She boiled at the core. I won—except I still have trouble balancing my checkbook.

At the start of Erich Muller's fourth-grade class I had been a pretty normal kid, pretty square and pretty straight—a midwestern boy of average stature, if that. By Christmas I had scabs on my nose from the treadmill. I had followed the rules. I had stayed out of trouble. But I could not follow Mrs. Guttman's rules so I rewrote her rule book. My Comedy Club in front of the class became my only goal. At night I spent more time thinking up ways to entertain the class the next day than on all of my homework combined.

Over Easter vacation I entered a chrysalis state. By the time school started again, the worm I had been had become a whole new creature. It was spring, time to come out—like the flowers—in bright and amazing colors. Erich Muller had been murdered. Mrs. Guttman had played Dr. Frankenstein. But I unleashed the monster on the world. The villagers would never be the same. I couldn't realize until after it fully incarnated, but on April 17 of Mrs. Guttman's fourth-grade class, "Mancow" walked the earth.

In school I wore the best (and strangest) outfits Goodwill could sell me for five bucks a week. I was a kid. I dressed like a cut-rate Sammy Davis Jr. The school administration wasn't fond of my new look or my new me, which is why I got shipped off to Christian school the following year.

$$\bullet \quad \bullet \quad \bullet$$

"How much money do we have?"

"You have eighty guilders," the dwarf says as he counts left-pocket bills. "Got a math problem for you."

"No way, buddy!"

"Mancow is in Amsterdam with eighty fairy-tale guilders. A woman costs fifty guilders. Pot costs eighteen guilders. You can get a good beer for four guilders. How good a time can Mancow have?"

"Fucking fantastic!!!"

"See! Math can be easy, Mancow."

"From my mom's side of the family, I have Cherokee blood. Cherokee lovers were legendary. Why? Because when a Cherokee boy started getting hard a widow of the tribe took him and taught him how to love a woman by patient practice. Sexual love was beautiful, evidence of the Great Spirit moving between two fleshly forms."

As I toke deep on our peace pipe, I realize I want a Cuban!

"So, what are you going to do? Knock on every door until you find one? Where's Irma when you need her?" asks the dwarf.

Irma! God. The show.

"Dammit! I mean a cigar! Cubans are legal here. You can buy them in stores."

Twenty minutes after the dwarf interrupts a sex-show hawker to get directions, we sit in a Red Light coffee shop toking fresh Monte Cristos like Che Guevara.

"Be My Lover" blasts through the sound system. Thank you, Jesus! Finally, a blessed break from the endless Bob Marley soundtrack.

Day Two

"Did you bring the pipe?"

"This is a steam room, Mancow. A flare wouldn't light in here."

"Feels good, doesn't it?"

"Ever do your show stoned?"

"Once, a long time ago. Man, I thought it was the coolest show ever until I heard the tape." As all my pores open at once, my hot body drips with sweat. I feel the salt in my eyes.

"I'm getting hot down here," cries the dwarf.

"Man, don't leave, the steam's just starting to work."

Hans, who runs the spa in the basement of the Amstel, opens the steam room door. "Would be willing to have a woman join, maybe?" he asks.

"Of course," I respond. Why they call this a basement I don't know, because the whole wall beside the Olympic pool is glass and looks straight out on the river.

"I'm doing the cold plunge."

"Don't drown, dwarf!"

"I'll meet you in the Jacuzzi or outside by the canal." The dwarf opens the door and he's gone.

All that door opening let out a lot of steam. I pull the towel I'm sitting on up over my legs and privates. The woman enters. She has a bath towel wrapped around her in that amazingly sexy way. How do designers know exactly how wide a towel has to be to cover a woman's breasts and then hang down just enough to cover her whisker biscuit? The woman's skin reminds me of my *Madhouse* female sidekick, Irma. No, it's not her skin. It's her tits. Double-Ds stare me down like they do every morning on the show. Those puppies hold that woman's towel eight inches out from her thighs—about the same distance my towel has risen off my lap. The woman sits. We smile at each other. Steam starts filling the room.

"Where are you from?"

"Barthelona." Ah, that Catalán accent. "You know about Barthelona? Eeth a crathy town." Before she disappears in the mists, Barcelona woman opens her towel. I open mine. Barcelona smiles. Ding! The Mancow Question flashes. A gospel jingle for the show explodes in my brain.

> Are you ready for the Mancow?
> Ready as I can be.
> Hey. Hey. Are you ready for the MAAANcow?

● ● ●

"I love this town! I'm not afraid of much anyplace, but here I'm not afraid of anything," I say as the dwarf and I sit canal-side with the Amstel gym at our backs. "You saw *Fearless*, right?" The dwarf nods as he tokes. "I want to see *Fearless* for the first time again. I was walking down the street in San Francisco when I looked up and saw *Fearless* on the marquee. How could there be a film I knew nothing about? Jeff Bridges was in the film. I was interviewing Jeff on the show in, like, four days. No such thing as coincidence. I went in to see the film. I walked out stunned. How can you make a movie about a guy who survives a plane crash and not have it be about death? But it's not. It's about life, about what it's like to live without fear. It's about suddenly seeing there's no guarantee we will live to see tomorrow—so get the fuck on with life!"

"Let's go see van Gogh." It's the dwarf.

We walk to Amsterdam's Rijksmuseum. The cold stone building assaults the warmth of the day. The lobby is as far as we get. Two guys in uniforms sell tickets inside a glass booth that makes them look like they work in a bank that's been robbed one time too many. The dwarf's Butch, and I'm Sundance.

Life is a flicker.

When life ends, it's like a library has just been burned to the ground, a library full of volumes it took a whole lifetime to write. We think we know that library, but we don't. We look at the shell and say, Yeah, that's my dad, but we know nothing of what's inside.

All those volumes, all those histories, all those names, dates, adventures, feelings, and relationships—the whole damn library with all its contents—burned to the ground when he died.

I thought I knew him, but I didn't know him at seventeen when he met the fourteen-year-old girl who would one day become my mom. I didn't know him at six when his dad ran out on him. I didn't know him when he went to join the Marines to fight in Korea, when the man with the biggest heart I've ever known got rejected because of his bad heart. I lived with the man who railed at my brothers for not wanting to kill America's enemies in Vietnam—but I didn't know him.

I entered my father's life in room thirty-four of the John Muller Library. Not page thirty-four. Not chapter thirty-four. Not volume thirty-four. Not even shelf thirty-four. Thirty-three rooms had already been built, one for each year my dad lived before I was even born. The whole vast collection, all those intricate stories, burned to the ground when he died. All disks erased. As if they never existed.

I am only a sequel to the man. A Xerox is never as strong as the original.

As we leave the tomb of van Gogh's body of work, I realize this whole bank-church-museum was built for a guy who didn't fit in. Who never fit in. Vincent van Gogh got thrown into an insane asylum and never made a guilder from his paintings. Today we call him a genius, a visionary, a prophet of a whole new way of seeing. Why? Because we're going crazy. In today's psyche (and marketplace), this guy's a saint. People pay phat for his relics. A renegade. An iconoclast. A crazy man.

Those who have ears, let them hear.

When I interviewed Jeff Bridges on *Mancow's Morning Madhouse,* I knew his dad, Lloyd, was sick. Dying. You can see how frail he is in *Blown Away* when Tommy Lee Jones trusses a bomb to him, and Jeff has to walk away and let his dad blow up and scatter into a thousand pieces. That was coming for both of us in real life, and we hated not being able to do anything to help save our dads. Deal with it! We talked about it on the show. Lloyd Bridges was ahead of his time—out there on the edge—like my dad. *Sea Hunt, Roots.* Picking the wrong day to stop smoking, drinking, and sniffing glue in *Airplane!* Seeing the man who was omnipotent at the start of your life becoming weak and feeble brings death to your front door, makes you realize how brief a time fifty or even eighty years really is. It forces awareness of how much, and how little, each life really means in the grand scheme of things—and, if you're very lucky, makes you fearless for a time.

We cab as close as we can get to the Red Light. The streets are full. Outside restaurants are packed with people drinking beer. Coffee shops are filled with smokers. Open-air corner bakeries and pizza and gyro places work to wake up your belly through your nose. In a porno shop I look through the hundreds of magazines showing women with animals—dogs, eels, and horses are the favorites. It's weird. I move up a shelf to S&M and bondage mags that would please the Marquis de Sade. Then I pull down a magazine from the highest shelf. "Dude! Have you seen these?"

"What is it?"

"Kiddie porn."

We leaf through the magazines together. Mostly it's just naked girls and boys, like photos taken at a nudist camp, but there's some other shit there that turns my stomach. I hate all rules. And I love Amsterdam's freedoms. But I hate that these magazines even exist! They're revolting!

"I dated a girl in college," I tell the dwarf as we suck down smoke and Heinekens in a coffee shop close to the Red Light. "Man, we had fun getting to that first time the shirt comes off and the bra comes open. Pop! Snap! Boing! Boing! Is there anything like that feeling of freedom the female breasts experience as that bra unharnesses?

"Whenever I move down to lick some tit, I always, always nibble, I just can't help myself. 'Harder,' Monica moans. I oblige. 'Harder!' Okay, honest to God, biting it is. When my hand snakes down to that velvety ax wound she's sopping-mop wet, ready, willing, and—

" 'Wait,' Monica says. In the faint light of a crescent moon, she slides off my pants, drops hers to her ankles, and lays across my lap on the couch. 'Spank me,' she says. All right! Spanking was something I'd always wanted to do. I gave her a nice swat! 'Harder.' Swat!! 'Mmmm. Harder.' SWat!!! 'Ahh yes. Again.' SWAt!!!! 'Mmmm. Yes! Harder!' SWAT!!!!!

" 'Take me!' she cried, rolling off me onto the carpet. You know me— I'm in there hard! After awhile I get my elbows on the floor and push myself up enough to get my fingers back on her breasts. 'Pinch them! Harder! Yes! Oh yes!' she pants. An excited woman excites me, and this girl is excited! She fights and bites and scratches while I ram and pinch and kiss. 'Yes,' she's moaning, 'Yes. Yes. Yes! Oh! Hit me! Make a fist and punch me. Hard! Oh please! Oh God! Hit me!' "

"God, Mancow, did you do it?" the dwarf asks as I take a long drag on the pipe. "You didn't. Did you?"

"Of course not! I couldn't hit a woman! But I pinched those nipples like vise grips while she beat the floor with her hands and feet until every muscle in her surged in a rhythmic wave and I exploded as well."

"Great story."

"There's more. When I woke up at dawn I could see my sweetie's creamy breasts were black-and-blue. Fuck! I thought, I didn't do that. It's what she wanted, but damn! Does she have a hundred other lovers, all more violent than me? Does she slam her tits in car doors for fun? What? When I ask about her breasts, she gets up to make us coffee. Christ! Her butt's black-and-blue as well! How did violence get mixed up with the pleasures of sex in this practicing Christian choirgirl?"

I take a long toke on the pipe. "You know, I'm beginning to hate Bob Marley," I say as the Saint of Amsterdam sings "I Shot the Sheriff."

"Dammit, Mancow! Tell me the punch line!"

"Weeks pass. Finally, Monica tells me that since she was twelve her father beat her up every time he fucked her."

"Jesus!"

Bob Marley starts singing, "Get Up Stand Up." We get up and leave.

The red lights aren't as bright in the afternoon. My burgundy Thai sweetie stands in her window. There's a very nice tingle to my body. I go in for twenty minutes. Mine is the first raincoat in her trash can today. Why does that make me feel good?

We cab it to the Leidseplein for rijsttafel. Indonesian food. Fourteen courses.

As the dwarf lights up in the open-air restaurant, other patrons look down on him with hard disapproval. Huh?

"Why," I ask, "after dating a woman for a couple weeks, does she suddenly want to know my whole day's itinerary? Where I'm going to be. What I'm going to do. Where I'm going to eat. Where does this idea that they own me suddenly come from? Honey, you're my girlfriend, not my jailer. It's a relationship, not a prison. You remember my bulldog Max? Why can't women be more like . . . gimme your pen!" I write on my napkin:

> Why can't women be more like bulldogs?
> All my bulldog wants is to be loved.
> My bulldog never pouts.
> My bulldog doesn't sulk.
> All my bulldog wants is to bury his head in my lap.
> And he loves heavy petting.

No games.

Just ass wagging

And love whenever I need it.

Day Three

I've been listening to the Kinks CDs I bought in Berlin for an hour: "Apeman," "Dead End Streets," "Celluloid Heroes," "Lola." I listen to "Days" three times. When the dwarf finally stirs, I turn up our Amstel Hotel sound system to proper, wall-shaking volume.

"Pull out your sleepy-time earplugs," I shout. "Time you got to know the Kinks! This is 'I'm Not Like Everybody Else.' "

"Sounds like your theme song," the dwarf says after listening.

"I tell you, buddy, Ray Davies and the Kinks are my voice. They speak for me."

"Mancow, you're not like *anybody* else."

"Thanks! That's a hell of a compliment. Okay. Next. This is sweet and so melancholy. Ray wrote this for his favorite sister, Rene, who was like twenty years older than he was and taught him piano. She knew she had a bad heart but she loved to dance. On June twenty-first, our mutual birthday, Ray Davies turned thirteen, learned Rene's heart had exploded on the dance floor the night before, and opened the present she'd bought him—his first guitar. This is *'Don't Forget to Dance.'* "

> You look out of your window, into the night
> It could be rain, could be snow,
> But it can't feel as cold as you're feeling inside.
> And all of your friends are either married, vanished, or just left alone.
> But that's no reason to just stop living.
> That's no excuse to just give in to a sad and lonely heart.
> Don't forget to dance. Don't forget to smile.
> Don't forget to dance. You can forget it for a while.

"When my dad knew death was coming, he put his house in order. Three months before he died, he gave me the Japanese flag my uncle brought back from the war. On some South Pacific island, a whole platoon finger-painted their names on the flag with their own blood. Twenty-two Japanese soldiers committed hari-kari as Americans took the island. He gave me his shrunken head too. It really used to be somebody's head, now shrunk down to the size of my fist. No eyes. Leathery skin. Lips sewn together. Like people who voted for Bill Clinton."

"You know why cannibals don't eat clowns?"

"They taste funny."

"Is there any joke in the world you don't know, Mancow?"

"No. After he died I found all the tapes of my dad and me playing radio. I never knew he had them, but there they all were, labeled and sitting in the stereo cabinet where they never were before. Lots of them."

My tongue tastes salt as I lick my lips . . . again.

"Sometimes I get afraid the art of communication is dying. It's not something kids get taught anymore. As we move more and more toward an electrified, computerized society, our ability to communicate is weakening. We sit around in our La-Z-Boy recliners holding our remotes instead of getting outside and living. We're evolving to a point where people will be born with remotes in their hands—a flesh remote. You remember the butt-headed people who could only communicate by blinking in the old *Star Trek* series? 'The Cage' was the name of that episode. That's where we're headed. Already we talk less and less. Kids today cannot communicate as well as we did."

"But with all the input they're getting, they might be smarter."

"Probably. But verbal communication skills are dying. We're losing them to the computer. We're losing them to Game Boys. We're losing them to television. Talking to a fifteen-year-old is frightening! They just can't talk. In the future the individual who can talk will be worth his weight in gold.

"The research guy at KDON radio in Salinas talked better to computers than to human beings. Instead of going out to the fields at 6 A.M. to find out what workers were listening to, he brought in test groups to listen to my show at 6 P.M. No wonder they didn't like it. Neither did my boss. They didn't understand emotion.

"We're people, dammit! Not machines! We *emote*! In the radio business today, a song doesn't get on the air unless it's tested, researched, put in the computer, and spit out. Nobody just hears a song and says, 'Wow, that's a good song!' The station sets up a test group to ask five hundred other people what they think. They check what other stations are playing. Then they sit around asking why radio's so boring today. It's boring because no one acts from the gut! No one's feeling! Radio is an art—not a science. Sure, you want to do the research. You want to study the product. You want to visualize. You want to merchandise. You want to capitalize. But you also want to empathize! Dammit! You have to feel! Joseph Campbell once told me, 'Follow your bliss!' You can't do that if you can't feel. Man is destroying his instinct!"

We do another steambath, another cold plunge. As I get a full-body massage, the dwarf heads up to write. Probably more relaxed than I've ever been in my life, I hit the room an hour later.

It's later afternoon. We're ready. Marta says good-bye as we walk through the Amstel lobby. Her smile, her outfit, her eyes, all sparkle. The smiling doorman in his fairy-green coat with gold piping opens the Amstel door. The grinning bellboy in his pillbox hat opens the taxi door.

"Can you recommend a private club?"

"Yab Yum is best," Cabbie says, handing the big brochure over the seat.

"Let's go," I say. "How much?"

"For a hundred fifty guilders you can drink with the girls as long as you want—and, well, you know."

I thought I did. Except I didn't.

Cabbie pulls up to an anonymous canal-side row house. A valet opens the taxi door and escorts us up ten steps to a big black door with a huge gold knob and knocker. Valet rings the bell.

"Welcome to Yab Yum," the fat man in the bad suit says as we enter a true bordello lobby—red carpet on the floor, red velvet on the walls. Huh. Not a single sensuous beauty in sight, just an old blond broad in a carnie ticket booth and the fat man.

"How much is it?" I ask.

"One hundred and fifty guilders," Fat Man says.

"Do you take American Express?"

"But, of course."

"You're on your own," I say as I put out my hand and the dwarf hands up the Amex Gold.

"That price includes drinks?" asks the dwarf.

"All your drinks. Yes."

"And the women?"

"All of our girls are Dutch."

The dwarf hasn't made a move for his Visa yet.

"How long do you get with them?" inquires the dwarf. I expect to hear Fat Man say seven inches, but he doesn't.

"To do whatever you like, gentlemen—only five hundred guilders."

Suddenly we're both staring Fat Man down.

"Five hundred guilders per . . . ?" It's the dwarf.

"Per hour, gentlemen."

Whoa! And no way to even see the girls without dropping a buck and half? I remember Berlin's live-sex show boulevard and nothing behind the curtain. The dwarf has already turned to leave. So do I.

"Waiting for your fucking cut?" the dwarf screams at the cabbie, storming by the cab still sitting outside. "We can have three Red Light women each for the price of admission!"

He's not picky. He never sees their faces anyway.

"Where do we go now?" asks the dwarf. "Order in?"

"How?" I respond.

"Hell, there are signs on the lampposts in front of the Amstel."

"Those weren't parking-limit signs?"

"Ads for escort agencies, Mancow."

"In metal? Damn! How much cash do we have?"

"Believe me, they take plastic."

Whore delivery to the Amstel is a freak show.

"Did you ask for a chick with a dick?" I yell at the dwarf.

"No."

"Tell the midget to stay dressed."

"I did."

"We only got two people here. I ordered three girls."

"Maybe the chick with the dick counts as two!"

I'm pissed. The dwarf cracks up.

"Get rid of them! I'm going to the Red Light. It's my last night in Amsterdam!"

The dwarf pulls bills from his pocket.

"I hope that's not my money. I'm not paying for a tripod woman!"

"This one's on me, Mancow."

"We didn't do anything! What are you paying them for?" I'm itching to get out the door. My last night in Amsterdam I want my pestle in a vessel. True fact! Forty-six percent of American women would rather shop than make love. Is that because what a woman laying down her body usually gets is fucked, instead of what pleases her? No wonder laying down her money at Macy's gets her more turned on. Suddenly, I sense a presence. Behind a beaming dwarf stand two of the most astonishing women I have ever seen in my life.

"How much is this gonna cost, buddy?"

"Do you care?"

"Right now . . . not a lot."

"It's your last night in Amsterdam, Mancow. I leave you with the good hands people. Go to work, girls."

The dwarf heads out the door but sneaks into the closet so he can watch.

The best! Making Dad laugh.

Home

Leaving Amsterdam, I feel like I'm leaving home, leaving freedom to head into the unknown. Without my dad, America's going to feel foreign. On Monday, for the first time, I will broadcast from a whole new studio to a personal audience my dad's not in. I feel the roller coaster rumbling. Is there track ahead?

"I don't have anything on me, do I?" I ask the dwarf at the airport.

"Not a leaf, not an ash, not a Ziploc bag."

"I hear they check you pretty closely when you fly out from here.

Wish they didn't." We hug farewell. "You are a brother from a different mother. See you in Chicago!"

• • •

The KLM stewardess is stunning. A real Dutch girl—no question. I've leaned my seat back, but she says I can't do that before takeoff. She leans over me and gets me erect. She plugs a set of headphones into the jack on the seat arm and hands them to me. A guitar plays familiar music—Leo Kottke.

• • •

Brainflash! Another seat. Another time. The very start of Mr. Cow's wild ride. I'm driving to California to begin the first ever Mancow show. Except I'm in Utah. Kottke's been cranking for hours when my U-Haul breaks down in Wendover. There's nothing around except salt flats, where people drive cars faster than anywhere else in the world. Ray Charles drove for a Renault commercial here because even blind, he couldn't hit anything. According to the rack of postcards with pictures of all the record-holding cars, 548 mph was the last record set here.

"Record's already been broken," the Dairy Queen guy says.

"So's my U-Haul."

"Where you going?"

"California."

"Oh, son! Oh, no."

"What?"

"You can't get there from here." I believe him. He laughs. "You see! Things could be worse."

"Why can't they fix my truck? Why don't they give a fuck?" U-Haul has offered me a replacement but not the crew to move my stuff, and I'm too tired to do it myself.

"Where you going in California?"

"Salinas."

"Steinbeck country."

"You been there?"

"Nope. Don't like Mexicans. What's your name, son?"

I decide to do it. Every other person in the world has met me as Erich. "My name's Mancow," I say. "Mancow Muller."

"What do you do, Mancow?"

"Well, I was a farmer back in Missouri."

"I guess you're going to the right place then, Mancow."

"Thank you, Chuck."

The Dairy Queen guy looks down at his name tag a long time, like it's hard for him to read upside down.

"Name's not Chuck, Mancow. It's Theodore, which I always hated. Started calling myself Chuck when I left home. Long time ago now. Changed my life. 'So he drove out the man; and he placed at the east of the Garden of Eden, angry angels and a flaming sword to keep the way of the tree of life.' "

"John Steinbeck, *East of Eden.*"

"Borrowed from Genesis, of course. You really a farmer, Mancow?"

"I'm going to California to do a radio show, Chuck, but I think the Joads made better time in their Model A."

"Hmmm. *The Grapes of Wrath.* I can see Henry Fonda and that truck right now. You'll get there, Mancow, just like he did."

Eventually, I did.

And found a place to live.

Salinas is one giant field of lettuce. Smiling Mexicans pick dirt-clodded bits of the American Dream. Their violent kids, drunk on that same American Dream, the locals call "salad shooters." There are eight times as many Mexicans as whites in Salinas, some of whose families have been in this valley for 200 years. To the ones who arrived today, I'm an old-timer.

That late October night was warm, so most of the inhabitants of Elysian Fields trailer park were sitting outside taking in the air. As the salad shooters skidded onto my street, they opened fire. They shot high. Most of the injuries in the drive-by came from flying glass. Actually, since anyone who ever enters a trailer park has to turn off the main road onto one of those endless goddamned concentric circles filled with aluminum boxes people live in, ours was more of a drive-thru shooting. They shot bullets into my quarter-wide and kept firing through the next four trailers. The salad shooters screeched to a halt, jumped out, ran into the whore Delilah's double-wide, and ran out with a guy everybody called Johnny Two Shakes. Delilah had told me how he got the name. Johnny must have pulled some bad shit to have six guys bust in and drag him out like that—naked—and screaming bloody murder. From the shadowy front of my mobile home, I watched as they hurled Johnny into the trunk of their burgundy '56 Dodge low-rider. It was cherried out. They pumped the shocks twice and peeled away. I ran to Delilah's and discovered she'd gotten her ticket punched riding over Johnny Two Shakes on her knees.

We should ban aluminum to save lives! But then, what would we use to make lawn chairs and beer cans? Trailer parks are positive proof that if there is a loving God, he has an evil twin who gets off skipping twisters—like boys skip rocks—to see how many trailer parks he can flatten in a single throw. Twisters are drawn to aluminum! The first tornado to ever hit California showed up the same week Kmart finished a six-acre aluminum roof for the wind to dance away with.

My trailer looked like Sonny Corleone in *The Godfather*: a connect-the-dots can-opener lesson with a line of holes I thought only Hollywood bullets made. Shit! I don't have anything to cover those holes in my house! Then it came to me—Mancow bumper stickers!

The police and paramedics pulled Delilah out of her trailer. My only physical solace in Salinas—and (until the last night at the Amstel) the best piece of ass I had ever had—was dead. As I sat in bed reading Steinbeck's *Pastures of Heaven,* I grew suddenly very happy that my first week in Salinas was over.

I met Carolyn, Delilah's sister, the next day. After we comforted each other, she decided to stay. While I prepped for the start of my KDON show, Carolyn searched for someplace we could live. She finds one. On Saturday we visit the most beautiful town I have ever seen in my life. I understand why Steinbeck left the fields of mice and men to live in Cannery Row. There are no more canneries on the ocean side and no more whorehouses on the uphill side. All the sardines are gone now, replaced by lots of Japanese packed in double-decker tourist cans with windows.

"What's the name of your morning man?" my future landlord asks the people at KDON radio over the phone. "It is Mancow? Okay! What's his real name?" I have to get on the phone to tell them it's all right to tell him. "Matthew Erich Muller? Okay. Thank you." That's his whole credit check, his whole application procedure. I count out money. I don't have much. "Do you have a pet?"

"Well, now that I have a yard, my dad can bring out my bulldog, Max."

"Okay. We have three days left in October, the November rent is $960. Gimme a grand and we'll call it first and last. I was thinking $300 for cleaning deposit and $500 for Max."

"Maxine, really. I've only got $800 left. Can I just give you the $500 pet deposit?"

"No! Are you crazy? You need something to live on. Give me $300 for Max and sign the fucking papers."

"I need a mail slot in the door," I say after papers are signed.

Sunday, with my new landlord halfway to Italy, we move into the tiny cottage he rebuilt and made as sweet as the town. We're the first people to live in it since it's been redone. And there's a new brass mail slot cut in the door and a new welcome mat in front of it.

"Come here," Carolyn says when she opens the freezer to slip in the corn dogs.

Two champagne glasses sit beside a fifty-dollar bottle of Moët & Chandon. And a note, "Welcome Home! Peace and love, the dwarf."

That night I dream of the silence that rested on rural Harrisonville, Missouri, until my dad shattered the Saturday morning peace to mow the lawn—at 6 A.M. When John Muller was awake, dammit, so was the world! Maybe I'm more like my dad than I thought. Fuck! That's not my dad's mower I'm hearing—it's the buzzer on my clock. At 3 A.M., I leave home to wake up California for the first time.

In a few weeks my KDON morning slot has jumped from a six to a nine share. I've worked hard for it. I deserve it. I'm giving myself a present. I open the door of my dwarf cottage for a fan named Carmen.

"My period isn't over yet."

What a time to tell me! Lucky I don't care! There's something about removing a woman's tampon I find sexy.

Carmen made love as easily as Suits shake hands. We did it. She left. I fell asleep. Perfect? I wake up gagging.

"That's not my Tampax! Is it yours?" Carolyn stands over me. She's pissed. "Why am I not enough for you? Why do you need . . . why do you . . . ? Fuck you!"

Carolyn races to the bedroom and locks the door. Fuck! I'm paying the rent here! I break the door down.

The dwarf's in town for Christmas. Carolyn stays at his place for two days. I'm pissed as hell at both of them. Then Carolyn comes back.

Guys—give a woman what she's hungry for and she'll stay. I don't think I'm God's gift to women, but almost every woman I've been with says no other man has ever even tried to turn her on. That absolutely amazes me. I love lickin' ladies. I love the wetness. Love the taste. Love the obvious pleasure I can give with my tongue. When I eat pussy I'm going home. I'm a salmon rushing back upstream to where I came from, to a place my nose and mouth remember—to where I grew up—to where I swam in warm, dark, comfortable water every day and the temperature was perfect, and everything I needed came in special delivery—where I didn't have to figure anything out, where I was blind and didn't care, where I breathed fluid.

Guys! Wake up! Get past that voice in your head that says women were made for your pleasure only. Don't be so selfish. You are not the center of the universe. Don't surround yourself with yourself. I want more men out there satisfying women. The more you please, the more you'll get. Wag those tongues! Women talk to one another. If you don't really care about giving them pleasure—fake it! In 1950 Hugh Hefner couldn't get laid, so he started dressing and acting like a playboy. He was pretending! And look what happened to him! I gotta tell ya, the rewards you'll reap will make you think you did it for purely selfish reasons. If you need to drop a load to fall asleep, don't use your girlfriend—use your hand. The secret to sexual happiness is on the tip of your tongue, guys. Literally!

• • •

"You write a lot," KLM Maria says as I stand up to pull out another yellow pad.

"Yes I do." And I'm on a roll.

Want to offend a flight attendant? Call her a stewardess. Or even better—waitress!

• • •

"Slackers! Slack-offs!" That's what my dad called my whole generation. But maybe we just don't want their world. Maybe we saw through the illusion until disillusionment took us. I mean, look at the world! Look at what those before us have done! Try to find a tree older than your grandfather! They cut them down. We can't create our world as well as our fathers did—they used the raw materials! They destroyed it! They plowed it down and replaced it with s-t-r-u-c-t-u-r-e! And Corporate America was happy.

> I know that I shall never see
> A Starbucks, Gap, or Taco Bell
> As lovely as a tree.

But isn't nature unruly?

Mankind can't predict a tidal wave.

Or create anything as beautiful.

All those 1960s idealists—the generation that was going to change the world—what did they change? They got stoned. They made love. They had babies. Then, they discovered they had to feed those babies, and

they became Corporate America. You know what? My generation is better. We're more realistic. We can't be fooled. We hate phoniness. We hate
fakes. And we can smell them.

Listen, man! This ain't no Shangri-la! When people say to me, "Have a
nice day," I always ask, "Why are you so selfish? I'd like more than a nice
day! How about a whole life?!"

When you're a kid, you taste everything. You touch everything. You
smell everything. You feel everything. You're alive! Then the world
knocks us down. It bashes us. It breaks us. It works to make us numb. As
a kid I swore to myself that as I got older, I would never lose the wonder,
that wide-eyed, optimistic, child's view of the world. And I haven't.

"You had a good sleep." My KLM stewardess is tapping my shoulder.
"Sorry to wake you, but it's time to bring your seat to the upright posi-
tion." I'm really not awake. She smells wonderful as she leans over,
pushes the button, and gets me erect. Through the window the blue of
Lake Michigan races to the John Hancock Building. Fuck! We're low!
We're going to clip the Top of the Cock and plummet to our peter graves!
Maybe I picked the wrong day to stop smoking grass.

"We are on our approach to O'Hare. Local time in Chicago is ten past
noon." It's the pilot. Eight hours of flying and in Chicago it's only one
hour later than when I left Amsterdam. "Temperature is thirty-five degrees Celsius."

How the hell hot is thirty-five degrees Celsius?

Like all Dutch people, the pilot reads my mind. "That's ninety-four degrees Fahrenheit. Humidity is eighty-six percent."

Damn!

The temperature in Amsterdam was perfect.

Out my KLM window I see Navy Pier. I see it every day from my apartment, but now I see it for the first time. It's not Navy Pier. In my mind,
it's the Cole Brothers freak show. I am there with my dad, up to Chicago
from Kansas City. I'm six years old and looking up at a woman so fat I

can't see her chair. There's a man with all of his skin different colors, with pictures all over his body. There's a guy sticking swords down his throat and driving an ice pick into his head! Wow! Doesn't he need that part of his brain? There's a guy with no legs, moving around on his hands. That's scary.

But the best, the worst, the coup de grâce, is Popeye. He's a big black man in a white sailor suit. He just sits on his stool looking normal. But he isn't. He tells jokes until a crowd gathers around, then he bends down to tie his shoe. While he's tying his shoe, I see things fall out of his head. As he raises back up, Popeye has no eyes. There's nothing in the sockets except a cord running down his cheeks. His fucking eyes rest on his cheeks below his nose. He asks for a business card. My dad hands him one. Popeye holds the card over his ear with one hand and lifts up an eye with the other. "Mr. John Muller—oh-ho—you're up from Missouri!" This Popeye doesn't need spinach to be special. I'm impressed. Terrified. Enthralled.

God, I'd love to see that show again.

It wouldn't be the same without you, Dad.

Two guys out on their own.

Adventures in the big city.

My trip through my fatherland is over.

I'm back in the U.S. without you.

• • •

"Mancow?"

"Yeah." It's a KLM stewardess, one I haven't seen before.

"I'm sorry about your dad."

I fight back a flood of emotion. It takes forever to collect myself. "Thanks," I say. She hears the emptiness in my voice.

"It takes awhile," she says as she tousles my hair. "You'll be okay."

"God, I hope so."

"Welcome back, Mancow."

"Thanks."

She gets my duffel bag down from the overhead bin. Every other passenger has already deplaned into Chicago. When I get ten feet down the gangway she says, "Love you."

I stop. I wait. I turn. "Thanks," I say, glad for these words from a stranger that make me feel less alone.

"Love your show."

Sufa gets me a ride on the stewardess shuttle to the Sheraton. We cab it to dinner at Shaw's Crab House. As we talk I have a strange realization: every man, every woman, every human, every creature that lives long enough, joins the Dead Dad's Club eventually–every one.

"I think we need a shower after our flight," Sufa says. "Do you have someone to scrub your back?"

Ding!

Sufa won't let me pay for her dinner, she insists we go Dutch treat. This is my kind of woman. We go back to the hotel. Sufa uses a loofah on my skin for over an hour in her Sheraton shower. Then the fun keeps flowing. At 9 P.M. Chicago time, which is like 3 A.M. in Amsterdam, I leave. I have stuff to do before tomorrow's meeting with my *Madhouse* crew.

• • •

"Patrick Duffy, you played Bobby Ewing on *Dallas.*"

"Yes I did."

"And now you're in a sitcom with Suzanne Somers."

"Yes I am."

I didn't want to talk about shows with Patrick Duffy or about acting either, although I knew I could learn a lot from *The Man from Atlantis.*

I brainflash to this interview when I find my mountain of waiting mail topped by a package from Patrick Duffy. My dad was still alive when I talked to Patrick, but both of his parents were dead. I wanted to talk about how he dealt with his own parents' death. I remember their deaths. Not because I knew them, but because one night they were butchered in Montana. It was a heinous, brutal murder and because of

Patrick, sensational enough to make national headlines and TV news for a long time. The murder affected me. It affected a lot of people. But it didn't seem to affect Patrick. I wanted to know why. He'd caught shit from everyone for not being more upset, for not cursing his parents' murdering butchers and swearing eternal revenge. He'd caught hell for staying calm, for not crying. TV shows had a field day: "Next on *Hard Copy*!–a brutal murder in Montana and the strange religion that keeps Patrick Duffy from being upset." I saw that program–pictures of butchered bodies, gore, and police–but nothing from Patrick, and nothing about his religion except that it was weird. The media played Patrick Duffy like a freak.

"How can you feel closer to your parents after their deaths than before, Patrick?" I asked him on the show.

PATRICK: I'd rather not talk about that.

MANCOW: I know you caught hell for not being really upset when they were murdered. I think the press was horrible. I'm sorry to bring up a subject I know you caught a lot of flack on.

PATRICK: Then let's just let it go.

MANCOW: I'm not trying to trap you or make you look silly, Patrick. It's just that I need to know.

PATRICK: There's nothing to know.

MANCOW: No, you don't understand. Right now my dad is really sick. He's dying of cancer. He's going to die soon, and I'm going to miss him I want to know what it is you know, what it is you believe, what it is that enabled you to let go of your parents? How is it possible to feel closer to them after they died than before?

PATRICK: My weird religion?

MANCOW: Well, tell me about it, because all I can feel is that when my dad goes, he's gone–and I don't like that feeling.

Finally Patrick Duffy opened up.

PATRICK: No matter how much anybody loves their parents, or how much they love you, there are always tensions between you, right?

MANCOW: Right. Always.

PATRICK: Those tensions, those feelings always interfere with really feeling close. You're always having to prove yourself somehow. My religion teaches that when people die, all those human tensions disappear, all the problems disappear, but the spirit connections stay. You still have all the things that were good without having to worry whether some new disagreement will push them away again.

MANCOW: But how could you not be mad at their murderer? If I could destroy cancer right now, I'd do it in a heartbeat.

PATRICK: Death comes to every one of us sometime, Mancow. When death comes, it doesn't matter whether it's knives or cancer that murders the ones we love. People are spirits, not bodies. Nothing changes in spirit when the body dies. Except that spirits keep in touch more easily after death without the bodies.

The package from Patrick is the book of his weird religion—a religion that teaches spirit is real and immortal. Okay. Teaches one God, an infinite creator. Okay. Teaches that a God-inspired mortal, or God in human form, brought the world a path to follow to get to the peace of heaven. The man who brought this good news to the world was a reluctant teacher-prophet who taught we shouldn't worry about the body or material things, but he wasn't a Jew from Galilee—his name was Siddhartha, the Buddha. Patrick's "weird religion" is one of the most believed religions on earth!

The sayings of Buddha that Patrick has underlined all have to do with death and the continuation of spirit.

• • •

It was dark and quiet as I lay in my bed in the family home in Missouri. My thoughts were troubled. I was far from sleep when I heard soft footsteps and the door to my mother's bedroom being opened. My panic dissolved into calmness and trust. This was no intruder. Those were my dad's footsteps. I listened as he checked on his wife and each of my brothers. He knew I wasn't sleeping when he opened my door, but he didn't say anything—and neither did I. In the dim light of the hallway, every bit of him was lighter, less burdened, more peaceful than I had ever seen him before. My father stood in my doorway a long time as we looked at each other. I felt his spirit blowing over me. Love, knowledge, lots of stuff, passed between us. When he gently closed the door I felt full, and I swear to you, I watched him walk softly back to the family room as though there were no door between us. My dad had been unable to walk for weeks, but I heard him and saw him walking the halls of our home while I knew his body was still in the hospital bed dying of cancer.

It was two more days before his silent, motionless, blinded, decomposing body finally died. He was hell to look at. As his body stopped functioning, his organs pulled water from wherever there was moisture to draw, turning his skin to jerky, stealing the flesh from his lips, turning his tongue to a small dark finger, hard and dry to the touch, unable to flex into language, if there had been enough breath to speak. Sometimes I knew his thoughts. The hands that had often squeezed mine in encouragement, lay on the bed like some huge eagle's dry, unmovable talons. I would squeeze that unfamiliar hand trying to reassure him. The skin of his face drew up so tight that paper-thin lips no longer covered his teeth. He looked more like the mummy he once took me to see than a living man whose body was being eaten by carnivorous cancer cells. This body was not my dad. This body made me cry, prevented me from remembering what he'd looked like. How could I forget my father's face?

The overweight man with the pot belly hanging over his belt, with the cigarette always hanging out of his mouth as he cooked knockwurst on the backyard grill, these images were lost to me. They would not come back until I looked through old family pictures after he died. This desiccated body on the bed was in no way related to the dad or the man I had known. Where were his mind, his spirit, his liveliness, tenderness, love, laughter—even his anger? Could any of these really have been inside this hunk of flesh? No. No. This flesh can be no more than his earth suit, which, like the salesman he was, he was required to wear while on call here on earth. This worn-out, threadbare earth suit made Dad look human once, every bit as much as the suits he wore to garden in made him look FBI. My dad bought all his suits too cheap. They all wore out too soon.

I resist going into my home office, but something makes me want to check my faxes. Just to the left of the office door, I see the photos: a four-shot photo strip taken so long ago on the boardwalk in Wildwood, New Jersey, that the pictures are sepia tones. Smiling, laughing, and staring at me like I'm the camera is my dad when he was my age, with my mom. And I don't feel sad.

I understand, Patrick.

The last fax in, the one on top, is from the dwarf at the Amstel:

> Images of my youth are always here in my mind.
> I know I'm a different man—but what will tomorrow find?
> Will I be my Father?
> I have no children now, but maybe I will someday
> They'll never know who he was—my father has gone away
> Will I be my Father?
> I'm looking at pictures now—of someone I never knew,
> A boy of sixteen years old—when Dad was a young man too.
> Will I be my Father?
> Will I love my children?
> My father lived on this earth—the flickering of an eye,
> Now I want an answer to the question why people die.
> Will I be my Father?
> I know that he tried to live the best way that he knew how,
> The things he got wrong or right—don't matter an atom now.
> Will I be my Father?
> Has he gone to heaven?

I go to bed.

It's quiet.

In the stillness of a hot Chicago night, I feel the hum of the world.

I hear the hum of life.

The hum starts with my heartbeat and my breath,

then grows until it includes the ticking of the clock on the wall,

the police siren out on the street.

A lone crow caws

and two taxi cab drivers fight with foreign tongues.

All the sounds collect,

until they become one in the hum.

My dad is now part of the hum.

Part II
One Step Beyond

Arrgghh!

The Inner Sanctum

CD players, DAT players, cartridge
tape decks, a reel-to-reel, a turntable, amplifiers, and more—two solid
walls of equipment—create the sanctum's left and rear boundaries. At
nut level in front of me, because I never sit when I work, is the thirty-
channel control board where my fingers will dance over volume pots for
the next five hours as I decide exactly how much people will hear from
every piece of machinery, every phone line, every microphone, every moment. Rising behind the control board, nipple-high glass creates the in-

visible wall dividing the inner sanctum from the larger temple of the studio. Irma, Turd, Phone Girl, and DJ Luv Cheez face me from the other side of the glass. Freak and the sports guy check in from across the street because even in this new, larger studio I helped design, there isn't room for them here.

Through a soundproof window behind my crew, I can see the waiting room. At the right-hand end of the control board stands a half wall of shoulder-high equipment. Between that pillar and the rear wall of equipment is the narrow entrance to my tiger cage through which no one passes during broadcast without permission. Outside this entrance to the inner sanctum stand five six-foot-high rolling carousels holding 360 different Mancow tape cartridges which we call carts. My tape runner hands me the five carts I want to start today's show. The crew puts on their headphones. As the second hand sweeps toward 5:30 A.M. I slide volume pot nine from zero to six, ready to broadcast the theme song. As the last of the night show commercials end, I punch PLAY on cart one:

> This is the theme to Mancow's show.
> The opening theme to Mancow's show.
> Mancow called me up—and asked me to write one.

Pots one through six all up for my crew's mikes. Everybody sings. Mike pots down.

> The opening theme to *Mancow's Morning Madhouse.*

Up on pot ten, play cart two.

"And now! From the cramped and dimly lit studios! The man who would be Cow! Mancow Muller!"

Mike pots up for live cheering, whistling, and applause from the crew, then I open my mouth to wake people up like a noisy cock.

"I just got back from Amsterdam. I'd read about the place. I'd heard stories. You know I've got a fertile imagination, but I have to tell you . . . never in my wildest dreams did I imagine anything as good as what

Amsterdam really is. Sure, I subscribe to *High Times.* Yeah, I knew they had pot there. But there is no way to describe the sensation—no way to imagine the feeling of absolute freedom and liberation—that first time in your life you buy marijuana legally.

"I remember my dad's anti-grass party line: 'If you smoke marijuana you'll move on to harder drugs. You'll wind up doing crank. You'll wind up doing heroin. You'll be mainlining tomorrow! If everybody smokes it, society as we know it will be utterly destroyed!'

"But in Amsterdam that isn't true. In Amsterdam that's not what happened at all! In Amsterdam the number of hard drug users has gone *down* since they started selling marijuana legally.

"In Amsterdam I saw a society where everybody is happy. Everyone is—stoned maybe—I don't know. But all of them are happy. I find that really interesting. Without laws confining pleasure, people are happy. With total personal freedom, people are happy. Even the Amsterdam cops are happy! And people actually like the cops, who seem more like Maytag repairmen, hanging out in their uniforms with nothing they need to do, maybe a little bored, waiting for a call that rarely comes. Deciding between glazed or sprinkled could be the greatest decision these policemen ever make—but you know that can't be true because none of them are fat. Unlike America, where cops are always eating, and always always busting chops for stupid stuff that in Amsterdam is legal!

"Maybe my dad didn't know what he was talking about.

"Or maybe my dad was a liar.

"My mother was a liar:

"I made a funny face—it didn't freeze.

"I ate my carrots yet I still wear glasses.

"I picked my nose and my finger didn't stick.

"I never washed them and yet, as I move my finger around inside my ear, no potatoes!

"What is it, Freak?"

"I told you you could buy marijuana on the streets there, Mancow."

"How often have you been to Amsterdam, Freak?"

"Well, never, but—"

"Then shut up and listen to someone who has. You don't buy marijuana on the street in Amsterdam, you buy it in coffee shops. They've got menus! For marijuana and hashish! And they've got rolling papers sitting in shot glasses on the tables, and little pieces of cardboard for making filters!"

"What about the women?" It's Turd. "Do they really stand in windows?"

"They stand in picture windows in sexy underwear, Turd. Yes they do. And what a variety. I saw tits as big as Irma's, and smiles as sweet as Phone Girl's. They even have fat girls, Turd, and every time I saw a fat girl in a window pudging over her lingerie, I thought of you."

"That's just how I like 'em, Mancow!" Turd's chortle grows into the deep laugh that rolls through his whole huge body until it shakes the studio.

"Irma, tell me—when you came to America, did you have to sign a paper promising to shave under your arms?"

"No, I didn't have to sign anything."

"Well, God bless you for doing it anyway, and God bless all American women because the most frightening thing I saw in Germany, which is a pretty scary place, was underarm hair on women. I mean that's just unnatural."

"There's nothing wrong with hair under your arms, Mancow."

"That's 'cause I'm a guy, Irma! I don't pluck my eyebrows or wax my legs or trim my bush either. Lots of women in Europe don't trim their bush, which I have to say I liked, but is seeing those headlights of pubie fuzz coming at me down the street worth having to look at that pit hair? And! And! Here's something I want your opinions on: I talked to a European connoisseur who said the taste in the pit tells you if the clam's worth eating. That sweet virgin who is my Phone Girl is answering your calls. I know we've got callers wanting to talk about Amsterdam, and there's a lot I have to say about Amsterdam—and Germany—and thank you everybody for the cards and letters and calls to Freak about my dad while I was away, they mean a lot—but right now I want to hear what you think about pit hair. I say let Europeans lick BO if they want. I want the tuna taco. And down there, I like it paved, not shaved. I like 'em big and hairy and untamed!"

Push PLAY on cart one.

PHONE GIRL AS WIFE: My husband. He's the best. He works hard all day, and still takes time to call me just to say he's thinking of me. He's great with the kids—and helps me around the house. I love my husband. So, sometimes when he comes in late, I put the kids to bed early, light a few candles, and give him a perfect dinner. Plus, I give him a delectable dessert he'll savor all night. I give my hubby a Whisker Biscuit. Yes. Whisker Biscuits are those lip-smacking late-night snacks that will have your husband begging for more.

SOUND OF DOOR OPENING.

LUV CHEEZ AS HUSBAND: Honey! I'm home! FOOTSTEPS. Say? Do I smell Whisker Biscuits?

WIFE: Serve 'em warm or hot. He won't care as long as he's munching on a Whisker Biscuit. And—don't forget—Whisker Biscuits come in three assorted colors. Whisker Biscuits! Give your man a box today.

MANCOW AS ANNOUNCER: Whisker Biscuits. Try new Frosted Whisker Biscuits! Or, Whisker Biscuits with cheese!

HUSBAND (WITH MOUTH FULL): Um. Uh. Delicious.

"I picked up a CD in Germany and I want your opinions on this too. I think this record's going to be huge in America." Push PLAY on the music cart Luv Cheez and I laid down this morning.

Cart plays polka music!

MANCOW: That's not it.

CART: "Deutscheland, Deutscheland uber alles."

MANCOW: That's not it.

CART: "Come to the cabaret old chum! Life is a cabaret."

MANCOW: Sorry. I thought I had it on top here.

Cart plays the Kinks singing "I'm Not Like Everybody Else."

MANCOW: Sorry. Here we go.

The undulating pulse of the disco beat begins.

MANCOW: This is it. This is the most popular song in Europe right now. Phone Girl? From me to you. "Be My Lover" with La Bouche.

Cross fade "Be My Lover" with what Luv Cheez and I recorded yesterday on reel-to-reel with ten gospel sisters after they finished Sunday service. A song I wrote in Berlin:

```
Are you ready for the Mancow?
Ready as I can be.
Hey. Hey. Are you ready for the MAAANcow?
Ready to brush your teeth?
Are you ready?
Ready.
Are you ready?
Ready.
Are you ready?
Ready.
Are you re-a-d-y
Are you ready to start the day? H-e-e-e-e-ey Hey!
```

"Okay! Got a trivia question for everybody: What was Martin Luther King's original first name? I'll give you one hint—it wasn't Martin. I saw Martin Luther's church in East Berlin. There's a scary place. The Wall, the Berlin Wall—the wall that symbolized oppression for thirty years—is down, but man, you can feel what oppression does to people. You can feel how it makes them all—"

```
Just another brick in the wall!
```

Press REPEAT and PAUSE on Pink Floyd in CD two.

"We have to tear down the walls, folks! Those walls that keep us divided from one another! Those walls that keep us divided from ourselves! Those walls that prevent freedom! I mean, who wants to be—"

```
Just another brick in the wall!
```

"East Germany makes America look like paradise, but, in comparison to Amsterdam, Americans are miserable. In comparison to Amsterdam, every U.S. cop's unhappy. In comparison to Amsterdam, the U.S. is a police state. In comparison to Amsterdam, everybody in America is—"

Just another brick in the wall!

"Since the War on Drugs started, America's prescription drug habit has shot up fifty percent. No one 'just says no' to Valium. Yet, *half* of America's jail population is in for drug offenses! All those prisoners are—"

Just another brick in the wall!

"Did you get a piece of the wall, Mancow?"

"No, I didn't, Irma, but I got lots of pieces of something else in Amsterdam. Fitty guilders. Mike in Highland Park, what's happening?"

Volume slider eight up.

"Hey, Mancow! Glad you're back. Love you, love your show."

"Thanks, man."

"Hearing the *Best of Mancow's Morning Madhouse* was great. Freak was playing stuff I never heard and I loved it, but I wanna tell ya, Mancow, we all sure missed you while you were away."

"Thanks, buddy. That means a lot."

"I just wanted to say, I lost my dad two months ago, and . . . uh . . . I feel for you."

"Thanks, Mike. How old are you?"

"I'm twenty."

"Yeah. I wanted to hear you were sixty. I'm sorry you didn't have more time with your dad."

"Thanks, Mancow. Me too."

I tell my tape runner to pull me a Kinks CD.

"How did your dad die, buddy?"

"Cancer, Mancow, just like your dad."

"Would your dad have ever smoked marijuana?"

"Fuck no! Not in a million years!"

Hit the BLEEP button, and be very glad for the delay.

"You can't say the F word on the air, Mike. But what if a doctor prescribed marijuana for your dad? My dad swore he would *never* do radiation or chemotherapy and he did both before he died because doctors told him he should. Coming up on *Mancow's Morning Madhouse* here on Rock 103.5–when will the doctor be on, Phone Girl?"

"Eight-thirty, Mancow." Load in the Kinks CD.

"At 8:30 we talk to a doctor who prescribes marijuana to every patient he has who has cancer. Wonder if he's been to Amsterdam? Mike–and anyone else in the Dead Dad's Club–it's helped me a lot to talk about my dad these last ten days. I want to recommend it. I recommend you tell stories about your dad to your buddies–especially the things that made you laugh. There's lots of who they were in each of us."

"Glad you're back, Mancow."

"Thanks, buddy. I'm glad I'm back too."

People are listening. People are feeling.

"This is for me, and Mike, and anyone else who's lost their dad. This song is a thank you to them for having lived and been in our lives. This is the Kinks with 'Days.' "

Punch PLAY on CD one, pot eleven up, treble down.

"This Thursday, Jonathan Harris is coming into the studio! Dr. Smith, the star of *Lost in Space*–my all-time favorite TV program–will be on *Mancow's Morning Madhouse* here on Rock 103.5. To anyone who thinks I'm strange loving *Lost in Space*–I give you Europe! Where a mouthful of underarm hair is sexy on a woman! Where every day, in every major city, they run a Jerry Lewis film festival. How can you respect a culture that finds Jerry Lewis funny? Irma, you know who John Williams is, right?"

"Of course, Mancow, he's–"

"John Williams, the football player?" That's Turd.

My tape runner slaps a cart into my hand.

"John Williams did the music for *E.T.*!" Thank you, Freak.

"And for the *Star Wars* trilogy—and for maybe a hundred other films—but before he did any of those, John Williams did the music for the pilot of *Lost in Space,* and I think it's some of his finest work."

Every day, like the Borg on *Star Trek,* I plug in and become my studio. If I couldn't do that, I could never do this show—things in the studio are too insane and move too fast. It's 5:40 A.M. I'm happy with the show so far. "Great kid! Don't get cocky!" Four hours and fifty minutes to go.

• • •

Yesterday I opened the box of tapes of my dad and me that my mom sent up. When I heard my dad's voice, I brainflashed to the dream I had in Europe of my dad selling Mancow CDs on TV.

"I know what I want on it," I tell the crew after the show. "Let's make a list. I need a Sharpie."

Everybody checks pockets, but no one's got one. This is not rare. This is unique. Everybody knows that without a Sharpie fine-point permanent marker—I can't write! Phone Girl opens a desk drawer.

"Here, Mancow. Have a whole box of Sharpies."

"Okay! The name of the first ever Mancow CD is *Box of Sharpies!* What goes on it?"

With the list finished, I open the sticker-covered file box I lug to work everyday. I pull a handbill. Whenever a circus came to my dad's boyhood town, he'd pass out enough of these to see the show for free. Mom sent me his whole collection of circus programs and flyers.

"Find me this banner, Phone Girl. I want to buy it."

• • •

As I drive my 1972 yellow Ford Maverick in perfect working order home from work, I fume at the soundtruck blasting "We are all freaks!" until

I realize there's no truck there. "We are all freaks! We are all freaks! We are all freaks!" I hear the crowd chanting at the show.

What show?

I don't know, but I'm dressed like P. T. Barnum in a ringmaster outfit and there are *a lot* of people in front of me.

I have to do a freak show!

• • •

"Carnie barker Johnny Meah's on line three," Phone Girl says Thursday.

"Johnny, how you doing, buddy?"

The deep rumble of Johnny Meah's voice rolls back at me. "I'm doing fine, Mancow." Johnny always sounds like a freight train, going slow.

"Johnny, there's a 1940s freak show banner with all the freaks painted on it—Johnny Eck, JoJo the dog-faced boy—"

"And a big figure that looks like it's kind of embracing them."

"That's it! Did you paint it?"

"No. I didn't start painting banners until the sideshows folded up and we all lost our jobs, Mancow."

"You were a carnie freak?"

" 'Geek' is the word in the trade, Mancow, and, yes, I was a sideshow geek. Did card tricks, swallowed swords—"

"So you can deep-throat anything?"

"As long as it's not too big around. Long is fine." If a train can chuckle, Johnny does.

"You're my man, Johnny."

"I know that banner, Mancow. I believe I even know where it is. I would love to own it—it's one of the great pieces of circus art, six-feet high and maybe fifteen-feet long . . ."

I must have it!

". . . but the reason I'd like to have that banner is because I worked with every geek on it."

"Johnny . . ." I can feel it. Like the train in Johnny's voice, I can feel it.

The Mancow Freak Show is starting to roll. "If I wanted to put on a freak show, would you be the man to help me?"

"Well, Mancow . . ." You could drive a train through every one of Johnny Meah's pauses. "I know every geek working in America to-day . . ." I could do my whole show in these pauses. ". . . and some geeks who aren't working but would love to."

"Johnny, I gotta go. Get me some names. Find out if they're interested. Find me that banner. I'll talk to you." I hang up. It's rude, but it could be Wednesday before Johnny finishes saying the word "good-bye." *Yes!* When Johnny Meah painted the ass end of a cow with its head turned and my face looking back, I had no idea it might lead to this: "Half Man Half Cow."

I'm bringing back the Great American Freak Show.

I feel like P. T. Barnum.

● ● ●

I'm in trouble.

Huge trouble. Management is furious at me—for doing something nice for the homeless people of Chicago. I thought it would be great to give them a decent meal.

Pigeons can't fart. Feed them Alka-Seltzer—they explode.

I send Turd and Freak out in Mancow Mobile One. They feed some pigeons, watch them explode, then smash their tiny pigeon heads between two bricks.

On Air.

It sounds revolting.

Coo, Coo, Coo.

BOOM!

SMUSH!

Screaming pigeons. Bricks into pigeon skulls.

Turd and Freak pull the pretty pigeon feathers off their birds. As Turd broils the meat in a portable cooker in Mancow Mobile One, my boss,

Sergeant Hairclub, barrels into the studio screaming, "You can't do this, Mancow." I guess he's right. Thirty seconds later, six Chicago troopers storm the temple of my studio.

"Turn off the tape, now!!!"

"You can't do this!"

"Turn off the tape!"

All of them are shouting. Six pistols point at me. Their eyes say they want me dead. Their faces twitch less than their trigger fingers.

"There is no tape."

"You can't kill pigeons!"

"We already have. But we won't kill any more."

I have never seen cops so angry. I don't like drawn pistols—especially pointed at me. Will these guys really shoot me for killing pigeons?

"Where's the pigeon van?" Trooper One demands.

"Mancow Mobile One is more like a truck, really, Off—"

"Tell us where the fuck it is!" I have to move fast to bleep the F word out of Trooper Two's demand before it broadcasts live.

"Turd?! Where are you?"

Phone Girl has him patched in live on the portable phone.

"I'm moving, Mancow."

"Where's he going?!!" Trooper One demands.

"Where are you going, Turd?"

"To feed some pigeon to the homeless people on Lower Wacker, Mancow!"

"You can't do that!" Trooper Four shouts.

"He's right, Turd. Better tell them it's squab. Not even homeless people eat pigeon."

"You can not serve them the pigeon!" Trooper Three screams.

"But it's already dead. It's already cooked! You want us to just throw away the food? These people are hungry."

"Stop the show!" Head Trooper shouts. "Stop this fucking show, now!!"

These cops act like somebody has a howitzer trained on their families. Maybe somebody does. Animal rights people on the phones are absolutely nuts!

"What's the punishment for killing pigeons?" general manager Mike Fowler asks, playing negotiator.

"Two hundred bucks a pop! What are you laughing at? Keep your hands where I can see them!"

"I'm getting my wallet," says program director Dave Richards. Everyone pitches in—except Irma who's been going crazy like we were crushing cocks between those bricks instead of pigeons. Every male bird is a cock, Irma.

"How much does Mancow owe you?" Mike Fowler asks.

In walkie-talkie consultation with the station, the troopers decide they've got tape-recorded evidence of six pigeons biting the plop-plop and fizz-fizzing into squab heaven.

"Twelve hundred bucks! You owe us twelve hundred bucks!"

We've collected six.

"Pay us now or we stop this show!"

I can't help. They don't take Amex Gold.

Finally, Irma opens her makeup case and pulls out a wad big enough to choke a pony.

"What have you been doing, Irma?"

"You owe me big time, Mancow," Irma says as she rolls six singles off and puts the wad away.

When Mancow Mobile One pulls into Lower Wacker, fifty armed and dangerous cops stand ready to keep the homeless people hungry. Finally, the troopers in the studio—money in their hands, pigeon-killing ticket in mine—decide they've done their duty. They decide to let Turd and Freak exercise their God-given right to feed the homeless, while fifty cops on Lower Wacker cry fowl.

Mancow's homeless pigeon blowout has cost me twelve bills.

I was trying to feed the homeless!

And rid the world of a few flying rats.

Everyone is going nuts!

If we'd thrown oily rags on homeless people and burned them alive, I honestly believe there'd be less of an outcry.

The phones will not stop ringing. Reporters. Lawyers. Animal rights nuts. They will not go away. I'm getting death threats for killing pigeons! Even pigeons enter the war. I parked my 1972 yellow Ford Maverick in perfect working order on the roof when I came in to work. Now it looks like Hamburg after an all-day Allied pigeon bombing. There's nothing else to do.

The next morning on the show, I reveal the truth.

There were never any pigeons!

Luv Cheez recorded pigeon coos, then laid in a muffled explosion from a sound-effects record.

In Mancow Mobile One, Freak held up the phone while Turd smashed two bricks together onto dead chicken heads Freak picked up from a voodoo priest he knows.

A guy on a portable phone supplied the live pigeon screams.

Wreeerrr!

Feather plucking was a guy on another portable phone ripping two pieces of duct tape apart.

Shhhzwick!

Phone Girl had every telephone line engaged as I slid pots like mad to create the live mix of elements.

None of it was real!

You heard the pigeons dying. You heard the homeless eating.

We did feed the homeless.

But not the squab we told them. Lower Wacker's hungry Chicago homeless people ate an all-you-can-eat Mancow buffet of KFC Rotisserie Gold—which cost a shitload less than the pigeons!

P. T. Barnum reared his head in me again: "six-foot man eating chicken."

I still had to pay the fine. The cops could only believe their ears. "We have recorded proof you killed six pigeons, boy!"

Must be true. Heard it on the radio.

I could never kill an animal. I'm an animal lover!

(I always use a condom though.)

Mancow's "Frog in the Microwave Day," I refuse comment on.

It's a radio *show*!!!

Not a radio fact!

What part of that don't people get?

Give me voices, sound effects, atmosphere, and I will make you believe I am anywhere, doing anything. I love radio. I love creating everything from nothing.

Mancow's Morning Madhouse is a P. T. Barnum six-ring circus every day. How much is real? How much is fake? You decide.

Two slices of heaven.

Radio Goo-Goo

Radio turns seventy-five years old
tonight. I'm going to the party. I feel honored to be invited. As I enter the
Radio Hall of Fame gala anniversary dinner at Chicago's Hyatt Regency
Hotel, I feel like a pimply kid at a gathering of the saints. My new girlfriend, Jenny, couldn't get out of a teachers' meeting, Sufa's not in town,
so Phone Girl came to the party. She looks stunning all gussied up, infi-
nitely better than Turd, Freak, or even Luv Cheez ever could.

Next to me at dinner sits Space Mom! June Lockhart! Mrs. Robinson from *Lost in Space*. June doesn't seem at all interested that *Lost in Space* is my all-time favorite TV show. I can't understand that. How can someone who was in it not love *Lost in Space*? On the other side of Phone Girl sits Jim Bohannon, the fill-in guy on *The Larry King Show*.

I was nineteen years old when I started in radio on KOKO. My boss told me that he hired me because I wore a suit to the interview. I got to work with Larry King and Jim Bohannon *every night*. They paid me minimum wage to do it—none of this working-for-free intern stuff. Each night I listened to every word Larry King said, live, in my headphones, waiting for those electronic beeps that told me to slam on local commercials, and then go live on mike to say, "This is KOKO Radio in Warrensburg, Missouri." At the next beep, I punched the button to put Larry King back on live. But on my first night on the job Larry didn't do his show. Cuing in and out of Jim Bohannon was my first paying radio gig.

"What was the name of the station?" Jim Bohannon asks me as the waiter sets down his dinner of french-cut green beans, whipped mashed potatoes with cheese, and (no lie) squab.

"KOKO radio, Mr. Bohannon," I say digging into my roast beef.

"Call me Jim, Mancow," says Jim Bohannon. Wow! "And, I'm sorry, but I've never heard of that station."

"Well, it was only your syndication station in Warrensburg, Jim." I just called him Jim! "On a clear day, KOKO's 1,000 watts of power reached almost to the end of the parking lot." Jim laughs.

"We worked nights together, Mancow," he says. "How far did the signal reach then?"

"Prob'ly to the Dairy Queen."

Jim Bohannon laughs. Again. Phone Girl's first radio job doesn't hold a candle to mine.

So there I am between Jim Bohannon and June Lockhart, and across the table sits Robert Feder, radio writer for the *Chicago Sun-Times,* who is way beyond me intellectually but likes my show. He still thinks Mancow is the Falstaff Everyman voice for a new generation, and I still don't know what the hell he means. And that's just my dinner table!

As dinner ends, people mingle. I meet Les Tremayne—a god—the voice of *Jack Armstrong, the All-American Boy,* of *Inner Sanctum,* of so many, many great old radio shows. I hang out with Casey Kasem, Paul Harvey, Harry Carey. Phone Girl takes pictures.

"How you doing, Eraserhead?" It's Rush Limbaugh. He remembers me! Hell, he even remembers some jokes and stuff I wrote for the radio comedy service he uses.

Then, it happens.

I meet my radio idol, the man who inspired me from the very beginning—the King of Radio Comedy—his royal and immaculate holiness, Stan Freberg.

Wish my dad could see this.

Jack Benny, Burns and Allen, all the radio dead folks are there live on tape. Celebrities gather around to listen to *Inner Sanctum, The Shadow, Jack Benny.*

ROBBER: Your money or your life!

Long pause.

ROBBER: Did you hear me? I said, your money or your life!

JACK BENNY: I know. I know. I'm thinking!

Brilliant.

When the Jack Benny tape ends, a very famous radio guy turns to me and asks, "What makes you so hot, Mancow?"

Another radio celebrity joins in, "How have you done it, Mancow? How have you captured Chicago?"

I'm blown away! At the seventy-fifth anniversary Radio Hall of Fame dinner everyone knows my name!

"What's your secret, Mancow?"

"You're a legend in your own time, boy. Tell us. We want to know. What do you do that's different?"

"What do you talk about, Mancow?"

I take a deep breath. "Sex . . . is what I talk about."

All the radio legends, all these people I admire, look at me in silence. They look at one another. Lips curl. "Ohhhh" someone finally says in that way that means "Eeew!"

From across the room I hear Paul Harvey say, "P-a-g-e two!"

"I'm only a twenty-seven-year-old man," I say.

Silence. The conversation is over.

Casey Kasem gets up, lays his napkin down on the table, and walks away. Everyone else follows.

"You're on a totally different wavelength than these people, Mancow," Robert Feder says, trying to reassure me.

"Yeah, well, I'm not surprised, Robert. They're old!"

The dinosaurs still want to think they rule the world.

Old-timers like to live in the good old days. Give them the present and they fall apart. I watched it happen live at the seventy-fifth anniversary radio gala.

Now is my time. I don't ever want to be a crusty hack looking back. "Now is my time," I say aloud as I walk past the dinosaurs to leave.

The saxophone was seventy-five when John Coltrane reinvented it. In this seventy-fifth year of radio, *Billboard* nominates Mancow as 1995's "Radio Personality of the Year" for rockin' Chicago. My dad would be— is—proud. I'm in Atlanta when they tear the envelope open. I'm excited.

"And the winner is . . . Mancow Muller!"

I walk through a crowd of 2,500 other working radio stiffs. They're applauding! As I reach the podium to say my thank-yous, someone races down the aisle shouting, "Mancow! Mancow! It's for you!" He shoves a portable phone at me.

"Who is it?" I ask the flunky, though I think I know.

"It's Howard Stern!" the flunky screams, turning to the audience expecting applause. Silence. I look at the audience, take the flunky's $800 phone, and throw it on the stage as hard as I can. Then I stomp it like a man possessed. On his show, "Coward" said unforgivably sick things about my dad. I'm not in Atlanta anymore. I'm looking at my dad's desiccated, cancer-ridden body. Then I hear his voice again, just before it went away forever.

"Be grateful for the publicity, son, really. Nothing anyone says can hurt me. Don't let anyone use me to get to you. If you let that happen, they win."

A roar like the waves of an ocean storm surrounds me. As I start to see bits of phone at my feet, I remember where I am. Storm sounds linger as I turn slowly to the mike to discover a sea of people standing, applauding, and stomping their feet. I let the sound wash over me, through me, into me. When the sound recedes, I say, "The only person I can thank today is my dad. If you give me another award sometime, I'll thank everybody else."

• • • •

I talk about Atlanta on *Mancow's Morning Madhouse,* about how I wish my dad could see my "Radio Personality of the Year" award. As I talk, I start to cry. I'm not ashamed.

"Chris in Kenosha, how you doing, buddy?"

"I hate you, I hate your show, Mancow. I'm glad your father's dead, you faggot!"

I'm stunned. Hurt. Is it so strange for a man to feel in America today? It should be normal! Human beings were designed to *feel.*

When I finish the show, Sergeant Hairclub calls me to his office.

"Look at these latest ratings, Mancow! The *Madhouse* has moved up to number four! Stern's fallen to number thirty!"

Maybe I should thank Mrs. Guttman. Without that demon teacher trying to steal my soul, I might let aggressive assholes run over me today instead of taking them on. Without that demon I would probably be a happier, less offensive person. But is it worth it? To survive Mrs. Guttman's hell I became "something." I'm not sure I've found the real me since.

• • •

It's March 16, St. Patty's eve. At 5 P.M. Jenny and I pick up the dwarf at O'Hare. In my 1972 yellow Ford Maverick in perfect working order, which the dwarf knows from Monterey days, I drive us to Shaw's Crab House. We sit on stools at a high table, slide down a dozen slimies, and eat a whole crab each. The dwarf buys dinner, which is a lot less than his plane ticket cost me. At home I show off all my stuff—the autographed Michael Jordan jersey; the *T2* poster with bullets; my Muhammad Ali boxing gloves that he had to sign with two hands; my original *Star Trek* photo signed by all the stars and framed with patches from every rank; my Bela Lugosi photo matted in red that's cut in the shape of a coffin; my Rush Limbaugh thank-you photo; the real shrunken head from my dad; Buster Keaton's death mask; the Beatles photo with all four signatures. The dwarf stares up for a long time at the Wildwood photo booth four-shot of my dad and mom.

"I've never seen even a picture of them before, you know that?" I didn't. "He looks like a sweet, happy man." He was. "In this picture your mom reminds me of Carolyn."

"You're full of shit, buddy!"

"She reminds me of Jenny too."

"Double shit!"

The dwarf opens the venetian blinds in the living room. "What's that down there all lit up?"

"Navy Pier. You're coming to the freak show aren't you?"

"Not for all the tea in Amsterdam would I miss that show."

St. Patty's Day in Chicago: 4:45 A.M.

"Take us to the Park West," I say.

"What's going on over there?" Cabbie asks. "There's a couple thousand people milling around."

"Is there a fat guy hanging from a crane out front?" I ask.

"I don't know. What's going on?"

"Mancow's Morning Madhouse is broadcasting live from the Park West for St. Patty's Day," the dwarf says.

"Mancow's what?"

"Some radio guys," I say. "Are we sure the crane's coming?"

"It's supposed to already be there," Phone Girl says as she hands an all-access pass to the dwarf, and (in case anybody doesn't recognize me) drops one in the pocket of my brand-new green velvet suit.

"Can't go no farther," Cabbie says as he stops at the police barricade. So many people have gathered, the police have closed the street. I like to take my time through a crowd if I can, but it's 5:05 right now. *Mancow's Morning Madhouse* starts broadcasting live at 5:30. I have a lot to do. We hustle through. When I see the crane, I'm pissed. It's there, but it's laying flat on the truck and Turd is not suspended eighty feet up in the air like he's supposed to be. Security opens the door to let us into the lobby.

"Why aren't you up on the crane, Turd?"

"I got no harness! Big-head Tony was supposed to get a harness an—"

"Where's Big-head Tony?"

"Haven't seen him."

"Damn!"

"I been here since 4:30, Mancow," Turd says like I'd fire him if he'd gotten there at 5—and maybe I would.

My friend Dewey—Lord of the Fat Chicks—is in the lobby, but he's only got one box of T-shirts.

"Big-head Tony's bringing the rest," Dewey says.

"Where's Big-head?!" I shout to the room.

"Engineer Bob Fukuda can't get rid of the static on the connection to the station," Luv Cheez tells me inside the hall. Damn! "But look at the bed!"

Okay! The bed in the cage onstage looks great. With porno women in there doing their thing with lucky listeners from the crowd, we have a show.

The Miller Genuine Draft guy tells me they can't sell beer until 7:30. The crowd outside ain't gonna like that news.

Vixxxen the porno star arrives with Misty Rain. Summer arrives with Amber and other girls from the Body Shoppe.

Big-head arrives with Turd's harness, but it's too late to hang Turd up; he was supposed to be up there an hour ago, and now I need him on-stage. At least Big-head has T-shirts for Dewey.

The Park West doors open. The place packs up as full as the fire laws allow.

"Bob got rid of the static," Luv Cheez tells me.

5:28 A.M.

Back at the studio, Prison Bitch pulls the six carts I want ready as Luv Cheez gives him the list. At 5:30, he hits PLAY. The Mancow show theme hits the airwaves.

"Wake up Chicago! It's St. Patty's Day. And *Mancow's Morning Madhouse* is broadcasting live."

The St. Patty's Day show is the first time I've been onstage in front of this many people since I stopped doing theater in college at Central Missouri State University. All the chaos convinces me that I must hire a production group to help me put the *Mancow Freak Show* on the boards.

Five hours later, it's over.

● ● ●

That night I head to the United Center to introduce AC/DC to thousands of fans. When I interviewed AC/DC on the show, they were prepping to premiere their new CD in London. I told them Chicago should be there too. AC/DC said that if I could set it up, they'd love a live simulcast to Chicago. In three days I rented a hall, found the satellite time, and pulled together all the electronic gadgets I needed. I could have really used my dad's electronic expertise. Giving away 3,000 tickets was easy: get hard enough to hang a Mancow hat on yourself in Mancow Mobile One, you get two tickets.

Tonight AC/DC is paying me back.

It doesn't go as planned.

Big-head Tony doesn't show with the promised thirty dancers. He doesn't show with any. He doesn't even show. The mini-Mancow show I had planned to introduce AC/DC evaporates. It's just me, by myself, playing emcee.

I'm so hyper I could spit nails. Twenty-six minutes later I feel weird, afraid. When I tell myself it's only paranoia, every cell in my body says I'm wrong. Danger lurks, danger to me specifically.

"I need to leave!" With Jenny on one side, the dwarf on the other, trying like hell to be inconspicuous, I race through the fans for an exit.

• • •

While I worked at KDON, Carolyn, Delilah's sister, worked at the Monterey Rape Crisis Center. "Ninety-five out of a hundred women who call say they had a weird feeling—sensed something odd, different, unsettling—as they left their office, or entered that parking garage, or went out on that date where their rape was waiting to happen," Carolyn told me.

Premonition? Female intuition? What Stan Lee calls "the tingly Spidey-sense" in the pages of his *Spider-man* comics?

Can women feel danger? Can they smell it?

Can all of us?

The strange feeling in my body and soul haunts me for two more hours. Nothing goes wrong at the AC/DC concert—no explosions, no murders, not even any car wrecks as people headed home. Doesn't matter. Had I stayed at that concert, I'd be doing radio in hell. I would have been killed. I know this.

I devoured Stern in Chicago.

P. T. Barnum Comes Again

Chicago's aldermen are aghast! They
han the *Mancow Freak Show.* They let 30,000 fans pack the United
Center to watch giants do amazing things with their bodies every night
the Bulls play basketball, but the *Mancow Freak Show?*

Wake up!

We are all freaks!

P. T. Barnum's discovery, Colonel Tom Thumb, got rich the same way
Michael Jordan did. People paid to see him! Come on down! See an amaz-

ing human! Sammy Salami can tie his dick in a knot. I want to see that! So do my listeners. But it ain't gonna happen in Chicago. America celebrates freaks every day, but today it's the tallest, the fastest, the prettiest, the strongest—to the exclusion of all the rest of us ugly people. Chicago's aldermen would welcome the Miss America Pageant, I bet—and that's a freak show. In this Barbie-dominated age, beauty is so media defined, so inhumanly industrial and plastic that overweight kids go to court so they won't have to shower at school. What the hell's going on? Does everyone who isn't media perfect have to hide in this PC age? I'm against it! We are all freaks!

• • •

"Don't look and stare!" your mother said.

Why is it better to look away from a disabled person instead of walking up and staring? Looking long. Looking hard. Looking at the freaky earth suit until you realize that it's just a suit. Bodies don't matter! They aren't what we are! We're human beings, not milk! We're not meant to be homogenized! We must appreciate diversity. Hiding the freaks away and standardizing what bodies should look like aren't the ways to teach this! Eli Whitney invented interchangeable parts, and now all Corporate America wants is interchangeable people. Welcome to public schools! Welcome to standardized testing! Welcome to the end of diversity!

Protesters call the show every day accusing me of exploitation.

"These are 'special' people," they scream.

"You're exploiting the handicapped," they yell.

What are they talking about? Scotty Pippin has to duck through normal doors—that's a handicap. If he shits on a normal shitter, he's scratching his ears with his knees—that's special. He's a freak. We are all freaks! Wake up, America!

What's the difference between Sharon Stone and a bearded lady? Where they keep the hair people pay to snatch a glimpse of!

I'd rather watch Johnny Meah deep-throat a neon sword than watch weightlifter freaks compete in their own Olympic sport. I'd rather see every inch of the tattooed guy and watch him nail his tongue to a board than watch Miss America contestants parade in gowns and swimsuits or hear them answer a question.

I waited for the school bus with a girl who had no nose—just a hole. I could see inside. I was thirteen. "Wow! That's cool," I said. "Lemme see!" I've always been nosy. Noseless Nancy was cool! Of course everybody else treated her like a reject just like they treated me. We talked every day for months. When our high school rich-kid gang came back from Christmas ski vacations with zinc oxide on their noses, Nancy and I carved a nose out of cork, put zinc oxide on it, and she wore it to school as a joke. She got invited to some parties after that. Once people weren't afraid of her, everybody wanted to know the freak. They still didn't want to know me, but sometimes Noseless Nancy asked me along as her date. I loved her differentness. I love the special people. Hell, if you don't know you're special, I don't want to know you!

Hitler had a normal body. Noseless Nancy didn't. Which one was the monster?

Until Americans turned into a nation of sheep wearing gray flannel suits and no longer wanted any freaks around to disturb the illusion, Grady Stiles Jr. was a massively popular sideshow attraction. Instead of hands with fingers his flesh divided at his wrist to resemble fleshy claws. This fifth-generation Lobster Man had feet of the same design.

When Mary Stiles (who was not a Lobster person) became pregnant, Grady Jr. was terrified his kids might look like her. When the children were born, he was thrilled to see they continued the Lobster line.

But with his lobster hands he beat his wife. Prob'ly what he got when he was a kid, but that kind of shit's disabling! Mrs. Stiles repeatedly threatened her Lobster Man husband, but he never stopped the beatings. One day she gave money to the Human Blockhead for a hit man who later shot the violent son of a bitch, twice in the back of the head. She's doing time in Florida for the murder.

What was he thinking? It's not like he could run away.

Kathy Stiles and her brother, Grady III, are the Lobster Twins.

We think of all freaks as genetic mistakes, but they could be flashes of ancient human races hunted to extinction or physically unable to adapt to environmental change. Ancient texts and myths talk about the little people as real. In the Old Testament, Jehovah instructs the Israelites to destroy the Anakims, the children of Anak, a race of giants. Goliath stood nine-feet six-inches tall. P. T. Barnum paid freakish people to strut their stuff. He celebrated the unique. I respect that. The great American sideshow, the freak show, is an American creation, an art form like jazz, the blues, and musicals. I'm proud to be bringing it back!

Tonight!! Saturday, June 29, 1996.

Once I found an auditorium, tickets to the *Mancow Freak Show* sold out in two hours. All the performers were willing to stay and do it again on Sunday night. Four hours after we announced the second show, every seat was sold.

We are all freaks!

I'm on my way to the Merrillville Star Plaza in Indiana, where the *Mancow Freak Show,* the fastest selling show in Chicago radio history, can take place without Chicago's aldermen. The dwarf flew in two nights ago, and Jenny's driving us out.

"The *Mancow's Morning Madhouse* live shows I do are never just live remotes," I say. "They're whole live shows. Performances. Halloween at the Hard Rock, St. Patty's at the Park West. You have to do them; it keeps you honest. I do them a lot."

"But?"

"They're free, buddy! I mean, I know I can give people their money's worth if they're not paying. But this audience laid down thirty-five bucks a head to come tonight. Do you have my ringmaster's coat?"

"Right here, Mancow."

"Do we have my top hat?"

"Right here, buddy."

"You're gonna get to meet my brothers, dwarf. Johnny's coming both nights. Mark comes tomorrow."

"You still disappointed your mom's not coming?"

"You heard me trying to convince her on the phone. Mark's still trying. Maybe she'll come tomorrow. I doubt it. I hope so. Do you have the stuff we wrote for the intro last night?"

"Typed and ready to go, Mancow, with the Rainmaker's 'Snake Dance' starting it off."

"Good. I want to run through it a couple of times before tonight. Make sure we find the time. You might have to pull me away from something else but—"

"I'll make sure it happens," the dwarf says.

"You got my cigars?"

"Yes. And your shoes. And your socks," Jenny says.

"Even if your mom doesn't come, your dad will be out there tonight cheering louder than any of them, Mancow."

"Thanks, buddy. Glad you're here. There it is!"

Off I-65 the Merrillville Star Plaza billboard flashes "Tonite," then "The Mancow Show."

"They refused to put 'Freak' on the sign. Can you believe that?!"

In the parking lot, a huge crowd of twisted and mangled protesters picket the show.

"Jenny, can I have the flowers the dwarf brought you? I'll get you some more."

"Sure."

"Stop here." I get out of the car and walk to the protesters. I hand each one a flower for as long as I have flowers to give. One guy is clearly a Vietnam vet who caught a shell or stepped on a land mine. His legs stump off above where he used to have knees, his left arm is mostly gone, his face is badly scarred. The butt of his M16 sits between his leg stumps, the barrel rests in the crook of his right arm, the one complete limb he has left. I drop a stem of freesias in the muzzle of his gun. With the only hand he has left, he pulls the flower out and throws it on the asphalt.

"Get away from me," he shouts. "You're Mancow!"

The mood of the crowd changes. As the business end of his M16 lolls toward my face I wonder if today is a good day to die.

"Damn, you looked like a Berkeley hippie facing down the National Guard!" the dwarf enthuses.

"Yeah? Thought it was smart to get out before it turned into Kent State. Why don't these people protest beauty contests instead of me? Why don't they protest the media snow job that cuts them out of the American Dream?"

• • •

It's 8 P.M. The ten-minute film loop showing freaks from all times and places stops running on the giant screens. As Casanova Ace, the black Chicago rapper, finishes his intro rap, my booming, distorted, electronic voice fills the auditorium. "I am Mancow! I am Mancow!" The Mancow logo face flashes on the screens, becomes my real face, then morphs me in to Pinhead from *Hellraiser.* Snakes crawl out of my eyes. The face morphs to a skull. The curtains open. Fog machines mist the stage. The steel truss I'm sitting on descends. Strobes cut in. The follow spot hits me. The audience goes insane.

When I get close enough, I jump to the stage and walk to the lip. I let the audience excitement fill me.

"The Suits said we couldn't do this show, but dammit here we are!" I scream into the mike. The audience cheers.

"We are all freaks!" I shout. "We are all freaks!"

I point the mike to the audience.

"We are all freaks! We are all freaks! We are all freaks!"

The chant builds until it's louder than what I heard driving home past Navy Pier so many months ago. Suddenly—and for the first time since I started this thing—I actually feel it might work.

> "This is the Lion's Den!
> I hope you knew that before you came in.
> This is where the angels and the devils fight
> and they are choosing up sides tonight!

"The angels and the devils are playing tug of war with my personality.

"Tonight we see who wins.

"Tonight we shine light in the darkness!

"From a world where we are all taught to be alike we come tonight to celebrate the unique!

"We don't want to be swallowed by the world!

"We want to be different!

"We are different!

"We are all *freaks!*"

Well of Souls, big winners in the Mancow Big-Band Beat-Off, plays Turd's theme. The audience chants, "Turd. Turd. Here comes the Turd."

Turd the bartender comes out to wild applause. He wants to show me his golf clubs, but he must have picked up the wrong sack at O'Hare. When Turd unzips, Baby B the midget jumps out with a bat and beats Turd in the nuts and off the stage.

I intro Johnny Meah, the Czar of the Bizarre, but Johnny's old carnie rap is way too slow for this audience.

"Stop the hype and swallow the sword!" I yell at Johnny. The audience cheers. Johnny opens his goozle and deep-throats solid steel.

"Drive the ice pick into your head and get off the stage, you old fuck!"

Johnny Meah sticks the ice pick up his nose, pushes on it so it sticks out straight, and uses my mike to hammer all the metal into his head.

"I sure hope you don't need that part of your brain anymore, Johnny!"

Wild applause as Johnny pulls the ice pick out of his skull.

Turd comes onstage wearing a thong.

"Where's the rest of the crew? Irma, Luv Cheez, Phone Girl, Freak—come on out here! Let this audience see you." The crew comes out as stagehands (all wearing black Mancow T-shirts) move Johnny's electric chair and neon sword into place. Turd gets the chair. When Freak throws the switch, Turd electrifies. The bulb in his mouth lights up. Johnny lights a neon tube by touching it to Turd's skin. When Johnny takes the tube away, a fire starts burning in Turd's hand. This is not planned.

Turd's hands are strapped to the chair. He's screaming by the time Irma slaps the fire out with her scarf.

Johnny lights his neon sword and opens his shirt. I call for lights down and audience silence. I explain how dangerous this gag is; two other performers died when the neon tube broke inside their throats. Johnny takes a few deep breaths, throws his head back, opens his mouth, and pushes that neon down until his whole fucking chest glows brighter than E.T.'s. He pulls the neon out. As the audience goes insane, everyone leaves the stage except the Mancow ringmaster.

"Before the show, Irma was backstage getting it on with this guy, until finally I told her, 'Irma, that's not a guy—that's Zenobia the Bearded Lady!' "

My introduction makes Zenobia testy. She hates the jokes I tell on-stage with her even more. The way she sasses gets the audience angry. They want to see her tits, her snatch—some proof she is a woman—but Zenobia won't give it up. As the Bearded Lady starts to juggle her bowling pins, I leave the stage for a break. I wipe dripping sweat off my face and neck with the towel Jenny hands me.

"How do you think it's going?" I ask.

"It's a great show! You got 'em in the palm of your hand," says the dwarf, shoving an open bottle of water into my hand.

By the time Zenobia finishes juggling razor-sharp Mohammedan swords, she's got most of the audience back.

Mike Wilson the Tattooed Guy struts his art museum body, then nails his tongue to a table.

Vixxxen the porno star's pet phython charms her out of her pants. Every man in the house wishes his snake was slithering over her cracks.

With T2 I walk to Vixxxen as she gets the python out of her box and back inside his basket. The audience loves Vixxxen.

"When I started pumping the *Freak Show,* I got lots of calls. Hell, you all know that! You're listeners. But maybe you can't listen every day. Maybe you didn't hear the call from this man, a listener who called up to say he'd like to be part of this show tonight in his first ever performance in front of a crowd. This is a courageous man. He lost part of his face to cancer but instead of crying about it, he discovered he could do things now that no one else in the world can do and he wants to show them to you. So, T2—take off those sunglasses!" Under the sunglasses, T2 has one normal eye and one gaping hole where the other eye used to be.

"Talk about a weird way to drink beer—here it is!"

T2 sticks the long neck into his eye hole and chugs. "Spit some out so they know you're really drinking." T2 does. The amazed audience breaks into wild applause.

"Get the camera in really tight. You can't see this unless you're close. Okay."

A thing like a worm appears in T2's eye hole looking like it wants to slither out.

"That's his *tongue!*"

I wish my dad could see this with me. T2's as good as Popeye.

"Okay. Can we have the lights down? Good. Thank you."

I shine a flashlight around the audience. T2 takes it, puts it in his mouth. Light beams from his eye hole. The audience gasps, then starts stomping as they clap and chant, "T2! T2!"

As stagelights come back up, the delight and satisfaction shining in T2's face has just made this whole show worthwhile for me.

"Wait! T2 wants to say something!" I hand him my mike.

Slowly, deliberately, each word separate, T2 says, "We ... are ... all ... freaks." I look at him in awe.

"We are all freaks!" the audience chants.

"Ladies and gentlemen—Fireman Ray Wold!" Ray runs onstage with his hat on fire. As he tries to wave it out, his coat catches fire.

In my dressing room I strip off my sopping shirt. Jenny takes it.

The dwarf wipes me down, then massages my shoulders like he's Angelo Dundee working Muhammad Ali. I'm glad these two hold my corner.

Luv Cheez comes in semihysterical. "When Ray came up out of the burning water at the end of his act, the flames went everywhere! It caught the curtain on fire! I beat it out!"

"Dad would have loved it, Erich! He'd be proud. I'm proud. It's an amazing show, bro."

"Thanks, Johnny. That means a lot."

• • •

Tree, the comedian who makes Marge Schott look like a Girl Scout, gets booed off the stage. We're going down in flames.

I take the Pumpkin Fuckers out. Dressed as European clowns, one of them has a dick that hangs to his knees. The audience likes that. They do some funny shit. Then, while one clown holds the pumpkin, long dong starts to fuck it. Third clown races up and Bobbitt's the dick with a cleaver. Blood pumps everywhere. The crowd loves it.

As the Nipple Man, another listener freak, lifts bricks using rings through his nipples, fights break out in the balcony. Maybe the show's all right.

Stagehands roll the Lobster Twins onstage. While I talk to Grady and Kathy, the camera comes in close so the audience can get a good look. Completely unplanned, Grady wiggles off the platform and (because his lobster legs don't work) swings himself to the lip of the stage using his arms. He wants audience members to see him close, shake his claws, touch him.

The audience goes nuts.

Lawnmower Man juggles bowling pins and knives. He starts up three chainsaws and cuts some wood with each. He juggles three running chainsaws! That's insane! He finishes the chainsaws. He starts a lawnmower, lifts it over his head, and balances the handle on his nose! Once it's steady, the whole cast of the show throws cabbages into Lawnmower Man's whirling blades.

"This is the finale, folks! Thank you all for coming!"

Joints flying from the audience mixing onstage with coleslaw.

Curtains close. The *Mancow Freak Show* ends.

For tonight.

Night number two is exactly like night number one, except I'm calmer, the curtain doesn't catch on fire, Turd doesn't catch on fire, and from the seat I'd reserved for my mom, the kid who sold us beer for tonight's party keeps screaming, *"I love you, man!"*

After the show, Mark tells me, "Dad would have loved it."

At dawn, as the raucous postshow party ends, I cab it to O'Hare.

On the plane, as I look at Phone Girl's gift, a biography of P. T. Barnum, I see the picture. P.T. stands on railroad tracks in Podunk, America, while the biggest elephant the world has ever known, the elephant Barnum loved and coined the name Jumbo for, lies on her side across the tracks—dying.

This image has haunted my dreams my entire life. I feel the elephant skin on my hands and on my cheek as I try to say good-bye. I always wake up crying.

Every man's weakness.

Fungi Jumping

I love Amsterdam: the foreign feel, the signs and newspapers in a different language, people speaking Dutch as they pass, the multitude of bikes, the silent trams, the lack of cars, the number of people who walk. Last year Amsterdam gave me the squirmies, showed me freedoms I have never experienced, freedom from everything that comprises my normal daily life. There's nothing like that surprise, that new door opening to adventure. We call America "the Land of the Free," but after experiencing Amsterdam, the United

States feels like a police state where everyone walks around miserable and afraid. In Amsterdam, eyes twinkle. Delight bubbles out of everyone. I love it. I'm back!

The dwarf and I wander the Voorburgwal until we arrive at Oudekerksplein. Inside a fence with menacing spikes sits Amsterdam's oldest church. In every ground-floor window of Old Church Square, Amsterdam's legion of whores tout their wares.

"God didn't put us here to worry!" I say. "He put us here to love one another and enjoy our brief blip of time. How did this nugget of truth escape modern Christianity? I love life. I crave liberty. I pursue happiness—all out—all the time. And I almost became a minister."

"St. Augustine said, 'Love—and do what you want,' " the dwarf replies.

"I stopped going to church when I realized Jesus says whores and sinners get into heaven before the churchmen who write the rules. America's churches don't want anybody hanging out with whores and sinners, but Jesus did. Jesus' best buddy was Mary the whore. How can anybody call someone else a sinner? I know I have a dark side. I embrace it. If I had become a preacher, man, I'd be in the bars, the porno bookstores, and Wal-Mart giving Jesus' message of love. I hang out with porno stars now, and I don't think I'll be denied heaven."

Across a canal, a photographer shoots a woman in a bathing suit posing on a boat in the bright sunshine.

"Look at her! If I were four feet taller I'd give her what for," moans the dwarf, probably with a boner. Thankfully, if he does have one, you can't tell.

"Oh, dude, remember the suntan babes?"

"Don't think so."

"Lowest point of my life until my dad died. Almost two years ago—I hadn't been in Chicago long. I was the first act at a professional wrestling bout, introducing the tanning-lotion swimsuit models. Their *Baywatch* one-piece swimsuits were stretched to the limits of Lycra elasticity, but their fleshy nipples, some the size of my thumb, pushed that manmade material beyond science. The ten most perfect-looking women I have ever been in the company of at once. My 501 jean buttons were pushing to pop. Then something goes wrong—they speak. They grit their perfect teeth through faux smiles and instruct me how to behave. 'No tits-and-ass comments.' 'Nothing sexual.' 'We're models, not prostitutes.' 'And keep your hands to yourself.' Yes, teachers! Yes, bleached-blond dictatorial wenches of perfection! I look in disbelief. How dare they give me attitude while they hang their bodies all over me as they walk through the crowd to the wrestling ring.

"I hold the ropes apart and watch little black hairs wave at me as they bend over and open their legs to step through the ropes. Black mounds, exercised legs, perfect asses right in my face. The crowd loves these girls. But when I enter the ring, the crowd goes insane and I think, ten thousand people here like *me* better than *you*, cheerleaders! It's Dork Boy's party this time! I'm cutting those old strings. You sexual Geppettos can't control me!

"When I grab the mike a voice I've never heard before escapes my mouth. 'Look at all the pussy I brought you tonight! Just look at that pussy! You want some? My God, look at those tits.' The fans go crazy! Cheering. Enthusiastic. 'Look at those perfect asses! Who'd start with their pussies? Who'd start with their tits? Which tit?' I walk slowly by the women. If looks could kill, I'd be dead. I rant. These future Stepford Wives are my props and that's all they'll ever be to any man. 'They're getting hot, folks. Ooooh, they're getting hot! Can I sniff your swimsuit when you get it off? Look how it's buried in there! Can we get a closeup of that? I'd like to ring that out in a mug and drink it!' "

"Jesus, Mancow! You didn't say that."

"I did. I'm not proud of it, but I did. And more. Fake smiles gone forever, all the women looked like the pissed-off stomping Marshmallow Man in *Ghostbusters*. A couple start crying. 'Don't cry, honey!' I spewed. 'We're all whores in some way. Did you really think you were selling suntan lotion?! You sell pussy. It's okay.'

"The promoter storms the ring and rips away the mike. 'I want to apologize for Mancow Muller and his dirty mouth!' When my eyes finally focus on the crowd, I see a five-year-old kid looking up at his mom. What the fuck had I just done? I leave the ring. Most of the audience is booing but some high-five me. 'Mancow's a madman!' someone yells out. 'What did they expect? The Suits tried to censor him, again!' Yeah. The swimsuits. I suddenly thought, Where does this stop? Everything that just went down is new. I would never have done that four years ago. Did I need to crush those holier-than-your-hole babes? Did I care? Was I going crazy? I didn't know. Police escorted me out, protecting me. The crowd was volatile.

"The next morning I began to wonder if everything I love I spoil. Some Midas touch of corruption. I loved radio so much I jumped in headfirst and it took my life."

The dwarf hands me the pipe. I toke, sitting on a bench across the canal from where the photographer shoots the girl.

"Today, I love radio again, but that day . . . God, I just hated everything. I hated my life. I wanted to be a minister! To be a moral man. I reach for purity all the time, but every time I touch it, I spoil it. The battle for this choirboy's soul is ongoing. There's temptation on every side. I don't know if I'll end up a Jedi knight or a Dark Lord of the Sith."

"Complete the training you must, hmm?"

"Bugger off, Yoda."

"You do ask questions," says the dwarf. "You are out there in the fight. Obi-Wan Kenobi is a hermit in the desert when *Star Wars* starts. He'd given up."

"And Darth Vader is a corporate Suit. And Yoda is a puppet with Frank Oz's hand up his butt."

As we walk we pass a man grinding his organ in public. There is one universal law in this life: Monkeys in people's clothing always make you smile. Don't know why that is, but it's always true.

• • •

In a Red Light porno shop I buy the dwarf a present.

"What's this for?"

"It's for the Three-Eyed Turtle, a sexual activity I invented. All you need is a man, a woman, some flexibility, and this cock ring with the little Vienna-sausage-sized plastic penis attached to it. It's called a rectifier.

"Three-Eyed Turtle—Step one: At least thirty minutes of foreplay. Get the ax wound slippery and her backdoor lubricated.

"Step two: Roll the rectifier cock ring to the base of the penis with the little plastic salami toward your feet.

"Step three: Lie on your back—and don't move while your sweetie saddles up. Facing you, she straddles your body and lowers wetness to hardness until the Vienna sausage is knocking on door number two.

"Step four: Insert the little sausage.

"Step five: This requires some flexibility. Take one of her nipples into your mouth to lick, suck, and nibble.

"Step six: Take her other nipple between your fingers and thumb.

"Step seven: Slip your idle hand down, and gently caress the clitoris with a fingertip. I should probably warn you here not to sprain your hand or hurt your wrist. Keeping your palm on your belly and raising a knuckle works just fine, but fingertips feel more than knuckles so work on your flexibility until you can get the palm up.

"That's it! But be prepared for a fucking bucking bronco show because the Three-Eyed Turtle excites *all* primary female erogenous zones at once."

"You invented this technique?"

"Yep! Lots of people have a bastardized idea of what it is to turtle, but I tell you, buddy, no woman I've been with has ever called me too creative. Every woman who rides the Three-Eyed Turtle calls it the most awe-inspiring orgasm she's ever experienced—or even heard of. So, spread the word. Spread the beaver!"

"You're twisted, Mancow."

"Not twisted . . . sprained."

[Since knowing the clitoris and how to treat it well is the very first step away from amateurish sex and happenstancial female orgasms, we won't discuss it here. Attempting the Three-Eyed Turtle without knowing the clitoris is not advised.]

The head shop is packed with pipes, hookahs, Singapore paper umbrellas, and a vast array of weird shit people could only buy if they're stoned. They also sell freaky, visual fun stuff people might buy when they know they're going to eat some psychedelic 'shrooms.

"We'd like to buy some mushrooms," the dwarf tells the guy behind the counter.

"Which mushrooms would you like?"

Five fungi into the menu we opt for psylocibin—Mexican origin—grown from spores here in Holland. The Hell's Angel pirate-bitch counterman disappears into the back of the store. He returns with a little plastic baggie packed with fungi that I think he just picked. As we eat the 'shrooms, I want ranch dressing. These babies kick ass.

In the Bulldog coffee shop I sit with the dwarf at a huge red Stratocaster guitar table that even Jimi Hendrix's spirit on LSD couldn't play. The table starts to squiggle. As I set my beer down on the giant guitar, the whole fucking thing is squiggling. The waitress squiggles past the bar in the other room, but the doorway suddenly jumps two hundred feet away. Now the bar is ten feet away again, but it's packed with insects sipping at people's heads like flowers. Waves of energy. I want to put my own drink to my lips, but my beer decides to merge with the table, with my hand, with the music. The beer won't come off the table. My hand won't come off the glass. Everything I see and touch changes and goes psychedelic.

The guitar starts to breathe. It expands to the size of a football field then shrinks to the size of a pin. I'd love to play guitar. The guitar tells me I can.

"I must ask you to leave."

Where the hell is that voice coming from? As I turn my head, a body forms out of the energy waves. It's a woman. She's holding a tray. She looks like a giant mosquito with her stinger in a beer. How does the beer stay on her tray? She's standing on the wall. Flares of red shoot from every hole in her squeeze-clown head. She's going to stick me on a tooth-pick and eat me as an hors d'oeuvre. What would that feel like?

"I don't know what your friend is on," Waitress says.

"He's on the table."

"Exactly! Customers are not allowed to hump the tables."

"It's okay," the dwarf reassures, outside. "You're in Amsterdam. It's legal to feel."

"Is Anne Frank's place around here?"

"Yeah. Somewhere."

"I want to see that secret attic room where Anne gave up her virgin-ity to Peter. Many times. Her dad cut all the sex stuff out when he typed up her diary. They found it in the original after he died. I want to see the attic that little girl grew up in, fearful and hiding from Hitler's Nazis. I'm glad she got laid, aren't you?"

"There's the house."

"What are all these people doing there?"

"Waiting to go in."

"Shit! I don't want to wait in line with two hundred Japanese tourists. This is a nice neighborhood. I always . . . hmmm . . . never thought of Anne Frank living canal-side. Listen! Those are the church bells. She wrote about those church bells. Do you think Anne ever saw them?!"

"She sure as hell never went outside."

The line of tourists ends at a walkway up to a house with four floors and a secret attic. When I look at the place, I laugh so hard I fall in the canal.

"Have a nice swim?" the dwarf asks as I climb the ladder. "What the hell got into you?"

"You didn't see the sign?"

"What sign?"

When I show him, the dwarf roars. The line of tourists looks at us really funny, but the joke's on them. On a huge sign, the Anne Frank House Trust announces in four different languages (but not Japanese), "Closed for Remodeling."

"How do you remodel Anne Frank's house?"

"I don't know."

• • •

No wonder the Dutch don't mind wearing wooden shoes—they're too whacked to care! I'm too flipped to care I'm soaking wet, but when the dwarf informs me we're half a block from home I want to shower and change. I'd really prefer a steambath, to see what might come out of the mist.

At the Pulitzer, beer and chocolate come out of our fridge. The Dutch know munchies.

EuroMTV plays something I've never heard.

"That'll never make it in America," the dwarf predicts.

"Oh, man, I disagree!"

"It's stupid."

"You're tapping your feet. It's gonna be huge."

When "The Macarena" finishes, I shower.

After twenty minutes I remember to take off my clothes.

11

Peek-a-boobies!

Own Yourself

"What's up, Mancow? You've been really weird." It's the dwarf.

"My contract was up the night of the freak show, buddy."

"Right. Explains a lot. These guys are smarter than KDON. They won't cut you loose. Sure, working without a contract, they could fire you any time. But you haven't worked a day for them yet without a contract, and I know Eatman's negotiating."

"Bob thinks we can get a million dollars."

"How much do you weigh?"

"What?"

"How much do you weigh, Cow?"

"I'd like to say 200, but I'm getting fat. Maybe 220."

"You told me to figure it out once. I did. At one million dollars, if you weighed 178, you, the man who can talk, the man who can communicate, would be worth your weight in gold. Lose weight or you're not there yet. Let's see . . . 16 ounces times 220 times 350 . . . you need $1,232,000 to be worth your weight in gold. But, of course, that's worth your weight in gold *every year!* Congratulations! This is a problem ninety-nine percent of the world would give their right arm to have, Cow. Can you make a quarter mil if you syndicate or do they buy syndication with the million?"

"Eatman's trying to keep syndication rights for Cow Inc. It might mean a lot less money in salary."

"But you stay independent. Toke on this. There is an answer."

Rudolph the brown-nose reindeer,
bottom of his reindeer class,
Rudolph the brown-nose reindeer,
always had his nose in Santa's ass.

Funny song. I wrote it, produced it, and played it for Christmas 1991 on KDON radio in the Monterey Bay area of California.

"We can't have this, Mancow! You've crossed the line. Listeners are complaining. You can't make fun of Christmas."

"Guys, no offense, but you're Jewish. You don't even celebrate Christmas. I guarantee, Rudolph *never* appears in the New Testament."

Didn't matter. "Ass" was on their list of words I couldn't say, lines I couldn't cross, rules I couldn't break. For thirteen months I stayed inside their cubicle and followed their rules. Attica! Attica! Then I got bored of being so fake. December 22 my ass fell out on the air—the darkest day of the year, the most frightening day of my life, a stomach-losing plummet on Mr. Cow's Wild Ride. "Merry Christmas. You're terminated!" My one-year contract had expired a month before, and KDON slung my butt in the snow faster than you can say, "Lick my balls raw."

I felt like a downsized post office worker who bought the American Dream and just had a nasty wakeup call. My stomach knotted and screamed, You'll never work again, asshole! I understood the frustration, the anger, the fear of working for a faceless corporation that gives you assurances and then throws you to the wolves. I felt the human being behind the headlines, the guy with a family who suddenly doesn't know how he can support them. I understood how he could take a gun to downsize the boss who fired him, and the coworkers who didn't stand with him.

Those are people!

Not numbers!

Not a thousand too many checks! People!

I sat alone that night in the cozy little house I couldn't pay the rent on anymore. Frightened.

Across the street, my neighbors' five-year-old son Li'l Donny had a pet rabbit. He loved that rabbit as much as I loved my pud when I was sixteen. Which is why I could only stand aghast in heart-pounding panic when Max showed up with a muddy white rabbit clenched tightly in her jaws the night I got fired from KDON. Max was the undisputed winner in the bulldog-bunny bout. The litany of silent prayers that raced through my head as I reached for that rabbit were to no avail. Donny's darling, the great white rabbit, was dead meat in Max's mouth.

What to do? What to do?

All possible options flashed through my head in an instant. This rabbit was much too special to just take by the ears across the street, ring the doorbell, and say, "I'm sorry to have to tell you this but my dog killed your Thumper." Besides, it was 10:45 at night and their lights were out. I kicked the possibilities around and found to my surprise that rabbits slide really well on polished hardwood floors. Well, I didn't want to touch it! That bunny flew like a puck on fresh Zambonied ice.

I thought of accusing the kid. "You stupid schmuck, look what you get for forgetting to lock the cage!" But finally there was nothing else to do. I put on my gloves and washed the rabbit until he was snow white. I gave him a blow job to dry him off. I had to use some hair gel to make sure Max's tooth marks stayed covered. I pushed the left eye back in his skull. I forced his little rabbit limbs around until it looked like he was lying peacefully on his stomach fast asleep. (Do three-legged rabbits think a rabbit's foot is lucky?) I stole across the street and placed the bunny back in the open cage, locked it, stood back, and admired him for a moment. It was a good job. Mortician Mancow. Thumper looked great. Li'l Donny wouldn't know he was dead until he reached in the cage to pet him. Death by natural causes in the night, locked inside a bunny cage. No one would be the wiser. There would be no questions to answer. Tears of course—but that's life—or . . .

I went to bed, slept the sleep of the dead, and woke up like Pavlov's dog at 3 A.M., just like I was trained. Across the street the lights of a police car flash silently in the darkness. The cop and Li'l Donny's parents stand around the rabbit cage. Going over to see what's wrong seems like the least guilty thing to do, so I do it.

"What's going on?"

As the policeman shakes his head and the mother cries and the rabbit lays there just like he's sleeping, the father says, "I don't understand some people. What kind of sick bastard would dig up Li'l Donny's dead rabbit and put it back in its cage?"

Oops.

Five blocks from home I remember I no longer have the job I'm heading to.

• • •

In college I worked for a company that sent guys out to jockey discs for parties, weddings, high school reunions. It was more money than I'd ever seen. It looked like freedom to me. My dad saw prison.

"The company takes fifty percent? That's highway robbery!"

"I can't do anything about it, Dad."

"You can get your ass out there and do it yourself! Shut up and listen for a second! People request you. You're making a name for yourself. You're good. If you did half as many gigs on your own you'd be making the same green."

"What do I use for equipment?"

"Buy the equipment!"

"I'm a college student! The only income I have is spinning discs for Ray—a job that if you give me the money, Mr. Loan Officer, I'm going to quit to go out on my own!"

"It's a great idea!"

"We both know going out on your own can be a whole lot worse than sucking it in and working for the Man." I didn't believe those words even as they left my mouth, but I saw the weapon they formed. And I saw him flinch as it hit. My dad could sell more cabinets in a day than any other salesman sold in a week. It took years, but eventually his employers grew unhappy. If John Muller could sell that much in a day—think how much he could sell if he worked all week! His bosses suddenly wanted I saw-John-Jones-from-3-to-5-today reports. Dad resisted. They insisted. When they got hard-ass, Dad told them to fuck themselves and went out on his own. "Put their thirty percent in my own pocket!"

Six months later he came to see my high school's production of *Death of a Salesman*. I played the salesman. "Dammit, son! You were good! You were . . . I felt like you were showing me my life. Damn. What a play. What a part. What a . . . you . . . you were great!" The next month he declared bankruptcy. Then—Merry Christmas—we left Missouri for New Jersey, where we moved in with Uncle Frank, Aunt Kathy, and the cousins for what turned into a year.

"Dammit! Erich!" Yeah, I hit him. Here comes the counterattack. "I can't have faith in a man who doesn't believe in himself. No one can."

The next day I worked on my résumé while my dad worked on his '39 Ford. I couldn't realize then what that old car meant to him. That car embodied the last of his boyhood dreams, dreams that slowed when he got married, dreams that cracked and changed out of all recognition when he had a kid. Somehow that old clunker my dad bought for thirty-five dollars was the memory palace that still contained all the dreams of freedom he had at seventeen. I think he would have liked to have been Jack Kerouac living a life of adventure on the road instead of the traveling salesman who drove those roads for money, for the green he needed to support his wife and sons. I don't know for certain. I entered my dad's life in the thirty-fourth room of his life's library. Johnny entered in the twenty-fourth room. I can't know who he was at twenty-three. I can't know who he was at seventeen. I do know he kept that clunker until he died. I didn't know until he died that he'd bought that car half a lifetime before I was born, two thirds of a lifetime before I turned seventeen.

When I went to the garage to show him my résumé, I found my dad lying on the front right fender with his feet off the ground and his hands and head invisible under the open hood.

"Erich? Can you hand me a nine-sixteenths?"

"Open or box?"

"Bring 'em both, but hand me the open end first. Prob'ly have to hand it up from the floor."

He laid on that fender working on his car for an hour while I supplied him tools.

"What you got?" he finally asked.

"My résumé," I said, holding it out.

He took it, glanced at it, and ripped it up without reading it.

"Dammit, Dad!"

"Don't swear to me, boy."

"I worked hard on that."

"Nobody gives a damn about your résumé. Yeah, it's impressive for nineteen, but no one cares where you went to school, or about your commercials, or *On Golden Pond,* or any of the other plays you've done. Where's your business plan? You have to show 'em where you're going, not where you've been."

"I don't have to be independent!"

"You'll wind up hating anything less, son. How many gigs can you get on your own in a month?"

"Ten."

"Really? That's two grand a month coming in." Mrs. Guttman would have loved my dad. "What's the total cost on the equipment?"

"About six grand."

"Dammit! I can't use it, you can't use it, nobody can use 'about'! Price! Make! Where you're gonna buy it. You need an equipment list with retail prices and a side sheet showing what you can really get it for."

I ran his Muller marathon. I found the equipment. Made his list. Knocked on the door of every bank. No gold. Not even any logs.

"Dammit, son! These people are crazy or stupid! There's a cash cow staring them in the goddamn face! This is a *good* business venture!"

Every Savings and Loan turned it down.

"Come see what I've done to the old Ford, Biff," my dad says, calling me the name of the eldest son in *Death of a Salesman*. I see a glint in his eye.

"You get it running?"

"You'll see." He opens the kitchen door to the garage.

A neon creature flashes up, up, and through a neon hole. "How's 'Holey Moley Muller' for a disc demon's name?" I'm stunned. My entire portable studio is set up in the garage. With my dad detailing all the electronics like an excited kid, I'm twenty minutes into looking over the setup before I realize my new-to-me DJ equipment sits where his '39 Ford had sat since he found good work, and Mom and I left New Jersey to join him in the Show Me State.

"Where's the car, Dad?" When he looks at me, he smiles kind of funny. "Jesus! You didn't sell it, did you?"

"Nah. I got it running! Took it over to Jake's so he can knock out some of the dings. Maybe I'll get it painted. Besides, needed some place to set up your stuff. Your low price was $400 high, Erich. You gotta work on that. Got everything here for $4,283–including the mole! Go prove me smarter than the banks!"

I did.

During my first months at KDON, I used the equipment to do live Mancow weekend shows from places like Garlic World. But when my dad brought Maxine out to California, I gave the equipment to him to take back to DJ for old folks in Kansas City. Now, as I sit in a yellow Ford Maverick with more bondo in the body than metal, with a sticky valve that knocks when it idles, with no job to go to, with that fist of fear clenched in my stomach hard, I wish I had that amazing equipment back. As much as I loathe spinning discs at parties, I know it could make me some green.

Christmastime 1991 proved to be dog days for local news—Monterey County's top news story was Mancow getting the shaft. I was on the news a lot. On January 6, three men arrived at my door. "We saw a star," they said, "bitching on TV. We're the owners of K-Soul, KSOL in San Mateo. Next month we move to San Francisco. Come with us. Change our name. Start a whole new kind of radio." This was wild! They offered me gold, an easy way to separate from my live-in girlfriend (she was incensed), and aloe-impregnated toilet paper in every stall.

My first day at KSOL, the entire staff walked out. They thought a black man was coming to save their station. Most of them came back. In six months, Wild 107 was neck and neck with KMEL, our biggest competitor. In a year we were kicking their ass. In two years we beat everybody.

Contract time.

When I don't re-sign with Wild 107 right away, Evergreen Media offers me work in Chicago. Jimmy DeCastro tells me he's certain Mancow will help their heavy metal station thrive—and getting Mancow away from Wild is the only way to stop the hemorrhage of listeners and advertising dollars from their SF station, KMEL. Jimmy offers more than Wild, but I can't say yes. I don't want to leave San Francisco. I don't want to leave a station I named, helped create, and took to number one. I don't want to leave the people who pulled my ass in from the cold. One guy is a really good friend. I can't fuck a buddy and still feel good about myself.

"Word on the grapevine has it your owners are selling. Stay there or come here, you'll be working for different people either way," Jimmy says.

I ask my buddy if the rumor is true.

"Hell, no! We're not selling. We're not planning to sell."

One week after I sign for two more years, Wild sells. I'm stunned to realize a man I thought was my friend must have lied through his smiling teeth because without Mancow, Wild was suddenly worth a lot less money.

I call Jimmy DeCastro. Chicago still wants me. They fly me in. They wine and dine me. It seems like what they're saying is true, that because there's no Broadway, no TV soaps, and no film studios, radio personalities get more respect in Chicago than in New York or Los Angeles, the only two bigger radio markets.

I call Bob Eatman, who's just become my first-ever agent. And Bob's a lawyer. (Man, he was disgusted at the contract the lawyer in Monterey drew up for me when I signed with KSOL. For two years Wild has owned my name, my syndication rights, everything—and I didn't know it!) Bob gets Evergreen to commit to a lot more money than San Francisco was going to pay.

When I walk, Wild 107's new owners file a restraining order to keep me off the air unless I'm on the air for them. I suffer a month in hell.

I left Kansas City with nothing but the name Mancow Muller. I left KDON with a more developed Mancow character, the name *Mancow's Morning Madhouse,* and a year of development on the concept. Now I have to leave San Francisco. It feels like I'm starting over. I hate it. But I can't work where corporate suck-boys lie through their teeth.

When the case hits court, my lawyers show the judge the plaque everybody at Wild signed wishing me luck in Chicago. The judge tells Wild's new owners to suck eggs. I'm free to work where I want.

I hate contract time.

Two months later my dad has a heart attack. Then the doctors tell him he has terminal cancer. I can fly to Kansas City in an hour from Chicago. I visit my dad a lot.

In the big view of things I know God . . . destiny . . . something was watching out for me; Chicago hired me in 1993 so I could be close to my dad through his illness and death. I hate what my ex-buddy did in San Francisco, but I'm glad I'm not still there going, "I should have been home!" I was.

• • •

Outside, the Achterburgwal, the Red Light main drag, is packing with people. Nightlife is starting to pump!

"Sleaze and filth, gentlemen! Sleaze and filth! All day! Every day! Come on in now."

"You look like a man who likes wet pussy, sir."

"I can see you love knowledge, professor. Come in for the education."

"Walk by two more times and I'll make you buy a ticket!"

"Look at the pictures. Wouldn't you like to see that live?"

Twelve different hawkers use twelve different come-ons to ply a thousand prurient interests in forty different tongues. My favorite is a long-haired guy who looks like a pirate. Partly, it's his earring. Partly, it's the rattlesnake boots disappearing into Brioni blackness. Partly, it's his black hair, black brows, and olive skin. We stop to talk. He claims he's not Italian but Amsterdam Dutch. His name's still Guido, though, and he's always selling—a hustler hustling all the time.

"It's a living, you know?" is all he wants to say about his work.

On a bridge over the canal the dwarf and I toke while we watch Guido try to sell a married couple on seeing his fuck show. Guido hooks them solid, reels them in, takes their money. Then, instead of opening the door to the theater behind him, Guido leads the couple down the street toward us. I don't know if this couple is from Chicago, Baltimore, or Gdansk, but something about them shouts Polish. Embarrassed and Catholic guilty, the couple sticks close to Guido and listens hard to his walking spiel, keeping their heads down just in case the pope or anyone from the neighborhood happens to be in the Amsterdam Red Light tonight. Guido flashes us a satisfied, toothy pirate smile as he passes.

Guido's good. He has to be. He can't just take your money and let you in because Guido's theater doors lead nowhere! The *real* theater is a block away and across the canal.

It's like radio in America. The Federal Communications Act of 1995 changed the radio rules. Now, instead of a two-station maximum in a single market like Chicago, the same corporation can own and operate eight. Nothing in the new law says those stations can't be the top eight stations in the market. Under the old law a single company could own a maximum of seven stations nationwide. *No* limits exist anymore nationwide. I can feel the change coming already and it is gargantuan.

So far, Evergreen has never successfully syndicated anyone. A syndication company has offered me a million a year but since they *only* syndicate, I'd have no home station. I need to see response. I need to feel the people. The syndicators want the show bad. If the old rules still applied I'd probably go with the syndicators. If Evergreen got mad and kept me off all their stations, well, by the old rules, that would only be seven stations. But Evergreen (and Infinity) have been eating up stations like carp in a feeding frenzy. And they're still buying. Syndicator's afraid Evergreen might keep me off *all* their stations if I leave. I have never worried about offending an employer before. Fine, I used to think. If I lose my job on this station, there's one across the street, one in another town, that wants to build its numbers. They'll hire me. It's not that way anymore.

Colgate sells Tide, Cheer, Era, Oxydol, Gain, and seven other detergents. But there's only one theater. General Motors sells Chevys, Buicks, Pontiacs, Cadillacs, Oldsmobiles, GMC trucks, heavy trucks, tanks, and Frigidaires. Own everything—but give the illusion of choice. Clever ploy. RJ Reynolds sells five kinds of Camels, as well as Winstons, Salems, and More. Democrats and Republicans run two candidates—Corporate America owns them both.

Play ball or lose your job.

When I came to Chicago, I took on all the morning radio legends at once. Screwing with the competition is a time-honored radio tradition. One day my Evergreen Media bosses called me in for a chat.

"We love you destroying the competition, Mancow, but you're going too far. You have to stop attacking Johnny B."

"Why?" I ask. "Trashing the competition is—"

"He's not competition, Mancow."

"He's on another station!"

"Mancow, we love you. But stop fucking with Johnny—*now*!"

My boss and the big boss, who owned my station and Evergreen, didn't warn me off "Coward Sperm" or "Danny Bonadouchebag," but I had to—*had to*—stop trashing Johnny. He was theirs. He made them money. Building my audience by taking listeners from Johnny didn't put a penny in Evergreen's corporate pocket. Good-bye competition.

• • •

Guido sells elegant offbeat sex shows. His buddy sells sleaze and filth. Ten other hawkers sell ten other ways. But no matter what you think you're buying, there's only one theater. Only one show.

Guido's coming back.

"Only one theater, right?"

"We like monopoly in the Red Light," Guido says. "Competition is destructive. Lack of competition increases the profits."

Well, it's coming to American radio and it scares me to death.

In a black-lit room, the white bra and panties of the beautiful blonde glow in the dark. A brown-haired Thai girl walks into blondie's room to visit. First time I've ever seen two women in a single Red Light window. They talk behind their first-floor picture window—where the view is all from my side.

"You like them," Guido says.

Am I starting to drool or is he reading my mind?

"Would you like to have them? You Americans like threesomes."

"Do we?"

"Oh, yes. I can arrange it. It would be a fantastic night. And, this Thai woman is really a woman."

"What do you mean? What else would she be?"

"Many Thai girls in Amsterdam were boys in Bangkok."

Whoa! Sweet burgundy Thai girl I slipped inside of twice last year? No way! That double set of magic lips could not have been swinging a dick in Bangkok. She couldn't squeeze like that when you're inside if she weren't born female, could she?

"When they get too old for the boy-fucker tourists in Thailand they come here, take the pills, change their sex. Sell themselves for ten more years as a woman."

Whoa!! Is nothing anywhere what it seems?

"How much?" the dwarf demands.

"For six hundred guilders I can give you a time like you have never had in your life," says Guido.

"How long do you get?"

Guido smiles. "For six hundred guilders, I can give you an hour with both these girls."

"I bought him two escort girls last year for three hundred fifty."

"Not for both. Maybe you paid three hundred fifty guilders each," Guido says.

"No. We paid two hundred fifty guilders per hour per girl. About three hundred fifty bucks for both. That's still only five hundred guilders."

"But you had no idea what they would look like until they came," Guido says. "Mancow is looking at these girls now. And he likes them."

I remember two beautiful women at the Amstel. And a chick with a dick and a midget. I take the dwarf aside. "How much is six hundred guilders in real money?"

"Three hundred and thirty bucks. The exchange rate's better this year."

"I want to do it!" The dwarf pulls money from both pockets and counts. The dwarf is always short. We're replaying lime-green fuck-me blondie on the Ku'damm.

"We have four hundred eight guilders, Guido."

"Your little friend can get more. Many automatic banks all along the Dam. Both real women, Mancow. I guarantee it."

"Four fifty," says the dwarf.

"Six hundred."

I hate contract time. The numbers remind me of Mrs. Guttman.

Negotiations continue until they settle on 600. The dwarf forks over 400 guilders and heads off for more. Guido takes me up the stairs and inside. He introduces Maria and Annanda. My first whores with names. Interesting.

"Show my friend a good time," Guido tells them. He closes the damask curtains and heads to hawk his sex show.

Annanda caresses herself while Maria strips me naked. With a real Thai tit in my mouth, long black Asian hair sweeps my belly. Maria pulls me into her mouth. I like this double-teaming vastly more than the one I got from the Suits.

That '70s Muller family!

Jack and Diane

As my serpent of exhaled marijuana smoke becomes a frog, I remember lying back on just-mowed Missouri grass making circus animals out of the clouds with childhood buddy Teddy Smith.

"Do we ever have friends again like we did when we were kids?" I ask the dwarf. "Growing up in suburbia every day was like a Pleasant Valley Sunday. Mom cooked Spam while my Willy Loman salesman dad worked on boyhood hot-rod dreams trying to restore his '39 Ford jalopy.

Neighbors hated Dad's white-trash metal wart in our driveway for contradicting their perfect-house-and-white-picket-fence ideal. My brothers spent their hours terrorizing me.

"Mark stole all my toys—Cookie Monster, Major Matt Mason, G.I. Joe, my *Planet of the Apes* action figures—spray-painted them black, and nailed them to a board for his seventh-grade history project on slavery. I got them all back, but Cookie Monster never seemed right again with all his fur matted down with black spray paint—and holes in his feet. Johnny would open the living room Hide-A-Bed, close me up inside, and watch movies on TV while he farted at me through the cushions. Brotherly love! Remember the pranks you pulled as a kid?

"I loved playing 'Ring and Run' with my buddies where you ring somebody's doorbell and run like hell. Old Widow Withers was the best. Sneaking out my brothers' secret stash of *Club* porno magazines always brought huge appreciation from the other curious tykes. Throwing crab apples at cars. Egging houses on Halloween. When I was a kid and we'd crash at one another's houses, we'd sit around playing games and telling stories until somebody couldn't help falling asleep. You remember how soundly kids sleep, right? Well, once somebody fell asleep, the rest of us took out our dicks and waved them in his face."

"That's rude!"

"No! It was fun! Once we thought of it, we took pictures. Our childish pranks were pretty harmless . . . ooh . . ."

"What?"

"Just remembered the nights my buddies and I painted our faces and sneaked out to drag railroad ties onto the freeway. While humid, moonlit Missouri nights corrupted our poster paint G.I. Joe camouflage, we waited for an unsuspecting car. Ka-thud! Screech! Blam! Crash! The cars literally flew. We all held our sides to keep from laughing out loud. We were causing car wrecks! It was big-time fun. Nobody was hurt, thank God, but even today I feel guilt about that one."

"What would your dad have done if he'd found out?"

"Turned my butt crimson! Spanking would have been first, then grounding for at least a week, loss of privileges for maybe a month—only to be undermined by my mom, who never followed through on his discipline and would let me off the hook as soon as my dad went to work. He would have told all my buddies' parents what was going on. Glad he never found out. Years later, when I started driving myself, I realized how sick that prank had been."

The dwarf passes the pipe. I take a deep toke, and remember gagging on my dad's cigarettes when Teddy Smith and I stole a pack of his Merits and went out to the woods to be men.

●　●　●

While the dwarf goes to the tiny bar for two milk coffees, I relax into my stool in the front window of Kadinsky coffee shop. We're three blocks from the Pulitzer in a normal Amsterdam neighborhood. Normal Amsterdam citizens walk by in the narrow street out the window. Moms and dads pass with their kids who sometimes look up to see people smoking pot. Kids. I've never seen kids in the Red Light.

As I suck down smoke and sip milk coffee, I see two women walking arm-in-arm. In Europe that doesn't mean the women are gay just friends. When two men walk by arm-in-arm, I wonder if it means the same. No one takes notice. A white girl walks by arm-in-arm with a black guy. They get no funny looks, no stares of disapproval like I see everywhere in America, though not from everyone. Is Holland hatred free?

Music drills into my brain. "This is 'Jack and Diane'! Oh man, the memories pouring into me with this song! It's summer. It's my birthday. The gravel roads of Harrisonville, Missouri, are dry and I'm driving my brand-new-to-me, $800, bright yellow 1972 Ford Maverick in perfect working order down the hick paths of my hormonal youth with a cartoon cloud of dust pursuing me. Just turned sixteen. My first time ever driving solo. I feel so free and manly. Hannibal humping elephants over the Alps could not have been more excited. I have that cheapie Spark-o-Matic radio cranked up and John 'Cougar' Mellencamp starts singing. 'Jack and Diane' cuts into my soul the first time I hear it in my life. Listen!

Hold on to sixteen as long as you can,
changes come around real soon
make us women and men.

"At sixteen, I couldn't realize how prophetic that would turn out to be. Do you remember sitting around with your buddies listening to albums all the way through?"

"Hell, yes, I remember. When I'd lie on the floor, they'd all use me as a footstool."

"I miss those times. God, that was fun. A week after I heard 'Jack and Diane' on the radio, the album hit the stores. My best high school hell-raisin' buddy, Andy, called me up all excited 'cause he'd snagged a copy. We laid on the floor and listened to that album all night. We could both sing it all before we fell asleep. Man. Later that summer Andy shaved his head and joined the Marines. His future looked bleak as hell in Missouri, but if he'd stayed, he would have had one. After the mad suicide bomber in Beirut decided he wanted to see Allah, all they found of Andy were his dog tags."

Oh let it rock! Let it roll!
Let the Bible Belt come and save my soul.

I wish I could have saved my friend.

• • •

Across the street there's a grocery store, a hardware store, and an import-export shop. No cars use this street, only people on foot and women on bikes. Huh. I never saw a bike in the Red Light. A Dutch girl comes out of the grocery and hangs her sack on her handlebars. As she hikes up her skirt to get on her bike, there's no flash of white—just a sweet, brown muff shot. No one giggles. No one takes notice. It's a normal late afternoon in a normal Amsterdam neighborhood.

I like it.

I wonder what bicycle breezes blowing up my beaver would feel like?

Whoa! Dave Davies starts singing "Death of a Clown" with the Kinks. I like this place.

"You should play this song when Reagan dies," the dwarf suggests.

"Roger Clinton spent time in jail for drugs, and I think I know who turned him in. If Tim McVeigh were my brother I think I'd still stand by him. I don't know. I just couldn't turn in a family member. If my brothers were the Unibomber and Ted Bundy I couldn't turn them in. Maybe that's wrong, but I just couldn't."

• • •

Outside the window of Kadinsky it's starting to rain. People huddle under awnings and talk, put up their umbrellas, walk in the rain without caring. I realize a five-year-old boy with a bowl haircut is staring up at me as I suck the pipe. I exhale. He smiles. I smile back. In a pause in the rain he moves away with his parents. A Thai girl skitters under the awning arm-in-arm with a blond girl. Huh. You don't see women in the Red Light either, unless they're working.

"Did you get laid a lot in high school?" queries the dwarf.

"I did okay, but it wasn't like it is now, that's for sure. In high school I was Ferris Bueller. I got along with everybody. I smoked behind the school with the stoners. I played football with the jocks. I acted with the drama fags. Friends in every group. Partied with them all. Always tried to talk the jocks out of beating up the stoners and the drama fags."

"Drama fags?"

"From my dad. No question being on radio helps you get laid. The peacock with the best feathers gets laid. The lion with the longest mane gets laid. The ram with the biggest horns—and I have got a really big horn—gets laid. But anyone can get laid. If you've got a mouth you can get laid! People who don't get laid don't want to get laid! Don't ask me why, I think they're insane. Sure, radio makes it easier, but all you need to get laid is the ability to talk!"

"Some heart helps."

"Women are a lovely distraction, but sometimes I wish sex wasn't shoved down our throats all the time."

"That sounds weird coming from you, Mancow."

"Sex is overused! Okay, I admit *Playboy* isn't sleazy enough for me anymore and I enjoy pictures of women spreading their legs so far apart you can see their lungs. But enough is enough! You know what sex is today? *Sex is novocaine for the masses!* We feed the poor images of sex to keep them happy enough not to riot. It's like whoever's in charge is saying, 'We won't pay you anything or put anything good on TV, but here's a nice ass for you to get lost in.' How else can you explain *Baywatch*? I'm sick of all of these man-made, phony women. Have you ever met a woman who was truly happy with herself?"

"Never."

"The media has done that! Hell, I've done it. But only in an over-the-top mockery. I like women. All women. Short, tall, blond, brunette, blue-eyed, brown-eyed. I like thin girls. I like heavy girls. I like *real* girls. Did you ever hug a woman with implants? Have somebody hold their fists against their chest, then hug them. That's what implants feel like. Eck! These daughters of Stepford Wives are not sexy. Who has more plastic, Darth Vader or Pamela Anderson? America's doing something wrong when all our women feel ugly! Will there ever come a time again when the un-retouched girl-next-door will be able to look in the mirror without fearing herself?"

"Not in our lifetime."

"That's so sad!"

"I agree absolutely. Time for the Red Light?"

"Nah. Let's see a movie!"

In the English-language entertainment guide, I discover every major movie house in Amsterdam is showing a big American film I've already seen. I don't know the European films, but usually I don't like them. Jerry Lewis in *The Patsy* is a definite miss. Then I see it. One of my all-time favorite movies, a film that just knocks my dick in the dirt, John Frankenheimer's 1962 masterpiece, *The Manchurian Candidate*.

"No. I won't take you," Cabbie says. "Leidseplein is four blocks if you walk and twenty-one blocks if I drive you."

"We're stoned!" the dwarf pleads.

"Come on. I take you."

We buy our tickets and take hits from the pipe before going inside. We didn't need to. When I was a kid, I had to sit in the side sections of the movie theaters so my dad could smoke his Merits. The only people in this Amsterdam theater sit on the sides—in a pungent purple haze. The lights go down.

"Commercials?!"

"Standard in Europe, Cow. But they can be good." As we take another hit on the pipe, toothpaste fills the screen. It's on a brush in a woman's hand. She looks at herself in the bathroom mirror while she brushes her teeth stark naked. She approves of what she sees. So does the naked man who joins her. Focus on the toothpaste tube. The voice-over's in Dutch, but I swear I hear "Clean teeth ger fut!"

The Manchurian Candidate starts. Laurence Harvey plays an American soldier fighting in Korea. His whole platoon gets captured and brainwashed somewhere in China—Manchuria, I guess. Back in America, Frank Sinatra keeps waking up with nightmares as the truth of what happened in Korea bubbles up in his dreams. Frank's dreams tell him that Laurence Harvey is not an all American hero but a man programmed—to do what? If he's an assassin, who's his target? Can Sinatra figure out how to break through the programming? Will he be in time?

See this film!

After you see it, ask yourself, How much of what I believe is really what I believe and how much of it is other peoples' programs running in my head? How much is me? How much is programming from Mom? Dad? Whomever! Programming, brainwashing, works. Always has.

In *The Manchurian Candidate,* the bad guys think fifteen moves ahead in a game no one in America even suspects is being played. But Frank is waking up.

"Bill Clinton is the Manchurian Candidate," I yell on Leidseplein.

"No way, Mancow. Richard Nixon."

"But look how Clintler is selling us out to the Chinese."

"I lost respect for Clinton when he went to Nixon's funeral. Then he praised the slimy son of a bitch instead of saying Nixon worked every day of his presidency to undermine the Constitution he swore to uphold. Nixon's raving anti-Communism got him the vice presidency just like the guy in the film. Old Vulcan saying, 'Only Nixon could go to China.' "

Yeah, and way too soon we have to go back to Amerika.

With Ollie North. Ain't America great?

Machine

Like deadly mosquitoes, helicopters swarm through sweltering summer air. Navy gunboats patrol the river.

Da Nang? Panama? Somalia?

No.

Chicago!

Preparations for a Manchurian Candidate who will come to Chicago for the Democratic National Convention—and stay at the Sheraton Hotel across the river from my high-rise apartment. "I love the smell of napalm in the morning." As I look out the window at helicopters buzzing at eye level and gunboats in the Chicago River, my inner Thomas Jefferson feels threatened. *Apocalypse Now*—home to roost. The Big Brother propaganda machine has sold us surveillance as necessity. We have been "conditioned" to *want* fortress airports protected by billion-dollar machines the military-industrial complex can build now along with tanks and smart-bombs. When I flew out to Amsterdam my luggage was X-rayed, I walked through the metal detector, and then—then—people at O'Hare, who were only doing their job, only following orders, fucking pat-searched me! In America.

On December 6, 1941, every aircraft carrier in Pearl Harbor was sent out on maneuvers. FDR knew the bombing was coming and let it happen so that Americans would clamor for war. When TWA 800 went down after taking off from JFK, antiterrorist legislation flew into law. Give us your freedom now! As helicopters hover outside my window, I know its black eyes can look through me. I know its computer can access everything about me. I remember the film *Blue Thunder.* All the technology in that movie was real—and that was twenty years ago!

I don't want anarchy, there have to be rules—it's just the more we use machines, the more we seem to become machines, and machines don't *feel*! I can feel the clock running out on the American experiment of freedom. Has it already happened? Aren't we already a fascist society?

Every cop in Amerika today—local, state, FBI, CIA, DEA, ATF, and the SS—can throw the Constitution out the window. Any cop can break down my door at any time without a warrant as long as they say the word "terrorism." Or "drugs."

Against the Bill of Rights?

You bet it is.

What's my fear?

Hitler. Stalin. *We the people* are supposed to be the bosses here. People in government are supposed to work for *us*! We hire them. We pay their salaries.

It's not the president who controls this country. It's not the Congress. It's not the Senate. People who believe that are delusional. That the

People control America is more of a myth than George Washington chopping down the cherry tree or Abraham Clinton never telling a lie. Corporations own America. And Corporate America controls the world. We're just the little Monopoly thimble. Sure we get to move around the board, look at property, maybe even buy some, maybe a house, maybe a couple of houses—then we can kick back and live off the rents. That's the life, isn't it? Only one problem! The whole damn game gets played on the Suits' board! The Suits make the rules. The Suits print the money!

And the head guys are moving the chess pieces.

You are a pawn.

Don't you hate it?

All the poor sons of bitches who went to Vietnam to fight for their country were pawns. Robert McNamara (Mr. Body Count, secretary of war to JFK and LBJ) admits in his book *In Retrospect* that Americans bought the propaganda, the intentional lies! McNamara now says this country never went to Vietnam to stop Communism. My war-protesting hippie brothers were right. My flag-waving father was wrong. Why pick now to say Vietnam wasn't the bad guy, Bob? Guilt? No. Profits. Before he became America's secretary of war, McNamara was CEO of Ford, one of the biggest industrial giants in the world, and now the United States of Corporate America needs someone to take the blame so the trade door to Vietnam can swing open, so American corporations can join the world to reap megabuck profits by pulling a country (that we tried to bomb back to the Stone Age!) into modern times.

No wonder Eisenhower warned the American people to beware the military-industrial complex.

Sleight of hand. While the government waves its left hand, its iron right fist crushes us.

Gore Vidal, who was raised by the same stepfather who raised Jackie Kennedy and is a cousin of Al Gore, calls the president the guy they hire to do the commercials.

• • •

The 1968 Democratic Convention turned into violent chaos in Chicago. I was a fetus, but I've seen tapes. Twenty-eight years later, Chicago wants to present a pretty face to the world. Free speech—where you want it, when you want it—will not be tolerated. No demonstrations like 1968! In 1996, while the Democrats nominate a draft-evading, joint-sucking, pussy-hungry, non–Rhodes scholar, demonstrations will be confined to a park a mile from the convention.

In a huge coup, my guy inside the convention is Roger Clinton. He wants big bucks—but he's exclusive to the *Madhouse*—and he's bringing back good reports. Yesterday Roger said he'd heard people saying that the Clintons had more to give the world than just eight years of Bill. The master plan is to put Hillary in the White House. Roger's comment hit America's news like a tidal wave and flashed around the world: as quoted by Roger Clinton on a radio show in Chicago. But the story disappeared as fast as Bill's LAX blow job.

Another coup! John Frankenheimer comes on the show to pump his latest flop, *The Island of Dr. Moreau,* but I ask him questions about *The Manchurian Candidate,* which climaxes at a presidential convention. I love this interview. And it leads naturally to a question for my listeners: How would you kill the president? Calls come in from all over. Lots of them. Most of the ideas are silly radio chatter—but one call brought down a governmental shitstorm.

The FBI pounced. They want to chat.

"We want records of the people who call the show!"

"I . . . don't know . . . if there is one."

Phone numbers, fax numbers, Social Security numbers, driver's license numbers, credit card numbers, addresses, zip codes, checking and savings account numbers, PIN numbers, ages, radio frequencies, radio ratings: I am more number than Mancow now. As they pump me for information, I remember the cult classic TV series *The Prisoner,* which I found in reruns. Secret agent Patrick McGoohan quits his job, gets gassed, and wakes to questions.

"What do you want?"

"Information," a disembodied voice tells him.

"Whose side are you on?"

"That would be telling. We want information . . . information . . . information . . ."

"You won't get it."

"By hook or by crook we will."

"Who are you?" the Prisoner asks.

"The new Number 2."

"Who is Number 1?"

"You are Number 6."

"I am not a number! I am a free man!"

The invisible voice of Number 2 laughs as the gates slam shut in the face of this independent thinker who decided he wanted freedom and wakes up in a place where everything is controlled. Until he escapes the walls of this hell he didn't make and never chose, the Prisoner can believe in and trust only himself. The brainwashing goes on every day, programming catatonic sheep people. I will not conform! Conformity is death! I feel like the Prisoner trapped in a global village from which there is no escape.

Helicopters never watched me from delft-blue Amsterdam skies

"What do you want?"

"Information."

The information the FBI really wants is the number of the guy who called the show to say he would fill a garbage truck with fertilizer explosives and drive through Chicago's sewers until his mobile bomb sat under the convention hall. When the two smiling jackal FBI agents leave for coffee, Number 3 (who seems like a nice guy, but may just be playing good cop in a prearranged routine) tells me the garbage-truck bomb idea could actually work—and even worse, no one at the Bureau had forseen it. "Now we have to scramble, find and close every Chicago sewer entrance a garbage truck might fit through. I hate being here. I listen. I think your show could be the spearhead of a real voice for change in America. But tone it down! It's hard to spearhead anything if you're dead!"

Perfect good cop routine.

Abraham Lincoln said this nation was "conceived in liberty, and dedicated to the proposition that all men are created equal." In the Gettysburg Address, Abe asks Americans to dedicate themselves to a new birth of freedom so "that Government *of* the people, *by* the people, and *for* the people, *shall not perish* from the earth."

Not just from America, folks. From the earth!

• • •

Think about this. Every revolution starts with the poor. The middle class is sedated with just enough trinkets that they don't fight. The rich have it all and don't care. Real change begins with the people who live on scraps from the big table. So what has our government done to keep them happy? Given them lousy houses, government cheese, and welfare, which encourages them not to work or to better themselves but to breed and be drugged-out losers. Think about it!

People with leadership mentality, the real leaders with that Sandinista mind, wind up getting the other flunkies to sell crack for them. If they could funnel or channel that energy, maybe they could change their situation. Change our government. Change the world! But instead . . . ?

• • •

At home, I open my mail. The IRS wants me in for another audit.

One IRS audit on the heels of my Bay Bridge parody of Clinton's blow job, another after asking my listeners how they'd kill the president. Coincidence? Don't you believe it!

Seams of my mind ripping, I decide to give myself *Head,* a brilliant little flick by Jack Nicholson and Bob Rafelson with Frank Zappa and the Monkees doing a parody of the Monkees. When I saw it in college I didn't quite get it. Now I get it a lot.

In his book, Mickey Dolenz says that anyone who can see the limelight in the distance should get a good lawyer. First, everyone wants a piece of you. Then, everybody sues.

Mickey was right!

Everybody wants a piece of Mancow.

"We want to be your syndicator!"

"I want to be your TV agent!"

"If you want to be big-time you need to go with the best, Mancow! We're the best!"

"Hey, we're Jam Productions. We want to put on all your live shows. Your *Freak Show* sold out! Our market research shows that just on your name alone, Mancow, we could sell out twenty thousand seats four nights running in Chicago. We're thinking about the Rosemont Horizon."

"Four nights? No way!"

"We mean it! You could sell it out, Mancow."

"Yeah. I understand."

"If you sell T-shirts, you'll make more."

"Okay. Let's have T-shirts."

"We get sixty percent."

Ray Davies of the Kinks told me a money story backstage at the Westbeth Theater in New York City when I flew in to see his show *Storyteller*. He tells the story in a song, "The Money-Go-Round." Here's a dollar, but he takes ten percent, then *he* takes ten percent, the overseas investors take another ten percent, and here it goes, and there, and back over somewhere else. And when the dollar gets back to you, you've got half of nothing. Welcome to the money-go-round.

Two weeks ago I flew to San Francisco to be deposed for the Bay Bridge class-action suit. The San Francisco county prosecutor is suing me for a suitcase full of money on behalf of his career and all the Bay Bridge commuters who got delayed when "Mancow shut down the Bay Bridge." I swung past my old San Francisco pad on Green Street and powered up over the hill. That first sight of San Francisco Bay still takes my breath away. But the city has changed. I used to get homesick for San Francisco sometimes. Not anymore. The place has tripled in filth. The whole town seems dirty. More homeless people. More hookers. Some of them look fourteen.

I feel like the goose that laid the golden eggs. People used to eating Spam are gnashing their teeth and frothing at the mouth for steak à la Mancow. *Everybody* wants a piece!

· · ·

The surviving members of the Memphis Mafia, Elvis Presley's band and party buddies, once told me:

"What killed Elvis was how even relatives came to him asking for money."

"That's right. Soon he felt like a piece of meat! It ate his soul."

· · ·

I busted outta my college dorm while I was still in college. When I tracked down a trailer park double-wide for fifty dollars a month plus utilities, I moved in with a drama fag buddy from Central Missouri State University. Thirty bucks a month each. Fantastic! I knew the place would be clean if I brought a girl home—and knew my roommate wouldn't try to steal her. We partied hardy.

Years later, I watched Clark do the funniest phone scam ever when he called the flashing number below a Fundamentalist TV preacher. He confessed how much he believed in Jesus and told whoever answered that he wanted to leave his eleven million dollars to them when he died. But—big problem since this ministry constantly called it a mortal sin— he was gay.

Please hold.

When the next guy comes on the line, Clark tells him he's decided that the only right thing to do is get his money in cash and have it cremated with him. Everybody works to talk my buddy out of his insanity. They assure him if he leaves his money to them, the ministry will stamp his pass

to heaven. Clark scams these people until, while the Fundamentalist TV preacher rants on immorality, his Number 2 comes on the phone.

"Jesus is with you. Jesus is with you now. Do you have a pen? Good. Here's the official name of our ministry. Write down your wishes on a piece of paper and sign it. That holographic will assure your wishes are carried out. And here's the phone number of the ministry lawyer. Contact him ASAP."

Get that autograph. Get those eleven million crisp green samples of what Jesus tried to beat from God's temple.

Clark stares in my eyes while he tells Preacher's Number 2 that he won't last very long. He breaks the news. "I have AIDS," he tells them at the same time he's telling me.

Years later, I attend the funeral of one of my closest buddies. Killed by "the gay cancer."

Flying back to Chicago, flipping mindlessly through a paper, I read that Pat Robertson just got caught using his ministry's charity-relief planes to ferry dollar-a-week workers to the African diamond mines he owns.

But the Christian Coalition will still sell you Christ.

Send us money now. Give us the rest when you die.

This is not Jesus' message. This is not what it means to believe.

Are we in the last days?

●　●　●

Hal Lindsey wrote *The Late Great Planet Earth* in, like, 1972. Dismissed as a kook when it came out, nearly everything Hal predicted in that book has come true. For his updated *Planet Earth 2000 A.D.* I get to interview him. We talk about the time Revelation, the last book of the Bible, says will come when no one can buy or sell without the mark and the number of the beast.

"The number 666 is already the computer entrance code to the international banking system," Hal says. "It's *already* true that no records of any accounts anywhere in the world can be accessed without using the number 666."

The opposite of bravery is not cowardice. It's complacency.

Are we in the last days?

• • •

I dated a banker's daughter, a girl whose father did her like Mrs. Guttman did me. Only worse. In her teens, whenever Lori got home at night—in from a party or from wherever she'd been—her drunken banker dad made her strip naked, then sat there and laughed at her. Called in the rest of the family, woke them up if he had to, and in front of them told this girl how gross she was, how ugly and fat. Not only did everyone let the asshole do it, sometimes her brothers joined in. The fact that her dad was a prominent businessman didn't stop him from torturing his daughter inside the sacred confines of his suburban Kansas City home. The family just followed his orders. I went out with the survivor, who thought she'd recovered from the damage. Then one night with everything getting really physical, really intense, and really exciting, she cries out, "Fuck me, Daddy. Fuck me!" I'm not from Arkansas—I ran to the toilet and puked.

Are we in the last days?

• • •

Bob Marley's Rasta pals saw the meltdown at Chernobyl as prophecy fulfilled. Revelation says that in the last days, water will turn to wormwood and poison a third of the earth. So? The Ukrainian word for the wormwood plant is "chernobyl."

ChiCOWgo graffiti.

Merry XXXmas

Christmas cards that celebrate Jesus and his message of Love get harder to find every year as Christ gets XXXed out of Christmas. Today we celebrate the good news Jesus brought with greed and a decorated tree. Hey, here's a bunch of crap. Doesn't seem right. At Easter, instead of remembering the resurrection, we bow down to ancient fertility totems of bunnies and eggs. Doesn't seem fair.

I don't put any trust in psychics, but Heather Harder is a cool lady. She's got a Ph.D in, like, physics. Of course we all know what BS means, and MS just means more of it, and Ph.D means pile it higher and deeper, but one day working alone in her lab, Heather started hearing voices. It took her a while, but finally Heather realized that it was dead people talking at her. They've been doing it for years now. I have her on the show.

"Your dad just keeps talking, Mancow. I can't get him to shut up."

"That sounds like my dad, all right."

"He's a very powerful spirit, Mancow. And he's not alone. There are lots of spirits with him, and all of them say you are going to be hugely influential."

"Like the president?"

"No, no. Not like the president. More than that."

"More influential than the president? Get outta here!"

"There's huge energy around you, Mancow. Huge."

"Great. What else?" Never tell a psychic anything.

"The reason I tracked you down, Mancow, is because you are the only person who can help me."

Here it comes. "What do you need, Heather?"

"Tell me how to get your dad to stop pestering me! He wakes me up sometimes!"

"Heather, I'm sorry," I say as I laugh. "I never figured that one out myself!"

"Well, maybe he'll go away or at least settle down a little, now that I've told you what I know."

"Can you talk to the spirits, Heather? Or just listen?"

"It depends. Why?"

"The next time you hear from my dad, tell him Gomer says hi."

"Your dad's coming back to earth, Mancow."

"As what?"

"As your first child."

"Wow! If he enters the world with a beer belly, wearing a Dago-T, with a cigarette dangling from his lips, and laughs hard at that joke about how the Chinese go to the dentist at 2:30 (tooth hurty), I'll know it's him."

• • •

I collect lucky totems—mine are autographs of famous, powerful men who have touched my life. I have a huge collection of autographs. Robert Conrad as James West in *The Wild Wild West* was the first signed photo I ever bought. It cost me $2.50 when a buck was a lot of money to me. I have photos signed by the Kinks, Orson Welles, Bela Lugosi, the entire original *Star Trek* cast, the Beatles, the Moody Blues, John Mellencamp. I have an amazing P. T. Barnum letter and just bought one Harry Houdini wrote.

"Lock me in your best jail, and I'll escape!" Houdini would announce when he hit a new town. I guess back then all locks were pretty standard, and Houdini slipped a simple lock pick under his lip or hid one in the cell when he went to "inspect" the jail. Whenever he went back to a town, he'd do some new astonishing feat of escape: bound in chains and locked in prison, put in a straightjacket hanging upside down from a flagpole off the top of the town's tallest building, manacled inside a chained steamer trunk. But for me, the most amazing trick was that Houdini did his greatest acts, his greatest feats, his greatest escapes— for free! Thousands would show up. When Harry finished his escape he'd say, "All right now, if you want to see the rest, buy tickets to my show." The "real show" could never top the setup. The same way foreplay is more important than climax, Houdini knew the setup was the thing.

Brilliant.

Two days ago I had a dream: Barnum and Houdini appeared to tell me there's more I must do.

Wish they'd told me what it was!

• • •

On the fortieth floor of the John Hancock Building, I put my John Hancock on the line. For the first time I really believe those people who told me I'd be making a million a year. I feel almost guilty making this much money doing what I love most—after sex. The salary increase is retroactive to the night of the *Mancow Freak Show.* After I put a chunk in my retirement fund, I spend two grand for my Houdini letter.

For seventy-five grand the original, handwritten Beatles lyrics for "Good Day Sunshine" and "Back in the U.S.S.R." can be mine. I'm interested, which makes me feel like a fool. Seventy-five thousand dollars is more than I made in a year at Wild 107. For lyrics? Imagine. In college I lived on fifty dollars a month—in a trailer, eating Top Ramen and Smuckers' Goober Grape. I withdraw. After I say yes, I say no. The memorabilia pusher is livid. He was going to toss in an Einstein letter as a sweetener. I'll just buy that instead. At three grand, it's relatively cheap. A little Einstein fairy dust can't hurt.

• • •

When I did *The Crucible* at CMSU the director went apoplectic every time I changed a word of Arthur Miller's dialogue. Given half a chance, I know I could have made *The Crucible* a *lot* funnier. But I played Reverend Hale exactly as written. After that I decided to go where I could write my own lines and direct my own fantasy world. That's why I hate radio program directors. I don't want to follow their script! I don't want to follow anybody's script but my own.

That's okay with HBO. They've offered to pay me $80,000 just to keep me from signing with any other TV company for the next year. It's called a "holding deal."

"So, it really is money for nothing?" I ask my agent, Bob Eatman. "Like Christmas?"

"Not to me. I'm Jewish," reveals Bob.

"Like Xmas, then. Where do I sign?"

"Wait. Fox is snooping. I think they'll make me an offer too. We might have a Merry double XXmas."

The next day I power-breakfast with John Davies and Bob Zmuda. John introduced me to Bob at the most recent *Comic Relief Show,* where all of America's funny people gather to strut their stuff to raise Hollywood bucks for the homeless and AIDS. Don Knotts—Barney! Mr. Furley! Mr. Limpet!—was there at the Universal Amphitheater. He was frail and had to walk with the aid of two people but he clicked on Barney for me, and it was hysterical. I've always gotten a kick out of Don Knotts.

Bob Zmuda is the insane, old, ponytailed, hippie fucker who produces *Comic Relief.* He was also comedian Andy Kaufman's right-hand man. I love him.

"If you're interested, Mancow, Bob and I want to produce your next live show."

"Well, *Comic Relief* is a ton better organized than the *Freak Show* was," I tell them.

"So when's the next one going to be?"

"Christmas!" I decide.

"Whoa! Tight. But possible," Zmuda replies.

"One night only!"

"You could sell out three."

"One night! We'll call it *Mancow's Triple XXXmas Show.*"

Zmuda loves the name.

I don't believe in coincidence anymore. Luck, I believe in. The luck card is very underrated. It's only luck I get to do radio, only luck we get to eat, only luck this planet has water and atmosphere and life. Oral Roberts used to say, "There's a miracle coming at you every day." Stop gypping me, Oral! Miracles fly past every instant. Somehow I'm lucky. I catch lots of them.

My preview copy of the January '97 *Playboy* has Marilyn Monroe on the cover. Wow! I get naked with Marilyn.

Nudestock, the largest gathering of naked people the Chicago side of the Pecos, takes place at the Ponderosa Sun Club in Roselawn, Indiana.

Summer of '96 *Mancow's Morning Madhouse* went to party, hang out, and broadcast live. Huh. Nudestock. Woodstock. Did you ever notice that— (Jesus, I feel like Andy Rooney on *60 Minutes.)* Did you ever notice that all the fun stuff gets "stock" added to it and "gate" gets added to conspiracies against our freedom? With our radio-mike packs strapped to our naked bodies, my *Morning Madhouse* crew are the only people wearing anything. Mirrors at naked places should be outlawed! As I entered the toilet to empty my bladder (in two streams), I saw a fat boy with pizza breasts looking at me from the mirror.

When I got home I called a personal trainer. A five-block run had me collapsing, gasping, and wheezing for air like my dad at the end—on a bench in (no joke) "Cancer Victims' Park." A diet change, nutritional supplements, and exercise exercise exercise have lost me ten pounds—and solidified ten more. I can run a mile without stopping to retch. Great! All great! But it can't change the fact that when I open my *Playboy* for a little stress relief, I see my fat-boy self naked at Nudestock.

Uh! Nothing kills a woody like seeing yourself naked.

Marilyn's great. I take her into my bathroom and car-jack until I realize my mind's having sex with images of a dead woman who'd be over seventy if she were alive. Whoa! I toss the mag in my closet, settle into a hot bath, pull up my bath tray with a yellow pad and Sharpie, and pump creative fluids on the page.

—As I shaved this morning it was my dad's face in the mirror.

—With each new bit of knowledge, is a bit of ancient wisdom lost?

—Don't separate thoughts from emotions. Siamese twins can live, but one must die if they're separated.

—I want America to feel that Amsterdam freedom.

—The number one fear in America is speaking in public; mine is not having an audience. As I change, people will leave, and I hope new ones discover me.

—Imitation is the sincerest form of flattery. Bullshit! Wrong! Every time a human being imitates someone, every time you steal from someone, a little piece of what makes you unique—a little bit of your clarity—dies.

—Why don't they teach us in school to accept the astonishing diversity that pulses through every fiber of us?

—We've lost the long view. We burn rain forests in Brazil because wealth is measured in cows.

—Name of the International Firefly Union? Lighten Up!

—*Mancow's Morning Madhouse*: you're soaking in it.

—Unless you've got Ritz crackers, what good is a yeast infection?

—Call some travel agents. Say I want a vacation in Chlamydia.

—Mancow Muller: a sick mind with a powerful tool.

A paramedic calls the show. He's at the end of his rope. On edge. Depressed. The world he's known has fractured. His pain is so strong I can feel it through the phone. No question I woke up feeling weird this morning as well. Cold Chicago depresses me. I've been feeling down myself, complaining on the air and playing "Alone in the Crowd," a lonely Chicago song I wrote that women love and men hate.

"When you get to the end of your rope, tie a knot and hang on!" I tell him.

"I have. It's slipping, Mancow. My wife left with the kid."

He yelled at her, called her a lazy bitch. Got sick of coming home to dry dog poop on the carpet. Well, that part of his life is over. He came home this morning to an empty house—except for the dog. He's been driving around in his paramedic van ever since. He's down an alley somewhere calling on his portable phone. He wants to kill himself.

He's serious.

Off the air Phone Girl calls my Chicago policeman buddy who puts out an APB.

"Job was tortured in the Bible. We all have bad times. Just hang in there, man, things turn around. My dad always said, 'This too shall pass.' "

Doesn't cut it.

"Your dad's dead, Mancow."

He can't find any light in the darkness, and I can't find it for him. We talk a long time. His portable phone starts beeping—someone's trying to call him. We encourage him to flash over to the other call. We keep his line open so he can come back to us anytime—and, finally, we cut to commercials. He never comes back on the line. Eventually our line goes dial tone. When the police find my caller, he's hanging from his belt in the paramedic van. Dead.

I didn't sleep for a long time after that. Sometimes at night I still hear that tortured soul inside my head.

Telling myself "I'm a radio personality! Not a shrink! Not a crisis intervention specialist! Not family!" is not enough.

Did I let this man die?

God forgive me.

Anonymous voices on the radio, the last place he could reach for help.

• • •

I did save Angel's life. She called the show after taking way too many pills. A cop buddy was able to trace her phone number as she talked, and the fire department and paramedics broke down her door and pumped her stomach in time. I was on the edge of my seat.

• • •

"Mancow. Mancow. Mancow." The rumble comes through the gangway as *Mancow's Triple XXXmas Show* begins.

Twenty thousand fans chant at Illinois' Rosemont Horizon as Casanova Ace starts things off. I get into Santa's sleigh with Baby B, my midget elf. Twelve stunning women in furry red panties and tiny bras hitch into reindeer harnesses.

Casanova Ace comes offstage in his pink satin teddy. Announcer Bill

Hainsworth starts a stentorian recitation of *The Night Before Christmas,* but Turd stops him.

The Mancow intro video rolls.

"Where's the knife?! Where's my Macanudo? I don't have my cigar."

"The knife's right there with the doll. Here's your cigar." It's the dwarf.

The cigar hits my mouth as the back curtains open and bubble-breasted boobies strain against red leather straps to pull me onstage in my Santa's sleigh. The crowd goes crazy! As I walk the stage I feel the rush of sound pressing on me, exciting me like a naked lover hungry for satisfaction. As Baby B the midget, eleven porno women, and the virgin Phone Girl dance, I feel emotions washing over and through me from the audience. I go back to my sleigh. I get the knife and the doll. I hold one up in each hand. The crowd cheers. I behead Tickle Me Elmo. I throw the head to the crowd—and the still vibrating body. The crowd goes nuts.

It's cold in the parking lot. As Irma reports live, her nipples visibly push for Nebraska even through her fur coat. Red Rogers, my Hollywood stunt coordinator, readies for the finale when the now defunct Mancow Mobile One will drop 300 feet through the air to crash on the Rosemont parking lot. With me inside. In a bubble-wrap suit.

How did Rudolph's red nose get into Vixxxen's panties?

Rudolph the brown-nosed . . . nah. This crowd doesn't know that story.

The audience boos comedian Dane Cook for coming onstage after naked pretty women. He leaves the stage. Pussy!

Give the audience what they want!

Bring on David Kremer early. Yeah! That's more like it! A man who balances bowling balls!

Freak introduces Jackyl, and the renegade Southern rockers perform an amazing set.

I introduce the Torture King. I want to see his act up close and personal! The Torture King swallows three feet of a six-foot rope. Then, with a sterile scalpel—I swear to God I'm not making this up—the Torture

King cuts through the flesh of his belly! He cuts through the wall of his stomach, reaches in, finds the end of the rope he's swallowed, *and pulls it out through his stomach!!* Holy moley! I want to vomit! It's real. I'm right next to him. When all the rope's out, the Torture King wraps a bandage over his cut—he practices yoga and has complete control over how the blood flows in his body—and the wound does not bleed. The Torture King cuts a piece of wire off a spool and pushes it through his arm! Then another! And—

When the Torture King finishes, with all the lights dimmed, my buddy Scott, aka T2, the Human Cyclops, puts a flashlight in his mouth and lets light shine in the darkness through the hole where his cancerous eye used to be. He's a bigger smash tonight than he was at the *Mancow Freak Show.* "T2! T2!"

A lucky audience member pours eggnog all over our "Miss Puerto Rico." Then, in front of 20,000 people, he licks her off.

Intermission.

"We're running late!" John Davies worries as I come offstage.

But there's so much more to come! Including me. In the toilet. It's relaxing. And she's cute.

"Cut the Mancow's favorite movie video!" I shout through the dressing room toilet door.

"We cut it yesterday!" Rusty Humphries yells back.

"No, we cut it down yesterday. Cut it out of the show! We don't have time! Keep it pumping!" The sweet thing on her knees picks up her tempo, but I really mean the show.

"And lose *Sausage Boy,*" I yell.

"Cut your first starring role in a porno flick?"

"mmmMMMM HMMMM!" I respond. The girl on her knees looks up. This girl would like fries with mayo. She licks her lips. She'd be a smash in porno films. I'll introduce her to Vixxxen. "Let's put on Pantera, and see where we are. They could run long, and I don't have to tell you they're important! Somebody tell Pantera they're opening Act Two. Check the chainsaws. How are T-shirt sales?"

"If we run ten minutes over, we're in Golden Time for breakdown!"

says Bob Zmuda. In Golden Time, union workers get paid everything you've just paid them for an eight-hour day for every thirty minutes—or any part of thirty minutes.

"Okay. We can't go over." I leave my LBJ toilet to continue the conference live.

"Steven Lasko is here, Mancow." It's the dwarf.

Ever feel like people are just in your way? I'm paying for three times the normal police force tonight because of this asshole's militant Mancow hate group. He worked to get a ban on the *Triple XXXmas Show.* He'll fire any of his employees who sees it, and if his twenty-two-year-old son comes, he's disinherited. Is this the face of Christianity today? This man claims to be a practicing Christian, calls me "the Antichrist," and hates and tries to destroy anything he can't control. This man would walk over crack babies to protest my show. That's not Jesus. That's not love. That's Fascism. Jesus tried to teach the world that God is not a dictator. God is Love. Suit mentality must be destroyed—until it is, the machine wins.

"His son brought him, Mancow. He's had a stroke. He looks bad."

"What does he want?"

"He wants to apologize before he dies."

"Find out if he'll do it onstage."

"Mancow—great show. I'm loving it!" It's Billy Corgan from Smashing Pumpkins.

"We're ten minutes into intermission, Cow!"

"Great show, Mancow," a cop comments as Pantera trails a cloud of marijuana perfume past him to the stage.

"Thanks, man." I've heard *The Blues Brothers* set was guarded by a police force who knew exactly what kind of cocaine was going on inside but were told to look the other way because of how much money the film was pouring into Chicago.

Pantera cranks their chainsaws. As they play their opening riff, I slice the head off a Howard Stern dummy. Boy, that's redundant.

After Pantera, we roll out the barrel and draw the ticket stub of the lucky audience member who gets to have sex with Vixxxen—onstage.

Her husband/director films the action while 20,000 Pantera, Jackyl, and Mancow fans look on.

We check outside with Irma. Everything's set for the Mancow Mobile One van-drop finale.

Steven Lasko's son wheels his father onstage, where—feeling like Saul on the way to Damascus, seeing his stroke as a sign from God—he stops kicking against the pricks, gives me absolution, and cries while his son holds his hand.

I climb into the cockpit of a twenty-five-foot penis. Holding my joystick I fly out over forty rows of the audience as they bang their chairs. I spray sweet cream into everybody's mouths as they sing *Jingle Balls* and other Christmas carols with X-rated Mancow lyrics.

The FAA is there when my penis hits the stage. As I climb off my flying cock, this dick from the FAA hands me a piece of paper.

"You cannot get in that van. You're too close to O'Hare. We can't let you raise a crane that high. You're not allowed to do it."

"Fuck you, Suit! You can't ruin the finale!"

"That's the injunction in your hand. There's your name." He points. "Right there! Where it says Mancow!"

Damn Suits! The audience is booing. What can I do? Then I see it. It does prevent Mancow. But it doesn't prevent Turd!

Turd's already out with Irma, waiting with Red Rogers to put me into bubble wrap.

"Turd, get in the van!"

"What?" It's Irma. Turd isn't wired up out there.

"Tell Turd to get in the van! We have to give this audience what they came for! We have to do the finale!"

The audience is cheering as Irma talks to Turd. Turd isn't sure. Irma's against it.

"Listen, Mancow, that van's set up for you!" It's Red Rogers, the Hollywood stunt coordinator.

"We have to do this stunt, Red!"

"Well—"

"Put Turd on headset. Turd. Get in the van!"

"I don't know, Mancow, I—"

"Turd, if you want to keep your job—get in the van *now*!"

As Turd heads to the van, scattered booing begins in the audience.

What the hell am I doing? Why is it coming to this?

With Turd inside, Red Rogers hoists old Mancow Mobile One to 260 feet, but he won't hit the drop switch. He won't finish the goddamn stunt! Probably thinking of the one that went bad with Vic Morrow. Red's indecision doesn't matter. Destiny takes a hand.

Shhhrinngg! One of the crane cables holding the van snaps.

Shhhrinngg! The second front cables goes. The van tilts nose down.

Shhhrinngg! Shhhrinngg! Mancow Mobile One plummets nose first to the ground with Turd inside. Jesus! In the auditorium we see it all on the big screen. Irma runs to Mobile One. The paramedics screech in.

Would you be happy if you dropped forty bucks to see this?

Was it worth it?

I stand on the stage a long time.

I drop my mike.

I leave the stage.

The audience is stunned. Confused.

Is the show over?

House lights come up.

The audience doesn't move.

Vogue!

Searching for Stinky

Three torturous days and nights I sit there, a broken gargoyle with a comatose Turd until he surfaces into nonverbal, eye-fluttering consciousness. Doctors order me to leave.

I flip on my TV. Nothing. The cable box is new. But where did it come from? Someone's raided my apartment without my permission.

I call the corporation.

"We'll get someone there in a week," the cable rep tells me.

"A man can't survive a week without cable in a Chicago winter! Get someone over here now. You broke into my apartment."

"Sir, it's Christmas Eve." After a long silence he continues, "I don't like what you did to Turd." Click. The line goes dead.

Not wanting to feel the Radio Union's wrath, my bosses insist I take my Christmas vacation. But Turd's starting to mumble. I can't leave him. He's not quite alive yet.

When Turd doesn't show up on schedule, his wife and mother call from their Corpus Christi vacation paradise. They fly to Chicago. They hear my story and demand I leave Turd's hospital room and never return.

I head off for the Heartland, where my family's Christmas heart pumps nothing but love for their prodigal son's return. Being taken into the bosom of my family proves the perfect cure for that "Alone in the Crowd" disease from which I've suffered.

Like a couple of Ruskies in the Polar Bear Club, my brother Mark and I soak outside in his hot tub with Leon Redbone's "There's No Place Like Home for the Holidays," the perfect soundtrack for this living movie. The steam rises, creating a warm cocoon, and icicles hang from my goatee. When is it exactly that brothers go from being cruel limit-testers to best friends?

My brother Mark is a haunted man. Haunted by our father's fearful, dying eyes. To me they only proved him human.

"When I die I won't let my kids see that. I won't bow to terror. I'm going out like the Duke, with a defiant scowl, reins in my mouth, guns a-blazin'."

"I almost killed a friend," I tell him.

"You didn't!" Mark argues with an intensity that would put motivational speaker Anthony Robbins to shame.

"I told him to get in the truck."

"He didn't have to go."

"I threatened his job."

He takes a swig of scotch as smoothly as most of us drink water. "You thought Dad instilled the work ethic in us. That's laughable. You're wrong. He never did the paperwork his bosses told him to do. He got the job done but he was never willing to jump through hoops. What he taught us is that just because somebody's higher than you on life's totem pole doesn't mean you have to do what he tells you to do. What—because they have a name tag? Look at their endgame. See their objective. He didn't teach us the work ethic. He taught us to question authority. He gave us independence."

My brother Mark was right. My dad could actually be talked into doing our chores, and would do them gladly, but the argument had to be Lincoln/Douglas-debate-perfect.

* * *

I call Turd daily, and he finally improves. His mother says she'll shoot me if I ever see him again. Even now, my body twitches every time I hear an ambulance.

I escape.

I change planes in Tampa. As I relax in my seat I feel the Key West sun on my skin already. I hear my barracuda-fishing buddy Captain Tex telling me how things were when Hemingway fished off his boat. I feel warm water surround and support me. But they are all just figments of my imagination.

"Mr. Muller?" says the stewardess, jarring me back to reality. "This flight is oversold. You have to leave the plane."

I refuse.

"We had a lottery," she says. "You are booked on tomorrow's flight and we're giving you five hundred miles."

"I'm in my seat! It's *my* seat! I won't leave!"

"Please, don't be a problem."

"This isn't *my* problem!"

"Okay, a thousand miles?"

"Pick another sucker, lady. I'm not getting off."

"Would any passenger like to deboard and fly tomorrow for a credit of two thousand miles?"

"Don't do it!" I scream. "You're on the plane! Who is this latecomer who is more important than us?"

No takers. Silence descends for five minutes.

Flashing lights approach the plane. The pilot comes out to see why he can't takeoff. Passengers start to heckle. "Get off the plane, asshole!"

"You get off!" I shout back. I'm shaking with a cocktail of fear, anger, and purpose. The woman in authority seethes.

The pilot actually seems amused. The opposition huddles.

"All right. Two free round-trips anywhere in America!"

There's a mad, deboarding rush. Yes!

Turns out souls are for sale after all.

Brainflash. Did I just miss my miracle and stay on a plane that will crash? Damn! Sometimes the fact that God gives us free choice is a curse.

Captain Tex meets the plane. When he sees my face, he drives straight to the water and takes me out. He has had my line in the sea for an hour before I even arrive. I'm happy with Tex as I hold my pole and look over and through crystal-clear waters. Whammo! When the fish chobs my tasty bait, it almost rips my rod away. I grab hard, and reel. As the fish comes up the back of the boat, I see the hook ripped through his mouth—and Mancow Mobile One reeling up with Turd inside unable to wear the bubble-wrap suit that was custom-tailored for me. Fucking FAA! The fish looks at me. "Nice job hurting your friend," the fish says, Mr. Limpet style. "Are you sorry you tried to kill me?"

"I'm sorry. Yes, I'm sorry. Sometimes I forget there's more to life than my stupid pranks."

"What's that fish saying?" Tex asks.

"Uh . . . nothin', Cappy. Nothin'."

● ● ●

I first met Turd as he tossed me drinks across the dimly lit bar Al Capone used to frequent on the deep South Side. I could feel the cloud of stupidity surround me in the infamous Pauley's Pub the night I arrived in Chicago. As I watched him work, I saw unconscious comic genius hiding in a man who could barely function in life—a comedic idiot savant with the smarts of toilet waste.

"Put aside your apron here, and join the Mancow Militia of love. Come fight forces of terminal boredom!"

"No," he deadpans. "I can't give up bartendin'. You're on in da mornin', right?"

"5:30 A.M."

"No problem! I'll stay up." He laughs. His belly shakes until the whole bar follows. "Hey!" he shouts to Pauley's, "I'm gonna be on the radio. Me an da . . . me an . . . me an da whosit."

"Monday you're going to pay a hundred dollars to any woman who shows her tits as she boards the train for work! Can you do that, Turd?"

"No problem!"

Things work perfectly. Turd willingly does what no human with a mind would do. Crash a wall to test an airbag? No problem! Hug Mayor Daley? No problem! French-kiss a pig? No problem! Take a bite from the snowball a woman's kept in her freezer for thirty years, the one that means so much to her now that the husband who threw it at her is dead? Just do it, Turd!

Fight that alligator! Castrate that bull! Just do it, Turd!

The only time he panicked was when I threatened to tell his mom he was a homo sapien. He denied he was one. He was right.

Big-name Key West restaurants turn me and Tex away because we look like locals, not visiting Suits.

"I remember when they bulldozed Tennessee Williams's house to put that restaurant up," says a saddened Tex.

"Where is the next Key West, Tex? Where's the next free paradise?"

"Nowhere in America, Mancow. Maybe nowhere at all."

Paradise Lost.

The serpent in the garden is a Suit. Every time a serpent sheds its skin, it's got a suit just like it underneath.

"Here! Know good *and* evil! Get rid of your bad Maverick! Buy a good new car!"

Paradise, lost in the corporate web.

On New Year's Day we hit the ocean again.

"Out here it's still the same," Tex says.

I feel the different rhythm until I hurl. I want to be Tex—Mr. Mellow Dude—living a slower life, hanging with Jimmy Buffett and Ol' Hunter S.

We eat our catch at a harborside restaurant, drink, and smoke cigars from nearby Cuba. The Vietnam vet who shares our table goes churching every day. He remembers games he used to play from his helicopter in Vietnam. He doesn't want to remember. So he prays to forget the times they used the 'copter machine gun to slice a running human in half. "Sometimes the legs kept running," he says, "after the top half tumbled to the dirt."

That night I wake up with my hands moving in the air working a radio console that isn't there. I can't leave at noon. I can't. Go back, Tex. Go back for me! Do the show! Trade me, life for life!

●　●　●

I return from commercialized paradise to the colder and older concrete jungle of Chicago. Butcher to the world.

Coming in from O'Hare I see a stop sign, but it's been taken down, turned over, rehung. Spray-painted on its octagon back are the words LEGALIZE FREEDOM NOW. Yes. Yes. I'm trying.

●　●　●

Turd has not recovered.

"He looks fine," Irma says, "and his body is fine, but, Mancow, something's shaken lose in his head."

"He's dyed his hair red," says Luv Cheez.

"He quotes Shakespeare and wants to be called, like, what's the name?" Freak asks, "George Michael Montgomery?"

"Jeffrey," Irma corrects. "Jeffrey Allen."

"His wife and mom don't want you near him," Phone Girl reports.

In my 1972 yellow Ford Maverick in perfect working order, I sit around the corner from Turd's house until I see him leave alone. I follow him to Denny's, walk in, and sit beside him. He doesn't know who I am. I'm the asshole who put you in this condition, Turd, that's who I am. But Turd *is* fine—except he's not Turd anymore. He's Jeffrey Allen, who seems innately more intelligent than Turd. This is more than serious. This is a huge problem! My circus has no clown!

Then a good thing happens. The biggest heavy metal band in the world will do one radio interview before their three sold-out shows at the Rosemont Horizon. Metallica wants me. Singing "Ain't My Bitch," I pump the interview all week: An Hour in Bed with Metallica.

The whole band surprises me. They're not bad-asses but nice guys genetically unable to talk without cursing every second.

As we talk about his dad's recent death, like mine, from cancer, James Hetfield opens to real emotions. "Everything changed when he died. Everything. I don't fucking like it in your Dead Dad's Club, Mancow."

We talk for over two hours. Luv Cheez changes tapes twice.

"Major coup!" Luv Cheez says gripping three tapes.

"Pull out Lars saying it's their best interview ever. We'll use it tomorrow and through the weekend to promo Monday's start. We've got two weeks of amazing stuff here."

In his little wizard's studio Cheez throws on cassette one. Tape rolls. Silence.

He checks all his console buttons. He fast-forwards, punches PLAY. Silence.

One more time!

Silence.

Tape two. Silence.

My heart breaks.

"Cheez?!"

"I don't know what happened, Cow! I don't. I did everything right."

Zip on three.

Monday's audience will feel just as cheated!

"Take your stuff when you leave, Cheez. Don't come back. This is one fuck-up too many. You're fired."

"I'm sorry, Man—"

"Not half as sorry as I am."

• • •

I sit in my hot bath at home with a yellow pad and a Sharpie like I do every day and let out whatever comes.

—Driving home today I saw a cop stop a tiny car. A clown got out. Then another. Then another. Twenty clowns jumped out of that tiny car and beat the cop to death.

—Turd, when looking for women don't start in the gutter. Start at the curb. Shit! Turd doesn't exist anymore.

—I know a pregnant woman who has vomited every day for twenty-four weeks. That's impressive.

After hours of writing like Jean Paul Marat, I fling my yellow pad and Sharpie on the basin counter.

• • •

That night Metallica plays the most powerful concert I have ever seen or heard.

January 21, 1997, 2:35 A.M. I roll over to kiss my honey and find nothing there. Right, Jenny's at a teachers' conference in Springfield. I brush my teeth anyway. Grab a shower. Speed-watch last night's news on tape: four-alarm fire in Chicago, another leak at Chernobyl, California mother kills her kids. I speed-read my faxes. What?? Dammit! Evergreen can't offer Turd's new alter-ego piece of Jeffrey Allen head-case crap his own show!

Listen to my messages.

"Hi, Mancow, this is—" Fast forward. "Hey, Mancow—" Forward. Forward.

"Cow! Irma! Turd—I mean Jeffrey Allen—asked me to come to work on his show. I don't know what to do. I mean, he is a friend "

"Jesus, Irma! Without me you wouldn't even know him. He's a friend?! What am I?!"

This is not good.

I'm screaming at a machine.

Mancow's Turdless Madhouse has been on air for too many weeks of emotional and programming hell.

I can feel it swirling.

I am caught in a shit twister.

Brainflash: *It's a Wonderful Life.* Frank breaks through the ice. His brother jumps in and pulls him out. I'm six and walking in the country with my sixteen-year-old brother beside the new cement canal to the sewage treatment plant in Raytown, Missouri. Next thing I know I'm over my head in shit. The pressure becomes intense. My face pounds the canal bottom as currents of swirling shit turn me over and throw me along. I have no idea which way is up. My life flashes before my eyes. Short. Dull. At the instant I die, I feel something in my hair, on my collar. Johnny's pulling me up. My head breaks free. My eyes see light. My lungs gasp air.

Johnny pulls me back from the other side.

He throws me up onto the wall, his left arm pushing me against the cement so I can't slip back. We pant and gasp and pant and gasp. It's a long time until Johnny gathers strength to haul us out. Thirty-feet deep, that channel gets; ten-feet deep at its shallowest.

We recover. Sit up. Look at each other, and laugh without control. Both so happy to be alive. Both just covered in shit.

He's pulled me out a few times since, but Johnny can't help me here.

• • •

Things can't get worse.

They do.

I turn the key in my 1972 yellow Ford Maverick in perfect working order. Nothing happens.

Cabbie to work likes the competition! "Can't stand that Mancow guy."

Chicago is cold today. Frigid.

Except for the night guy doing his show, no one else is in yet.

I enter the morning show office and lock the door. The painted "Crush! Kill! Destroy!" looks down at me from the wall.

I've been Zig Ziglered and Anthony Robbinsed. I've read so many self-help books Brian Wilson would say, "Wow!" Right now nothing helps. I'm on the cliff's edge overlooking the abyss.

"The Secret Service wants to talk to you."

Write another joke.

"Your competition is praying for your dad's death."

Scam someone on the phone.

"You're being audited again for talking about the IRS."

Do something crazy on the street.

"Your girlfriend just left you."

Write a parody song.

"You're being sued—again."

Write a funny commercial.

"You lost $1.5 mil for the Bay Bridge haircut."

Take some listener calls.

"Your bulldog, Max, just died!"

Be funny.

"Your cable is off."

"Your dad's dead."

Be a wise-ass. Millions are tuning in.

"It's 5:28."

Time to make 'em laugh.

For three hours I do.

Then the darkness swallows.

MANCOW: Irma, you knew me for years before you knew Turd, or Jeffrey Allen. I think you need to make a decision.

IRMA: No. I don't. I don't need to make anything.

MANCOW: Well, I'm asking you right now. This is it. I'm asking you to make a decision.

IRMA: Cow, please don't make me do this.

MANCOW: Irma, I think you'd better leave. Leave and think about it. You let me know when you're ready to stand for what's right.

IRMA: Cow, come on now. You know that you, you—

MANCOW: And when you're ready to say whose side you're on—

IRMA: I don't want to pick sides!

MANCOW: Well, good-bye. Bye-bye. See the hand. It's waving at you.

IRMA: I need to get my coat.

MANCOW: Okay. Get your coat. We're in a battle here. Every day is a battle. I need someone who's going to stand up and say, "Yes." Our listeners do. I think people next to me should be able to stand up and say, "Yes! I stand with this program!" I'm going to continue to do this show with just me and Freak if need be.

MANCOW: Ed. Hello?

LISTENER ED: How you doing, Cow?

MANCOW: Hey, Ed. What's going on?

ED: Love you, love your show.

MANCOW: Thanks, buddy.

ED: Freak is kissing your rear. He's trying to get rid of Irma, maybe moving into her spot.

FREAK: No.

ED: Or your spot. I don't know.

MANCOW: You think so?

FREAK: No.

I hear it! The new jingle:

The Mancow and Freak Show!

MANCOW: You know what? You're right. Freak *is* kissing my ass and I think he is moving in. Freak, I want you to leave. I'm going to recast this show. I don't need any ass-kissers around. Good-bye. 'Bye!

FREAK: See ya.

MANCOW: I can do this alone. I'll do this alone. Jeff, hello?

LISTENER JEFF: Mancow, love you, love your show.

MANCOW: Hey, man.

JEFF: Just wanted to let you know that even though I thought Turd was really delusional trying to be a sellout with Jeffrey Allen—you're even a bigger sellout.

MANCOW: I'm sorry, I didn't hear that. Hello? Jeff? Are you? Phone Girl, if you can't answer the phones without screwing them up, if you can't do it right . . . Okay . . . 'Bye.

Now I'll lock the studio door, and we can be alone.

Irma left her . . . this is where Irma used to sit . . . I'm sitting in Irma's chair. I'm just a little bit hurt that she would not choose sides.

And this is her makeup case. And mirror. This has to be the hardest face you'll ever look at, folks. Your own face. Because you know what you're all about. I look in this mirror . . . and I don't recognize this face . . . I don't recognize the lines . . . Where did these come from? This hair. I don't recognize anything. I don't recognize my soul. I don't recognize me. Who's in there?

Sergeant Hairclub, the boss, just walked up to the . . . uh . . . just tried the door and then walked away. But they can't get in because I've locked it from the inside. Maybe I'll just start cursing!

I can't see my whole face in this mirror. I have to look at myself . . . in quarters . . . and then . . . I've got to put the puzzle that is me . . . gotta try to place it together. Guess I've been trying to do that a long time.

How the hell can you use this thing for makeup? And why do you make up for the radio? I never understood that.

Oh, crap. There's seven years of bad luck.

Right now Irma would giggle to fill up the pauses, but Irma's not here, folks. You missed it. I asked her to leave.

And Turd's not here.

No traffic because I got rid of Freak.

There's no Phone Girl because I asked her to leave with everybody else . . . and—I can see the lights on the phones—but . . . Hello? Hello? You asking for me? 'Cause I'm not here. Is anybody out there? Hello?

You know what? I'm in the mood!

(empty air)

The CDs are across the room here—so you'll have to wait. This isn't going to be the fast-paced show it normally is, but you people can deal with it, can't ya?

You'd think a rock station would have Pink Floyd right here where I could find it.

I feel like Frankenstein. I've created a . . . a monster. When I used to look into Turd's eyes I could see a soul. Now when I look at him—or the last time I looked at him—there's no soul. Or if there is . . . I see a soul I don't like. You know what I mean?

"He's an old friend." And what am I? Huh? What am I?

A commodity!

Owned by the corporation.

Something they can just throw away if the ratings dip, right?

I don't like feeling alone.

I don't like feeling abandoned.

Welcome—to—MACHINE. Finally! Pink Floyd.

Why is it skipping? Oh well. Set it on repeat! And—

Welcome —to— MACHINE

We're all part of it.

Michael Corleone dying in the dust. Huh.

Welcome —to— MACHINE

I gave the order to have my brother killed. Yeah! Put Turd in the van. Make sure he doesn't come back. Give the audience what they want! Naked women and blood!!

Welcome —to— MACHINE

Hi, Mancow. Love you, love your show.

Hi. How you doin? Hey, here's something for you.

Welcome —to— MACHINE

You know that monster I created? That fat kid I met from the South Side of Chicago and decided to put on this radio show? The monster is not him. Because . . . the monster in Irma's mirror . . . is me.

When was the moment I gave up?

That I gave up my ideas, my ideals?

Was it that split second when I sent my friend in my place?

Shouldn't Thief have been nailed on the cross instead?

I threatened his job!

I said, "Get in the van." And I was with that guy for two weeks in the hospital. Drugged up. Then he's wandering around the country. We hear he has a gun.

And I said,

Do it, Turd!

Do it, Friend!

Do it, Guy I stood up for at your wedding.

Do it!!

And that's the day . . .

I haven't slept.

I've lost weight.
Because that's the day
my soul died.
And I,
I cannot live without a soul. I cannot.

And I don't know that I'll get another chance to be in front of this microphone. I may have shot my wad. But we had fun. Didn't we?
Skyrockets in flight.

My soul is hungry. My heart is heavy. And if a tree falls in the forest and no one hears it, does it make a sound? I mean there's actually an answer to that question. Ummm, what is it?
I mean, who cares?

If I have a program and nobody listens, do I make waves?
No. I die. That's it.
And that's the answer.

Maybe I should never have done the Mancow thing.
Ever.
But I was tortured as a kid.
And the innocent I was . . .
I was brutalized.
I had to create Mancow to escape or I would have gone insane.
Which is what I'm doing now, I think.
Am I?
Am I going insane?
Please answer me.

Maybe if I'd just stayed . . . uh . . . Erich Muller . . .
Maybe I'd have friends and be happy. Maybe I'd still have you.
I'd have a show that could make dirt sleep, but . . . hell, I'd be selling shoes . . . just like my brother.

Welcome —to— MACHINE
I'm embarrassing myself.

Will this radio show ever end for me?
Welcome —to— MACHINE

I was having such a great time at that Christmas show.
Until . . .
Anyone remember that newscaster . . . that . . . uh . . . I don't know . . .
the guy in Florida who had some happy-talk BS show and then went on
one day, came on, and put a gun in his mouth?
Pulled the trigger!
Live. On air.
Inspiring.
Welcome —to— MACHINE
That empty place you go to if you commit suicide is lonely, so I'm not
going to kill myself, don't worry.
I'm trapped.

Bosnia.
Rwanda.
Where else is there a war right now? Zaire.
Kosovo.
Turkey.
Iran.
The Suits. The battle.
Welcome —to— MACHINE
Eighty percent of Zimbabwe is dying right now.
And what do I do?
Pull another dick joke.

I can see myself at the gates of heaven,
"What have you done with your life?"
Well I . . . I made some people laugh on a radio show.

"Go to hell. Go straight to hell! It doesn't matter. Go directly to hell. Do not pass go. You have no Get Out of Hell Free card!"

Hello, McFly, anybody . . . Bueller?

I was a Christian. You were a Suit. I was not. And . . . and . . . and there I am . . . I'm staring at a nasty afterlife, folks.

What am I doing for the world?

Nothing.

Welcome —to— MACHINE

I studied to be a minister . . . not to . . . not to peddle this kind of smut. That guy who called to protest my show . . .

Maybe he's *right*!

Sometimes the answer is the question.

Are you ready for the Maaancow?

Not ready enough, folks. You are not ready for this.

I mean . . . Fred Goldman, Ronald Goldman's father, is going to star in *Touched by an Angel.* Huh. Fred Goldman who would kill O.J. if he got him alone, and now . . .

I didn't mean to kill anyone's son. But I put a guy who used to be my best friend in a van and dropped him to his death, basically.

The phone lights on the console are going crazy.

Hello? Hello? Hello?

Hi. Hi. Hi. Hi. Lights blinking and I can't answer 'cause Phone Girl's gone.

Nobody's here!

No one's home. Hang the sign outside.

Welcome —to— MACHINE

How am I going to walk out of here? God. I am so embarrassed, folks. I apologize. It just gets to ya.

I just want paradise . . . inside. You know?

I'm a flake.

A sugar-coated cornflake on life's milky sea. That's me.

(Uncontrollable laughter.)
And I've got the penis pump going and I'm making more milk!

Self-loathing and Fear in Chicago. That's what it's about, man.

Why do you keep looking at me?
The program director's outside banging on the door. The door is still locked, 'kay?
Someone's just standing there . . . and . . . I have no idea who this is. Some Suit. I can't hear you, sir. This is a radio station. This is a sound-proof room. I can't–
I tried to fight the Suits.
Muzzle me? Never!
I don't want to live in a world like this.
Where the god is money.
Where everyone has a price.
I didn't used to think that. That everybody had a price.
But maybe I do.

And I promised you people when I started this show that if I had a price I would stop. I would quit. And . . . did I have a price? Did I get bought off to put my friend in a van 300 feet in the air and let him crash because that was the FINALE!?!
Did I become a Suit . . . to Turd?

Look! The door is locked! I will come out when I want to come out. Get an acetylene torch and burn me out. I don't care!

You ever look in a mirror and see a skeleton face?
Ever see your father?
When my dad died I lost my rudder.
When I was buried alive on the show . . . I was fighting the loneliness. But I could take you people with me . . . so I wasn't alone.
I loved you.

I loved this show.

Then I shoved a guy in a van in my place and changed everybody's life. Including yours.

I can't wipe this away. I can't wipe this out of my brain no matter how much I scrub.

No matter how many pills I take . . . I can't sleep.

I am insane.

Welcome —to— MACHINE

Noise! Noise, noise—everywhere noise. Shut up in my head!

Huh. That's all radio is, right? Background.

I am you . . . people's . . . background.

Radio is nothing to people who have a car. Yeah, give me the radio, I'll find something to listen to in the morning.

It's an accessory.

I'm an accessory!!

That's what I am.

Welcome —to— MACHINE

An accessory in a car.

Imagine having your life controlled by millions of strangers.

Imagine it.

I do.

I am.

I'm an accessory in an automobile.

That's my life.

All you Suits outside my studio window—you guys didn't care about me yesterday . . . when you were yelling at me.

They're very concerned. They're holding up a sign that says they want to help me.

Okay.

You should have thought about that as you were twisting the knife in my back.

Just a radio show, right?

Well, it's not my life.

Not anymore.

Oh, I'm sorry, is the accessory not entertaining?

Is the accessory not . . .

sorry . . .

not dancing good enough right now?

Does Pavlov's dog need more spit on his lips?

They are urging me to pick up the telephone! Why? They don't work!

All right! I'm picking up the phone, 'kay?

Sergeant Hairclub? Security? Police? Who is this?

"Hello?"

I recognize that . . . Jeffrey Allen?

"What am I doin' in Hammond? What the hell am I doin' in Indiana? I'm in the middle of nowhere here."

I don't know Jeffrey Allen, I—

"Jeffrey Allen? Mancow, this is Turd."

Huh . . . Huh.

This is . . .

Nah. This is too . . .

Yeah, this is too freaky for me even.

Welcome —to— MACHINE

After two hours of mental breakdown, after running half an hour over, I open the studio door and storm through the Suits, past Irma, Phone Girl, and Freak, past the 100 people who make the station run. The express elevator drops me forty floors of the Hancock Building in seconds, but it's a controlled descent. I fell farther faster today on the air. And I broke a cardinal rule of radio. I lost control.

Could Turd really be okay?

Surfaced from his insanity as I plummeted to mine?
I walk the frigid Chicago streets for hours.
Will I ever find work
or my mind
again?

Part III

I Want Freedom Now

Before the crash.

Tuesday Mosaic

I calculate about life,
but it doesn't add up.

Searching for an answer in the shallowness
a murky depth is discovered,
The answer does not lie in the past:
A faded picture reveals a rented elegance
with a rented smile

in a rented world that could not be bought.
The background is mock
and
she is wound from gears of Mylar not flesh and feeling.

Then—the chemicalization soars,
the program
is erased,
my table screams in agony and echoes of wood
but in reality is simply xerography
of a tree
much like the cybernetic crowd with Formica faces
and stainless smiles and the polyester wardrobes.
The sex symbol of lore is long since dead
and we step down to a standard impostor.

I for one am not impressed.

Old men flee with thoughts
of past days now replaced with replica joys.
I have my memories trapped on celluloid
and with each glimpse they fight
the fading that time will eventually impose.
Even something as natural as a kiss is tainted by colored chemicals.
Mimicking voices mask the melody of that old song on the radio.

We bulldoze
perishable life to construct our nonperishable.

We've got substitute trees for our makeshift yule.
Around the aluminum log a dull spouse plays chess with a stale mate.
I follow their lead and keep the pace that surrounds me.
People aren't people but blurred carbon copies
of what they'd like to be
or what they think they could be

but can't obtain.
My starched clothes replace skin, and leave my senses dulled.
From the fruit basket I grab an apple,
but all that meets my hunger pangs
is a mouthful of wax.

Do these icon apples fall from acrylic trees?
Epoxy friendships border on hoax?
Searching, moving blindly, you strain reaching
out for something yet all you feel is nothing
—at all.

I can see the plastic penis
—modern man of the future—
walking mechanical mutt.
Here rover, he speaks
—slow and in monotone—
roll over and play meltdown.

Boxers punch computers now
and walk away scar-free
at least outwardly.
With all of this computer-generated madness
comes terminal illness
that can destroy a man's heart.
I'll feast on imitation bacon bits
I'll top my salad from a plagiarized pig.

We don't look anymore
we analyze.

It takes hydraulics to lift our spirits.

Big brother picks out a book
as push-button people push me around.

Graphic people light the sky
as wires become the umbilical cords of today's society.
Sitting in our easy chairs
we remote-control our lives away watching a video image of life
too frightening to live for ourselves.
I'm on a television diet, I lost seventeen hours just last week.
Media morbidity
a thousand people with two thousand eyes
focused nightly on slow death
It started in France and now it's overflowing and sinking.
The overweights attach to their life-support machines
—their refrigerators.
The microchips are down, and
no one seems to care.
Even the mounted police are stuffed at the local museum
And some son of a glitch plays hangman with a noose of red tape.

If Orwell were alive today
he'd smile and say I told you so.
We are the ones here today
remembering yesterday and dreading tomorrow
so outside I go,
breaking away from the stale electrical stench
into the natural realm.
Grass devours the mud on my toes
like hungry children eating chocolates.
The geese pluck each blade in the meadow
inspecting it like old ladies
inspecting items at a clearance sale.
The horse,
although without jockey,
runs his daily race to the feed bucket.
Frogs sing serenades to lovers.
The sun hides

behind the hill
until we seek it.

I can't enjoy these
seemingly simple
childish pleasures
I scrutinize instead.

So I miss the bliss.

I wonder if the sun is going down
or the horizon is going up.
I notice the wires behind the trees
plummeting
the virgin soil
and the metal chariots fill the highways and the bypasses.
Innocence
is
always
out of reach
for me
so I hide away hoping no one gets too close to my idiosyncrasies.

Outside contains pagan truth
while inside is the sterile substance
of nonexistence.
We hide somewhere
between putting up the emotional smokescreen
and choking our souls.
I sit halfheartedly listening
to women complaining that they're Barbies
in this G.I. Joe world that I've made.
Aren't we both plastic?
Does any of this make any sense? I mean

does any of this compute?
We try to feel so hard that we become
numb in the process.
The things we think are real are nothing
more than images of our hopes
that we've processed and made and created.
We continue in our listless battle as the shells
crush and become sand
on the endless beach fading to sea.

One shell waits
to tell stories of the ocean to me

But I have no time left.

Healthy lungs.

Connecting

Only god knows why he walked in, but after an hour of Jeffrey Allen obnoxiousness, Turd's old buddies broke the mirror at Pauley's Pub with Jeffrey's head. Eight hours later Turd woke up in Hammond. Shakespeare, the red hair, his own show—all the insane delusions—disappeared like the hum in a fridge when you know just where to kick it. God . . . luck . . . destiny—one of them, all of them—cut Turd a break by smashing his smelly, South Side, bad-boy self back from the other side. Now, God . . . luck . . . destiny—one of them, all of them—pull me back from my own dark abyss as well.

I have a clown!

Luv Cheez, Freak, Phone Girl, Irma all come back. Even the Suits are happy. Mancow's On-Air Nervous Breakdown becomes continuing big-time news for every Chicago newspaper and TV station. Radio guys on other stations do parody after parody helping the bored majority of their listeners wander down the dial to find my show. Thanks, guys! Good. Bad. I don't care. No talk is death to a guy like me.

Battle lines are drawn. General Burnside fights Stonewall Jackson. Was Mancow's On-Air Nervous Breakdown real?

The tide of talk doesn't ebb.

The jump in *Mancow's Morning Madhouse* ratings is as miraculous as Turd's resurrection.

I book flights and hotels. I'm taking my crew to Key West.

Three days.

Easter weekend.

Check out syndication in Phoenix!

$$\bullet \; \bullet \; \bullet$$

Ninety-nine percent of the world is calling me a fool, but under the noise I hear my dad, like a Jedi, telling me I can do it, telling me not to sell my show no matter what, telling me I would wind up hating anything less than syndicating myself. "You can do it!" Telling me this time around, if he could, he'd buy the whole family steaks instead of feasting on his T-bone in such exquisite pleasure while the rest of the family ate Spam. This time, I don't have problems getting a loan to buy equipment. But it's suddenly an impossible market for a cowboy out there. Infinity Broadcasting has bought a third of America's radio stations. They won't pay rent to Mancow when they *own* the puppet Coward Sperm. Evergreen Media (now called AM/FM) has bought another third of U.S. radio. They could put me on all their stations. That they haven't makes me angry. When I arrived at Evergreen, Jimmy DeCastro (a man I think is so used-car-salesman slick he could enter a revolving door behind you and come out in front of you) was head guy for six stations. He brought Mancow here to protect a sixth of his empire and keep Wild 107 from destroying KMEL. Now Jimmy's so busy buying stations he doesn't have time to think about what's on them.

There's heavy talk of putting my show on KMEL to steal back audience from Wild. Otherwise Evergreen is doing nothing to help me. So, Cow Inc. syndicates the old-fashioned way: we earn it—one station at a time.

Fort Wayne, Indiana, starts calling the *Mancow's Morning Madhouse* nationwide toll-free telephone number, 1–888-2MANCOW, the day our billboards go up. The weekend before we hit the air, bevies of milkmaid beauties pump our coming—hand-jobbing live cows at every shopping center. The buzz is huge.

The Free Speech Radio Network hits the air on Monday, March 3, 1997.

On March 17, amid all of the shenanigans of another Mancow St. Patty's party, the Free Speech Radio Network expands again. Today, that freedom farmer I created eight years ago goes home to pump Missouri from Independence. Lots of people in Kansas City remember the Mancow birth. Everyone is talking. My brothers Johnny and Mark and all our friends have gathered in groups for the 5:30 A.M. launch. Old friends will be listening. Hell, my mom's tuning in at the restaurant while she serves biscuits and gravy and coffee to her girlfriends.

Are you ready for the Ma-an-cow? Ready for what a critic just called the radio equivalent of a broken-glass enema?

Ready as I can be.

My old Kansas City boss, who made me feel I was nothing and always would be, who condemned every skit I wrote, every promotional stunt I created, called me when he heard I was coming. "This is my town! Nobody fucks with me here! I'm going to blackball you, Muller!" Today, I go head-to-head with radio's Mrs. Guttman and kick his ass! I know current listeners don't care jack how much he sucks, but everybody's had an asshole boss they would love to go back and beat.

I'm ready for Independence.

The clock in Chicago sweeps 5:30. The *Mancow's Morning Madhouse* opening theme starts to play. As I work a live St. Patty's Day audience of 2,500, the studio hotline flashes. Prison Bitch patches my brothers through on Luv Cheez's portable phone.

"We can hardly hear you for static down here, Erich!" Johnny and Mark shout. My engineer Bob Fukuda tries everything, but nothing dims the noise. My whole first show to Kansas City sounds like I'm shouting through a megaphone from Atlantis.

After the show, my mom calls. "Erich, you can't talk about anal sex on the radio!"

Families, girlfriends, bosses—anybody—can hold you back. Base your life on what others think you should be, and you never find your own voice. A buddy of mine named Jonathan Livingston Seagull told me that those around us want us to soar—but not too high. And never any higher than them. Loving God and your neighbor is required, but Jesus also said to love yourself.

"I told all my friends to listen, Erich," Mom reports. "They called me during the show. They were all disgusted."

Great!

Through Atlantean seas of static, sixty-five-year-old matrons heard enough to get disgusted. Okay!

Reactions from my brothers and boyhood friends are terrific.

On Tuesday, the noise is gone, but different static replaces it. People from the Show Me State break my Mancow concentration to talk about Erich. The hands-down, pants-down, hottest girl in the Missouri high school I attended after New Jersey exile calls the show.

"When you came to the school with your shirt collar turned up in the back, you were the hottest thing. Every girl in the school wanted you."

"Like John Travolta in *Grease*?"

"Exactly!"

"Did you want me?"

"Absolutely."

"Then why did you call me 'Dork Boy'? Why did you say you didn't want Dork Boy at your parties?"

"Well . . ."

"That still hurts. I went home and cried!"

"I'm sorry, Erich."

"I never understood that young-girl psychology that if you like a guy, act like you hate him. Are you still the same hot number you were in high school?"

"I'm married now."

"And fat as a hippo, right?"

• • •

A buddy sends his copy of the yearbook I never got when we graduated. There's no posed picture of me. I'd like to say I refused to have it taken, but I transferred in too late to have the honor of refusing. Still, my Dork Boy mug dominates the yearbook.

Wow! I'd forgotten I had sex with so many of the hottest girls in the school. Up to six, and counting, I kept my mouth shut. Attracted to the loner, the unknown newcomer, they opened theirs. While the big studs masturbated nightly thinking of stolen panty glimpses during school assembly, thinking of when America's beauties jumped high enough to give a glimpse, I talked to those beauties. Even the most aloof ones opened up, told me how those puffed-up studs lasted under a minute.

I like lovemaking to last. And last. I love, and have always loved, the female form. And I'm gentle with my fingers, always trim my nails to protect soft inner flesh, and I love exercising my tongue. Why do guys not know that climax is really anticlimax? No theater training? No story classes? Guys, that long, slow climb up the mountain is the fun—not planting the flag. I never told my lovers' secrets. They, however, told one another of the gentle loner's silent ways until a line stretched to the back door of my 1972 yellow Ford Maverick in perfect working order.

Thankfully, I learned the vital Three C's of dealing with the female species early in life. I may have learned C numbers one and two from my dad. He was a charmer.

Always tell a woman how much you love her hair. They work hard on it. Talking about their bodies rarely works because so few women ever like their bodies. Feed the need machines that women are with C number one: Compliments.

Women have always had to nurture the offspring. The pill has been with us for thirty years, but there are millions of years of women seeing sex as creating the lasting obligation of children. Hold them after sex. They want to think you'll be around. Even ferocious femi-Nazis crave this; it's ancient biological wiring. Man the hunter's wiring says stick and move. Lots of married guys get hit on fiercely because women think he has C number two: Commitment.

Women like to feel cared for. To do that best you need C number three: Cunnilingus.

Actually, all three could be cunnilingus. Yeah. When you get C number three down cold you can skip those first two.

Guys, the three C's are *not* Come-on, Capture, and Climax. Get over it!

● ● ●

Who is Number 1? "You do not give up, Mancow! Faceless enemies fight you, but you won't stop, and they don't know that. You are a radio Terminator!" You are Number 6. Glynis McCantz makes no claim to psychic powers. She claims everything in the universe has a number. Glynis the numerologist has just run numbers for my birthday and my name. Names. "Changing your name to Mancow set you on the road to success," she says.

Names make a difference. Martin Luther King changed his and Junior's name after visiting Berlin and seeing Martin Luther's church. Would anyone have followed Mike "Buddy" King to freedom? Or swooned for Norma Jean? Could Roy Scherer ever be as sexy as Rock Hudson? Bobby Zimmerman. Samuel Clemens.

My cart from *The Prisoner* TV series plays Patrick McGoohan's Number 6 screaming, "I am not a number! I am a free man!"

"You're never serious are you, Mancow? You're playing *all* the time. Mostly, people don't get it, do they?"

Everything Glynis says is true until she runs Jenny's numbers. "This relationship doesn't work."

"Wrong! We're very happy."

"Were you introduced as Erich?"

With Mancow numbers everything clocks into place. She details the relationship like she lives inside it.

She runs numbers on Johnny, Mark, and Mom. She nails all three.

"You've had incredible turmoil and tests in this last year," Glynis says at lunch. "Make it through the next two months, you're on top. This is a really tough period right now—a million pounds of pressure."

"Glynis, my soul is living in a vise."

"Yeah. It gets worse before it gets better. In four months you'll start seeing changes. There will be a shift. This is a year of unbelievable success for you, Mancow—really amazing. Won't be easy. People will want to make you feel guilty for soaring so high. Stay up there. And get ready. As big as your success this year will be, it's only the start."

None of the numbers of any of my names comes out to 666.

• • •

The dwarf's psychologist used to ask him, "How much good can you accept?" How many people spend their lives denying the gifts a generous God tries to hand them?

• • •

At dinner with Mark, my agent, Bob Eatman, expresses his opinion that laws should be passed to keep people from eating meat.

"One more law to limit my free choice?!" My brother goes ballistic, screams for ten minutes, and savors each succulent piece of his Morton's steak all the more.

When Bob asserts guns should be outlawed, I take over.

"The Chinese sell guns to American gang members right now. That's already illegal. Will another law stop it? 'For the first time, a civilized nation has full gun registration! Our streets will be safer, our police more efficient, and the world will follow our lead to the future.' You know who said that? Adolf Hitler! In 1935. Bob, you're Jewish. Percentage-wise, Jews contribute more money to gun lobbies than any other group in America. Why? They remember that as soon as Hitler knew where every gun in Germany was, he sent goon squads to collect them. At Central Missouri State University I attended a lecture given by Jewish Holocaust survivors. I touched the Nazi-forced tattoos on their arms. One old lady cried as I felt the numbers in her very flesh. Branded like cattle! These survivors said the prime reason Jewish people were murdered by the Nazis was because they didn't have weapons to fight back.

"Bob, if you outlaw guns, only cops, soldiers, the FBI, the INS, the CIA, the ATF, the thugs of DEA, and the rest of our government goon squads will have them. Thomas Jefferson said it best, 'What country can preserve its liberties if its rulers are not warned from time to time that the people preserve the spirit of resistance? Let them take up arms.' People have been sending me tapes of Waco, Bob. For a man they could have arrested anytime they wanted, because David Koresh went jogging every day, Janet Reno sent in tanks! Those tanks sprayed flammable goo inside the Branch Davidian complex, and set it aflame. This man wasn't even under arrest, Bob! We must be able to fight back. But what do we have to do? Buy tanks now to be safe from our own government? While you're out of town could your wife fight off a rapist and save your kids with a rolled-up newspaper? Hell! Gun laws are sexist!"

• • •

The next morning on the show I get a call from a guy driving around with a carload of guns.

"I'm going to kill some people," he snarls.

"Why?"

"My girlfriend's been fucking around."

I'm not telling this guy not to swear on the air. I bleep as I need to and keep him talking. One thing I know. No matter how many guns he has in his car or how furious he is at the world, if he's driving and talking to me on a mobile phone, he's got no hands free to shoot anybody. The guy's been on an hour when 10:30 comes and goes, but I have to keep this unhappy son of a bitch talking until I talk him down, until he's ready to move ahead with his own life and leave other people theirs, until he understands he doesn't need to kill anybody. Slowly, my caller settles out of insanity into a frustrated, angry, jealous human being who feels abandoned. We will all feel like this at some point in our lives. The show runs forty-two minutes over.

"Jesus, Erich! That's the most dramatic thing I ever heard on radio," my brother Johnny tells me when the show finally ends. Chicago, Kansas City, every station of the Free Speech Radio Network let the show play. All of them are reeling. I'm reeling."

"If you ever get to the pearly gates, and they want a reason to let you in," my brother Mark says, "give them a tape of that show."

60 Minutes is getting old and haggard, but it's still a consistently fine TV program I watch every week. Today they're in town. I'm stoked. Amazed really. *60 Minutes* is here to interview *me*. No. Wait. It isn't *60 Minutes* that's interviewing me. It's *48 Hours*. I always get them confused. After makeup and introductions I sit down in my chair across from Bernie Goldberg. "William Bennett, you know who that is?" is his first question to me.

"I just finished reading his newest book," I say. "I bought ten copies and sent one to everybody I know who has kids. I think William Bennett is a modern hero. He's certainly a hero to me."

"Wait, Mancow! William Bennett talks about how to educate children, and you do a radio show kids shouldn't listen to."

"The race today is between education and catastrophe. I am filled with foreboding for a culture whose primary form of recreation is watching more and more mindless television. The world needs more people like William Bennett who think about how to teach children moral values and how to pick right from wrong. I say every day on the air that my show is for adults. It's not intended for kids. I'm not a parent, but I know being a parent in today's world is maybe the toughest—"

"Wait, wait, wait! Cut!" It's the producer. "You're coming across too intelligent, Mancow. We want the ranter. We want the crazy Mancow radio guy."

Huh. I either do this televised Mancow ad—or I get cut. Well, maybe some people who tune in to see "Mancow" will wind up actually watching the rest of the show.

When tape rolls again, I burst in ranting like the Mancow everyone expected.

"Great, Mancow! Perfect!"

Did I just do *60 Minutes* or *48 Hours* or *The Jerry Springer Show*? Are they all the same show today? Is there no news anymore? The Modern Othello Morality Play that was the O. J. Simpson trial hypnotized the media, that in turn hypnotized Americans into brain-dead "sheeple." It riveted our attention while giant corporations merged into behemoths and our Government silently stole away more freedoms.

Who watches the gatekeepers? Nobody.

It's a controlled cluster-fuck.

I feel like Toto in Oz trying to pull my friends' attention away from smoke and mirrors, from propaganda and lies, from fear and illusion.

I'm getting way too serious. Time for a dick joke.

If you suck on a fag with a British buddy it's okay. You're just sharing a cigarette.

Phone scam the Roy Rogers museum. Find out if he really stuffed Trigger. How often did Dale get stuffed? Is Roy?

• • •

A new study on workaholics says we tend to be happier and live a bit longer than others. Is it true? When people tell me I never stop, I never slow down, it makes me happy. That serious cancer heart-attack gene that hides in my DNA tells me to stop wasting time. My dad lived longer than any man on his side ever has. Mom's family live until they're old. Which side am I on?

A listener told me, proudly, *"Mancow's Morning Madhouse* is my only source of news and information." What? That's terrifying. Don't be so stupid! Don't be so lazy! Free Speech is the right to disagree, not to have no opinion. Sure, I have the Fist Full of Steel, but unlike all other radio shows I don't want worshiping dog people wagging tails and barking praises. I don't want followers. Hate me! Love me! But question everything I say. I could be wrong. My view is just that—my view.

Question authority! Question reality! Question everything!

Free speech carved in flesh.

Liberty, Destiny, Paradise

"*Those never come off,*" my dad in-
formed me as we looked at the tattooed lady in a freak show. Doesn't
matter. I have to do it. In his cover art for *Fat-Boy Pizza Breasts*, Tony
Fitzpatrick created something I want forever in my flesh. Two hands
shake across a red heart. Printed on a red, white, and blue ribbon blowing under the heart is my motto:

FREE SPEECH FIRST

Perfect. "Tattoo right there," I tell the artist, touching my left arm above the bicep, and hoping his needles are clean. The tattoo artist settles onto his stool. I hear my dad's voice in my head, "That's dumb, Erich." Ouch! Man! Why didn't you tell me how much it hurt?

• • •

I escape frozen Chicago. Under a broiling Caribbean sun, just like Papa Hemingway but with a better beard, I fight a fish for an hour and forty-six minutes. I land the second-biggest permit fish ever seen in the Florida Keys. Proclaiming it a good eating fish, Captain Tex doesn't want me to cut the hook and throw her back. I have to.

"Where you from, Tex?" the dwarf asks, stoned.

"Texas."

A school of dolphins swims past. The dwarf strips off his swimsuit and jumps in. When he hits the warm water the dolphins are with him. Happy and naked, they swim together until I dive in too. Swimming with them, I absolutely know dolphins are divine, godly creatures. I just hope they don't think dwarf dick is food.

After the dolphins swim away, we get back on board and the dwarf pulls a zip-top bag from our beer cooler.

"If the Coast Guard shows up, they take my boat," says Tex.

"For two joints?"

"Find marijuana on board, they take the boat."

Fuck! What happened to due process? What happened to innocent until proven guilty? What happened to the Constitution? What happened to the Bill of Rights? We're not drug smugglers—we have two joints for Chrissake!

When there's nothing but water as far as the eye can see, Tex lets us toke. I lie back, look up, and drift to a different time. I'm nine again looking at clouds with neighbor Teddy Smith. The sky is filled with circus animals dancing.

"Another boat's coming really close!" the dwarf screams. I snap awake. Damn! He's right. And it's big!

"They're gonna hit us!" I scream, jarred to reality. The dwarf pops the joints in his mouth, ready to chew.

"Cuban fishermen, Mancow, relax," Tex says. "They won't ram me. Never have."

The boat pulls up beside us. Tex talks Spanish. "Want some lobster?" Tex asks us.

"Abso-fuckin-lutely."

"How many?"

"Uh . . . seven!"

Huge eight-pound lobsters get handed over. They are beautiful. The dwarf finds forty bucks. What a deal!

"Tex! Cigars!" I exclaim.

Tex talks Spanish.

A gnarly-handed fishermen gives me a cigar with a big smile. "Hombre Vaca!" he says. We really are all the same. We just serve different masters.

"Oh, my God! This is the best cigar I have ever smelled in my life! Bueno! Molto, muy bueno!" I tell the Cubans. I want to say more, but "Me gusta l'asta mis huevos," the only Spanish phrase Luv Cheez taught me, relates to breakfast.

"Want more of those?" Tex asks.

"Oh, God! They have more?"

"No . . . Let's go to Cuba!"

"That's illegal," the dwarf worries.

"So's drivin' eighty on the highway," says Tex.

"*Yes!*" I scream.

• • •

The island looms on the horizon forever. Bigger. Bigger. I feel like Ulysses. Columbus. A whole new land before me. I can see rocks, trees, and people in the distance. We approach the little beach town as the sun starts setting. Clouds stack up on themselves. Their flat bottoms etch to brilliant scarlet. Awesome. Tex cuts the engine. My lingering eyes leave the clouds. Children, men, and women line the dock. Most people don't come to Cuba to watch sunsets from new angles. They come for women.

"How much cash we got?" I ask the dwarf.

"Whatever you've got is enough tonight," Tex says. "If you spoke Spanish you wouldn't need any. These people love good stories."

I remember creative writing class. I remember Buster Keaton. I remember that monkeys in people's clothing always make you smile. I start acting like a monkey. I stub my toe. The dwarf comes over to help. We are wasted! I yell at him in pig Latin. He chases me around the deck until I'm balancing up on the gunnel. I tumble into the bay. My head crests gentle waters to applause. We're a hit!

When I'm up on the dock, Tex arrives with the cooler full of lobster.

"We're not going to need all these." I put my hand in the wet box. I scan the people watching. "Ouch. Ouch." The lobster has me. The audience laughs. I give one lobster to a little boy, one to the prettiest woman. I give them all away.

In the yard of a fisherman's house, we eat dinner with the town. Lobster girl brings cigars. She gives the first to me. Using my hands, my eyes, and my gift cigar on the table, I ask in mime if she rolled it. She nods and touches her thigh. Ding! The Mancow Question flashes. In her long, colorful dress and white scoop-neck top, the sweet dark beauty with the long black hair delivers cigars to everyone. When she comes back I'm still smelling her gift.

After dinner, in a village house, my nose and mouth follow fine tobacco aroma rising to a musky scent. Two hours later, as I lie contented on the narrow bed, there's a knock on the door. Maria goes. Speaks in Spanish. Comes back. Kisses me. Smiles. Picks up her clothes and walks naked into the night. Her friend enters. Strips. Comes to bed. I don't get any sleep all night.

When the dwarf wakes me up, I'm alone.

He hands me a box of cigars. "Found this on the porch."

Life is in the moments. There's no great payoff. Magic only comes one moment at a time. Always in the surprises.

As we head to the boat the little town seems deserted. All the men out fishing, all the women in the fields. Very young children bounce around us as very old people watch them. Glynis was right. It's been four months. My universe is shifting.

The boat ride back to Key West seems unbearably long.

• • •

I have never understood the black-white battle. I just don't get it. B. B. King was on the show last week. When the show was over he wanted to do a promo, "This is B. B. King saying listen to *Mancow's Morning Madhouse* and you'll never have the blues again." Bo Diddley was in last week too.

But I also had a guy on the show who believes the answer to black problems is to kill all white people—sneak into rich white neighborhoods and cut all the housewives' throats, kill the white devil so the black man can— I mean it just went on and on. I don't understand it. To refuse to accept other people because they're different is insane.

Why does it happen? Maybe those who really run the Matrix controlling the sheeple have a vested interest in keeping us fighting. Think about it. As long as blacks and whites fight, or Mexicans and Chinese, or whomever, it keeps us from seeing the bigger picture. It prevents us from thinking how we're not getting paid enough or treated right. Right? Okay, yes, I make lots of money, but in the world of real money I'm a pipsqueak. Some corporate execs in America made 600 million dollars last year. As a bonus! $600,000,000. The power elite don't care a damn about skin color. The only color they care about is green. After giant company A buys jumbo company B, the behemoth throws 30,000 people out of work. I don't know math, but couldn't *all* those workers live for a year on the $600,000,000 tip the corporation gave the boss? If people ever wake up, they'll say, "My God, we're all getting screwed!" We can all dine at the big table. Why do we settle for scraps? Because—who will fight? No one will as long as the owners of the chess set keep the little guys fighting among themselves.

Jail any minority daring to question what's going on. Give the rest just enough of the novocaine of wealth to keep them numb.

Malcolm X came back from his travels in the Muslim world preaching against violence. He was assassinated immediately.

I interviewed James Earl Ray (he's not the voice of Darth Vader, that was James Earl Jones) on *Mancow's Morning Madhouse* via telephone. Having done radio as long as I have, I know a lot about voices. As we talked I felt—even if there were other gunmen from the misguided ultrasecret government hit squad he's now claiming he was part of—James Earl Ray *was* the man whose finger pulled the trigger on the gun that killed the best hope for real equality America has possibly ever seen.

Martin Luther King, Jr. was shot dead the first time he stepped away from winning blacks their civil rights. He didn't go to Memphis for civil rights, he went for economic rights—he went to support black garbagemen striking for a decent wage.

On the thirtieth anniversary of Martin Luther King Jr.'s death, I want to honor him by broadcasting live from the Lorraine Motel.

Independence Day. Fourth of July in Kansas City! My family's all-American celebrations are always perfect. I never miss the family Fourth of July. When the sun goes down, fireflies twinkle like magic. Black snakes ooze. Pinwheels whistle. Roman candles spew. Kids with sparklers carve their names in the night. Mark pulls out the cannon. Boom! Boom! Fireworks shoot above the lake for twenty minutes. Thanksgiving and Independence Day are the only American holidays still free of the corporate doctrine of buy, buy, buy.

My God! That's repulsive! Let's float a mall!

On July 5, with Jenny and the dwarf, I sail away on the whorish

Carnival Destiny. But outside the room from pastel hell, our private deck awaits. Four-feet wide and twelve-feet long it's all the heaven I need. Always thank God for the little things.

In the lingering sunset of a warm Caribbean evening we toke on a tin-foil pipe I've created. Via my traveling CD player, from their album *Question of Balance,* the Moody Blues ask:

> **Why do we never get an answer when we're knocking at the door?**
> **There's a thousand million questions**
> **About hate and death and war?**

I love our paradise deck. Jenny goes to a higher deck to get a tan, but the dwarf and I stay. Blue days float to azure evenings. Cooling evenings float to starry nights. Earth turns through inky darkness until it finds the yellow fire of our own local star. Time, the boat, and the earth move. I don't have to.

Four clouds collide on the horizon. Macho dudes before fists fly, they push against one another, separate but together, two armies that never mix, massing for a war. Jumbo clouds push together until, a long time later, a cauliflower thunderhead of gargantuan proportion fills an eighth of the sky. The foot of the cloud continues to darken. The head stays yellowy cotton-white, lit by the sun. In the midst of the gathering darkness a brilliant stream of molten silver sears my eyes. My mind questions what my eyes saw. Then it comes again. Again. Lightning, clear as a river, flashes *inside* the darkness of the cloud. I have never seen this before. Lightning flashes *only* inside the cloud. Every inner flash compacts the cloud. Flash. Compact. Flash. Compact. Slowly the dark and flashing part of this giant thunderhead looks more and more like a human brain. Waves of thunder roll through the cloud, visible to my eyes long before my ears can hear it. Electrical rivers flash inside the cloud a very long time. When it comes, that first connection from cloud to sea creates the largest and longest lasting bolt of lightning I have ever witnessed. Things have shifted. Electrical activity continues within the brain cloud, but the overriding objective now is connecting with the sea.

Universal intercourse.

I lean out into the rain. I feel I'm part of it all. Connected to the world. A vein on a god's hand perhaps.

The Moodies invade my mind:

> Hear the morning call of waking birds
> When they are singing, bringing
> Love—love.

Kids who grow up with an adult at home have more active brains than kids who are left alone. Brains of kids who are touched and caressed work better. Studies show this. Despite a Dot.Com-Game Boy world on a planet where machines appear to be winning, human creatures still need touch and love.

Brainflash—first ever cruise of my life. I stand on deck with my dad as we watch a storm over Grand Bahama, thunder beating like a steel-drum band.

I'm over my dad's death. I'm not affected anymore, not even a little. Not in any negative ways. Maybe Father's Day will mean something to me again when I have kids, but it's meaningless right now. As a son, you go through a time after your dad's death when everything hurts. Any question that you are alone when you enter and leave this world disappears. When my dad died, a two-ton sledgehammer smashed my soul. That feeling's gone. Last month, in Missouri, suckin' on a chili dog outside the Tastee-Freez, I inched down the paper like he taught me. We become our fathers. Sometimes that first look in the mirror while half asleep becomes a reunion. I wish I could just see him one more time, hear his voice again, talk to him face-to-face. The line has gone dead, but I haven't stopped talking. The conversation continues, albeit one-sided.

On Miss Puerto Rico's island, we walk around Old San Juan on a dark night. Built 300 years ago, the city is quaint, friendly, and Spanish— except for the assaultingly bright KFC across from the magnificent church. The old god stares at a new god of corporate greed. In an old bar on old town square in Old San Juan, we drink Old Stick rum. I convince a Puerto Rican couple to sit down with us. He's a putz, she's stunning. My girl, Jenny, storms out. The dwarf goes after her. I stay. The dwarf comes back alone. The rum revealing hidden jealousies, perhaps, Jenny's gone back to the boat because I was flirting with the woman.

"It doesn't mean anything. I just like people, okay? She's my girl-friend, not my jailer! We're not married. I haven't promised fidelity."

"Neither has she. If Jenny had a fling right now, what would you do?"

"I'd throw her out. You didn't just fuck her, did you?"

"It pissed her off you didn't come after her."

"Buddy, I don't play that game. Three, four weeks ago she got mad about something and started yelling. I started to yell back and thought, This is stupid! I sat down and put on *Hellraiser*. When she stormed out she slammed the door so hard I worried for the windows."

"That's cold."

"Is it? I'm me. I'm not going to change for her. If she doesn't want to stay, I can't make her. Take me or leave me. In three minutes she came back in. 'You're not going to follow me?' she asks. NO. I told her, 'If you want to leave, that's what you should do.' We haven't had any problems since. Guys should never follow a woman who runs out! It's a trick! Do it once and you'll be chasing her down forever! Tomorrow Jenny will start her period. On this day every month she has a meltdown. Why can't women admit their period affects them? You worry too much. She went to the boat, not the airport, right?"

Back on paradise deck, as night gives over to day, Jenny storms inside for Tampax. I pack grass in a bong I just created out of a one-liter plas-tic water bottle, a straw, and the bowl from our tinfoil pipe. I am the

MacGyver of bongs when I have to be. In college we made one in a guy's fake leg.

St. Croix: hot, flat, uninteresting. "Can I go anyway?" asks the dwarf.

"Asking for permission means wanting a no, buddy. Forgiveness is easier to ask for. Always. Don't ask. Do."

At night the harbor comes alive. Bells ring. Juices flow. Music plays. Intercourse, between those who come and those who want them to, continues for hours. Spent and happy, we pull out. Tomorrow, another tourist ship will thrust in, coming with tourists.

From my CD player the Moody Blues sing:

> Wake up in the morning to yourself
> and leave this crazy life behind you.
> Listen we're trying to find you.

Next morning we ease into one of the thousand virgins that make up the Virgin Islands.

Cops in Puerto Rico looked like Jackie Gleason cowboy rednecks from *Smokey and the Bandit.* The one cop we see on St. John wears shorts and looks like a summer camp counselor. Our taxi lets us off at a beautiful beach with an old hut renting snorkel gear and selling icy brown bottles of Red Stripe lager, the Caribbeans' own. Giant houses out on the point to the left belong to Liz Taylor, Mick Jagger, and Jon Bon Jovi. To the right the sea caresses the mounds of five more virgins. Straight ahead, a hundred yards off the white-sand shore, the rocky breast of a tiny island thrusts above the water. We swim to it. Purple fan corals wave to me. Giant alien heads of brain coral think at me. Tiny silver fish laze in congregations so thick I can't see through them. Large iridescent blue fish swim beneath me, jet-black fish with yellow shoulders wear red epaulets; fish the size of my hand change color as they change direction.

Amazing. Exhilarating.

Lying on the beach, I feel the sand embrace me, the sun warm me, the sea cool my legs, the wind caress me. Pressure and fear absent, I feel the balance.

As we leave this Eden, a tourist warning sign, BE CAREFUL OF WILD DONKEYS, makes us all explode in laughter. What? Seems wild donkeys attack and kill on this island. Are these the kids from Donkey Island in *Pinocchio?*

A *Fantasy Island* taxi with a red-and-white-striped canvas top picks us up. Driver's a happy, no-souled black guy in khaki shorts and an Izod shirt. Everybody here is happy. Except the dwarf.

"We're going the wrong way!"

Driver laughs so hard that invisible donkeys bray. "No, maan! Not pauseeble. Whare you going?" This disturbs the dwarf. I laugh like an evil ass. "Twanty mile of rood in St. John," Driver says. He talks so slow I could shove an hour of *Mancow's Morning Madhouse* inside one of his sentences.

"Relax, buddy. What are you worried about?"

"Missing Destiny, Mancow. Can we smoke?" the dwarf asks.

"Deepend whaat you smookin' maan. Eye dean muuush like de to bu coo," Driver responds.

The dwarf pulls out the last of our joints, rolled on board in JAH, Lion of Judah, papers from Old San Juan. The *Fantasy Island* driver stops the trolley.

The dwarf panics. "What are you doing?"

"End of de li-ine, maan. Turn round heaah."

Dirt roads go off in two directions into nothing but nature. I offer the driver our joint.

"No, maan. Ooonly taiste de pay-pa." He produces a monster spliff.

"Holy shit!"

"Yaas, maan!" Driver takes a long pull. Looks around. "No pee-ple," he laughs. "Oookay den! I git you to de church on ti-ime!"

Whoa! Mr. Toad's wild ride begins.

It took ten minutes to get to the end of the line. In three minutes, we fly back past our secret bay. Blowing a horn that sounds like Road

Runner's beep-beep on repeat, Driver swerves the curves until he hits town. Scattering tourists in the crosswalk, he skids to a stop dockside.

Can we do that again? Oops! The ferry's twenty feet out to sea.

It backs up as we try to shove a twenty in Driver's fist.

"Keep eat, maan. I haad fuuun! Ruun now. Ruun!"

I look back at paradise. Driver waves, pulls from his spliff, and . . . is that the cop he passes to? A metal badge flickers in the sun. No gun hangs from his waist. I could stay here forever.

• • •

On paradise deck the Moody Blues speak to my soul:

> And he felt the earth to his spine,
> And he asked, and he saw the tree above him, and the stars,
> And the veins in the leaf,
> And the light, and the balance.
> And he saw magnificent perfection,
> Whereon he thought of himself in balance,
> And he knew he was.

It's Formal Night. Jenny looks smashing in her baby-blue, scoop-neck, full-length velvet dress that dips enough to show a tempting valley of cleavage in front and almost in back. Underneath she wears only a tan.

I'm wrapping my black cummerbund when the dwarf pulls out an outfit from the toddlers' section at Goodwill. By the time the dwarf is fully dressed, the pinkest ruffled shirt I have ever seen won't matter. No one will see his shirt because—under the two-dollar tuxedo jacket he borrows a Sharpie permanent marker to blacken the moth holes in—the dwarf wears black Bermuda shorts. White tube socks rise to knobby knees from black dress sandals.

"Nice ensemble."

"Hoped you'd like it," the dwarf squeaks, missing my bitter rebuff.

My dinner jacket is deep burgundy with faint black paisley woven in, and black satin collar and lapels. Fits me better than anything I've ever worn in my life. I tried hard to buy it from the rental store, but they refused to sell. It cost me $400 to purposely lose it into my closet.

As we walk to dinner I turn to the ninth group to stare at us slack-jawed or giggling. "Please! Don't!" I say, explaining the dwarf. "He's our boy. He has progeria, the aging disease. He's only nine years old, you heartless bastards!"

• • •

For the fifth straight night, an old couple from Ohio competes with their table partners to create the best videotape of the dinners our Transylvanian waiter, Viorel, has just served. As he serves us, Viorel tells us again, "You are not like other Americans." Nice compliment.

As soon as desserts are on the table for filming, the waiters disappear. They reappear as the hideous music I liked in Amsterdam starts. Even on mushrooms I could never do *any* job that required me to dance "The Macarena."

• • •

"Shooting star!" Jenny says, pointing into a starry black sky.

"P. T. Barnum's autobiography was a gargantuan best-seller, most popular book of its time," I tell the night. "Barnum published an update every year for four years. Then he published a completely new autobiography with different parents, childhood—everything. Brilliant. We could do that. Really ironic, rereading what we've written so far, that four days after I bury my dad I'm in Amsterdam doing shit he would never have approved of. I suppose, on some level, his death set me free."

"It's more fun living life than figuring out what it means all the time, Cow. I'm learning that from you."

Jenny whispers, "There!"

Three dolphins arc through the midnight water. Again. Again. Again. Free. A freedom we humans never have.

"Did I tell you? I'm taking the crew to Amsterdam to broadcast freedom back to America live."

"That's the end of the book!" the dwarf screams. "No wonder we couldn't find it—it hadn't happened yet. It's perfect!" The dwarf turns my CD player up loud. He sings with the Moodies:

> Just open your eyes,
> And realize, the way it's always been.

I see Jenny on her chaise. The female form, breathtaking to behold.

I toss a blanket out to the dwarf, who dances like Richard Simmons on crank leading aerobics in Liberace's shirt.

"Stay outside tonight, dwarf. Gonna get noisy." We slept outside in Berlin. If that creepy little bastard wants to watch—tough. I pull the curtains on the Tool Gazer!

• • •

Later on paradise deck I ask the dwarf, "What do you think? Are the nine insights of *The Celestine Prophecy* the commandments for a New Age?"

"If they are, I guarantee there'll be a tenth one."

The Moody Blues sing:

> Listen to the one
> Who sings of love.
> Follow our friend,
> Our wandering friend.
> Listen to the one
> Who sings of love.
> Everywhere, love is around.

Dolphins arc through the water. Again. Again. Just playing together they move three times faster than Destiny.

My brother from another mother: Ray Davies of the Kinks.

Past Perfect

Girl, you really got me going!
You got me so I don't know what I'm doing!
Oh Yeah!

Dave Davies, cofounder and lead guitarist of Rock 'n' Roll Hall of Fame band the Kinks, the group that inspired me to go into radio, the guy who invented distortion and grunge with a swipe of his guitar, is on *Mancow's Morning Madhouse.*

Yes!

"Your brother Ray told me you don't like radio people, Dave, that you walk out on interviews. Will you walk out on me today?" It's my first question.

"I will if you're an ass," Dave says. "Yes."

"Don't you just love his Cockney accent?"

"It's sweet," Irma responds.

"Don't you just love Irma's breasts, Dave? Get your knee pads, Irma, Dave looks like he might enjoy a little cock-knee action."

"Mancow, stop it!"

"Dave Davies of the Kinks—was the song 'Muswell Hillbillies' really inspired by *The Beverly Hillbillies* TV show?"

"Yeah, it was. London's only a city, but it's very old and very class divided. Each little London region has its own accent and sensibility. When our family moved from the East End to Crouch End we looked and sounded as out of place as the Clampetts in Beverly Hills, without the money."

"Play us some of that song, Dave!"

"I don't have a guitar."

"If you did would you play us some?"

"Well, yeah, sure."

I pull the guitar from under my control board, and hand it across the glass wall to Dave. He pulls the pick from the strings, and gives it a strum.

"It's in tune!"

"Of course! I don't keep that Aerosmith, Megadeth, Metallica roadie Freak around just for traffic!"

Dave plays the intro and sings thirty seconds of the song. I sing along in silence. Interviewers who think they're more interesting than their guests should be shot. Johnny Carson, always so great on *The Tonight Show,* never stopped being a fan.

"Some people sleep through their lives, don't they Dave?"

"Too many! All the poor sods should wake up! Sorry."

"For what?"

"Can I say that word on the radio?"

"Sod? Sure. In America it means dirt."

I'm on the air to eighteen states on the Free Speech Radio Network with one of my living gods. I'm in heaven.

Dave turns the tables by asking me to sing Kinks songs he names. I dee-dee-dum the intros and launch into even the most obscure songs the Kinks ever put on vinyl.

Dave's amazed. "You know every song we ever sang!"

"You can't stump me. I'm the Kinks' preacher quoting my scripture."

Dave relaxes his guard. We develop a relationship. We talk about Grisold Arms pub—across the street from the Davies' old house in Crouch End—that's become a Kinks shrine, a pilgrimage site for fans.

"When my father lost his job, he headed out of the house like he was going to work every day for seven months. He was too ashamed to tell the family," Dave tells me.

I see my dad. I see him bottling the honey, rebuilding the world's first Jeep, working on his '39 Ford. I see him at six years old, losing his dad, and know how lucky I was. I see his spirit in the hall before he died.

Dave and I talk about our dads, about what it feels like to be in the Dead Dads' Club.

"The Kinks song 'Days' helped get me through my Dad's death, Dave. It always reminded me of who he was, how he'd lived, and of everything he meant in my life. We shared wonderful, blessed time together."

"Let me sing the song for you, Mancow."

"I'd love that. For everyone in the Dead Dad's Club, here's Dave Davies."

* * *

"In your book, *Kink,* you talk about some relationships you had with men. Did a whole lot of sex go on between members of different bands?"

"It was the sixties. Everyone slept with everybody. It's how it was back then."

Dave tells me, the *Madhouse* crew, and listeners on the Free Speech

Radio Network that at parties Mick Jagger, Dave's brother Ray, and Pete Townshend of the Who don't drink. "They all watch other people drink and loosen up and reveal themselves, but they don't reveal anything. All of them like to get into other people's heads and play games."

"Sounds like you, Mancow," Irma interjects.

"When I was going through that weird part of a man's life, when you're not a man and not a child, the Kinks were the voice of reason in a world that didn't make sense, Dave. There was always reason in the lyrics, in your voices, and in your common-man music that wasn't common at all. You looked at life with humor, acceptance, irony, and smart-ass sarcasm. I would have died without you."

The sweep second hand on the clock passes 9:58. Damn!

"Dave Davies, everybody!"

While everyone in the studio cheers and applauds, I push up volume slider six and punch PLAY. We go out with the Kinks singing "I'm Not Like Everybody Else."

I could go on forever.

"That was the best interview I've ever done, Mancow," Dave Davies says. I'm amazed how many people have told me that over the years.

"This interview was for me, Dave. If I can't get excited about meeting my idols, what's the point? If I can't toss Mancow aside and be a kid again, I don't want to do this. Did you have fun?"

"I did. Seriously, Mancow, I really did."

"You English guys are so weird. How can you have fun seriously? Huh? I enjoyed myself to death today, Dave. What a treat! You tie for gold with Jonathan Harris, Dr. Smith on *Lost in Space,* for the most fun I've ever had on my show."

Later, Dave's management calls. He expects to see me before his show at Chicago's House of Blues. When I arrive, Dave, my idol, hugs me. Calls me "brother." Validates me. Before he starts his show, he does it again in front of the crowd. Life cannot get better than this!

Yes it can.

My full-sized *Lost in Space* robot arrives from the L.A. prop shop that made the original. I have my own bubble-headed booby in my living room. Life cannot get better than this!!

Yes it can.

At Nudes-a-Poppin', America's biggest nude event, porno star Hypatia Lee tells me she'd be happy to set me up with anyone there. "Or we can do it," she says. Hypatia Lee. That long, black, straight, beautiful hair. Life cannot get better than this!!!

Yes it can.

Mancow's Hell-o-ween Spectacular is set for the United Center. Twenty-seven old buddies from Kansas City have chartered a bus to come. *And* my mom's coming. Life cannot get better than this!!!!

Yes it can.

The Free Speech Radio Network shoots our Iowa affiliate from last place to first place during *one* ratings book. Never happened in the history of radio there. Life cannot get better than this!!!!!

Yes it can. Yes it can. Yes it can!

Planes, hotels, broadcast space—everything gels. On November 20, I take my crew to Amsterdam to broadcast live from the City of Freedom.

Life cannot get better than this!!!!!!

John Records Landecker is inducted into the Radio Hall of Fame. "Whooo Whooo—you're a teen DJ" and "Boogie Check" were two big things he did. When he accepted his award he mentioned Mancow several times I'm told. "Nobody works harder," Landecker said. "Radio is in good hands."

NBC sees a video—me doing the show in Chicago. When I find out the seven-minute film included me just hanging out, doing nothing, waiting to go on the radio during commercials, I'm furious. I was showing them Mancow, not me. Terror of what people see if they get a peek behind the mask grips me. Surprise! NBC likes Erich better than Mancow. Huh? Huh.

I get my left ear pierced. My dad wouldn't care that left means hetero and right means homo: to him any earring was gay. But when I hang a gold pirate loop through the hole, I feel like I did when I grew my goatee, like my face is finally complete.

The Kraff Eye Institute performs laser surgery on my eyes. My dad wore glasses all his life. Mom still does. I fear going blind when my left eye goes weird for four days. When the healing's complete, my vision is perfect. No more steaming glasses when I walk inside on a snowy day. No more blind man's hunt for specs after making love at her place. After twenty years of slavery, I'm free!

• • •

A woman I took out once really turned on my webmaster buddy Dewey, Lord of the Fat Chicks. I set them up on a date. I prepay their Magnum's dinner. I tell Dewey, "Don't pay for anything except the cab to the Swiss Hotel! Don't spend money!" He listened, but he didn't hear. Took her sky-diving, bought her a drive around the park for, like, ten bucks a foot. She left, went home, and Dewey got nothing. Women know in five seconds if they'll sleep with a guy. Why waste our time with dates when they know they'll never give it up? That's right! Free dinners.

Ding! The point is to get laid! For me now, often, the icebreaker is sex. "Won't you at least buy me a drink?"

"Sure. I'll buy you a drink. Or I'll give you two hundred dollars. Or what is your price actually? Can't you just do it because you want to, and because it's why you came, and why I'm here as well? If you don't want it, there are lots who do. I'm not interested in a relationship, just a frolic in the hay." In San Francisco women begged me to take them to bed because every other interesting guy they met was trying to score another guy. San Francisco is paradise for a straight guy—the women are starving. My life right now is better than it was in San Francisco! Overwhelming—almost! Blinded by the light, success draws women like car grilles attract deer.

Sure, Jenny suspects, but we're like today's military: don't ask, don't tell.

I roll a nineteen-year-old, giggly, bob-cut redheaded virgin. I feel like John Travolta in *Grease* doing Olivia Newton-John with a dye job, but hers is natural. I don't make a move on her. She puts them all on me. Tickly everywhere. Candy. Cherry flavor. You *can* feel those walls giving in as waves from inside bid you deeper. She may be the first virgin I've had since high school. But I was a virgin too back then, all hormones and humping with no idea at all of the paradise of pleasures that really lay before me. Way too many women tell me they've *never* been with another man who even paid attention! Sure, the peacock with the biggest feathers gets the most hens, and I do love radio success for increasing my plumage, but mostly I like radio for keeping my tongue well exercised and limber.

Wake up!

Nobody likes a selfish lover.

Some people claim the female orgasm is overrated.

Wrong!

• • •

I meet a girl on a promotions gig in Des Moines. White Linen, Cuba, I don't know that I've ever seen a woman more beautiful. Any man who's been to Amsterdam knows what it's like. That long, thick Asian hair sweeping down your chest and over your belly is like those lamps with the hairs that beam light out the ends—only these beam out sensation. Astonishing! She went animal. So did I. At one point she's up on all fours while I ram in with that hair in my hand like I'm riding a rodeo bucking bronco and waiting for the bell to ring. And ring. And ring.

"I've never experienced anything like the passion we lived last night." The fragile male ego loves to hear it, even when it's not true.

I live my whole life with passion. Sleep through this life? Why? I don't know if I get another. And why would God give me a body this time unless I was meant to use it? We hooked up around 10:30. We didn't stop until 5 A.M. How many hours is that, Mrs. Guttman?

• • •

"And it came to pass, when men began to multiply on the face of the earth, and daughters were born to them, that the sons of God saw the daughters of men that they *were* fair; and they took them wives of all which they chose." Genesis, chapter 6, verses 1 and 2 make it sound like we all evolved from some enlightened alien race that came to earth and played among themselves until the women of earth got up to Amsterdam whorehouse Yab Yum standards.

On every level women are *designed* to make men want them. Modern man tries to deny it, but it's always there. Many will condemn me for being a man-whore, but salesman, priest, or webmaster, there is no man who would not feel desire in the presence of the women I've loved.

My dad taught me the birds and the bees. At Muller Apiary, hundreds of beehives churned out pure, clear honey I sold door-to-door to make money as a kid. I recently found a letter he wrote me years ago.

> *No matter how much a bee thinks he's getting, the flower's got no way to put her two things together without him. But—you never hear of a bee getting so attached to one flower he never leaves, and you never hear of a flower chasing after a bee. They each live their different lives and each fertilize the next generation in their different ways. The bee moves all over the flower until the flower's ready to do something new. And, the bee—the damn worker bee—goes back to his hive, and uses all the sticky stuff on his fingers for things the flower never thought of and doesn't care about. The flower's already satisfied. The flower doesn't care if the bee flies back and transforms what he's gathered into honey to feed the hive. Flowers are content if one bee pushes himself inside one time*

a year. The more the merrier, sure, because the flower's just sitting there, open, waiting, full of the stuff the bee needs, the golden stuff he transforms to nectar just being himself. But you gotta go back to the hive. You gotta go back to work—you can't sit around on a leaf looking at the flower and wondering if she loves you. And, you can't spend your life moving around inside her. There's more you have to do. The flower doesn't have to do anything but sit there and look pretty but you gotta fly back to the hive—and then, you gotta do the dance that gives complete directions to all your fellow bees on how to get to those open and waiting flowers.

It's like women were made by Aphrodite, with beauty and whole-ness and silence, while men were made by Ares, always something else to do, a new field to conquer, and always a stinger sitting there in the tail. God of war and work. Goddess of love and beauty. I don't know about the women's rights stuff, son. I know there's union, I do know that. But how can you say a bee and a flower are equal? Why would a flower want to be a bee, and why would a bee want to let her?

Hell, son, you're a man, and the two of us will never be equal. I will never have your voice or your knowledge. Your awareness birthed at a later point than mine—I have 35 years of experience on you, and that can never change no matter what books you read, no matter how fast you run.

So, that's what I know of the birds and the bees, and I can feel you aching to tell me there's not a damn bird in it.

I'm not trying to prove anything. I'm a bee going from flower to flower, and loving getting my head inside.

I worry about my lust.

And sexual addiction.

If I put notches on my rifle for every woman I've been with I wouldn't have a gun anymore.

Bragger!

When a good-looking woman is looking at me, and she's ready, and I'm ready . . . I feel like not to accept that miracle spits in the face of God.

Sure, I hear Paul and the rest of the rule makers shouting I'll go to hell unless I color inside their lines. But the reason Paul wrote to the churches condemning fornication was that some early Christian churches had become orgy centers. Paul condemns fornication, but in the Gospels Jesus never does. The only thing Jesus ever condemns is a tree that bears no fruit. He never condemns a human being. Jesus is all about Love. I want to grab every good I see as it comes. I want to use every talent I'm given, and prosper them into more.

• • •

I go to L.A. for a weekend of meetings. The girl from Des Moines flies in. We spend a totally passionate weekend at the Four Seasons, the only hotel in America close to that Amstel feel. With hot women around, men do better. Testosterone pumps us into pure-winning-alpha males.

She sends me letters that say things like, "I think about you every day, every night for an hour before I go to bed." Partly, I'm flattered; she's drop-dead gorgeous. Partly, I want her to let me go and discover her own life. Partly, I worry Jenny might pick up my mail.

• • •

There is no such thing as coincidence.

On Friday, before I flew to L.A., the Simon Townshend Band played live on the *Madhouse.* Jenny was there. They signed a copy of their new CD, *Among Us,* for her. When I open the door to my Chicago apartment, the walls shake with cut three of Simon's CD.

> The way I'm feeling now I don't know how I will survive.
> Like this. But that's the way it is
> It's not what you want, it's what you've got

> You can't hang on to love. Best admit
> That that's the way it is.
> It's the way it is—not the way it could be—
> The way it was—or the way it should be.

Jenny's whole face is pain. Her shirt is wet. Her body limp. I sit on the glass-top coffee table facing her. She can't look at me. "The Way It Is" starts playing again. I know it's been on repeat all weekend while I've been talking TV deals and screwing my dick to a Hollywood nub.

> 'Cause that's that.
> That's just where it's at.
> Like it or not—it's what is what and there's no turning back.

Both of us are crying now.

> Soakin' up the rain—to wash away the pain
> Can somebody explain—why it's driving me insane?

From my shoes, Jenny's eyes move slowly, slowly upward.
Jenny's eyes meet mine.
"I do love you," I say.
Impossibly, Jenny bursts into even more tears. Echoing, so do I.
"Do you love her?"
"No."
"But you fuck her."
"Yes."
"How many others?"
"It doesn't matter. It doesn't change how I feel about you."
"It changes how I feel about you! About us! About myself!"
I love this woman to death. I would do anything to ease her pain, her feeling of betrayal.
Except betray myself.
But who am I if I make a spirit so beautiful suffer so desperately?

Dammit! I hate this feeling. This is hell.
Sex is different than love. My rendezvous were "masturbation plus."
The woman I love does not share this view.
Was I getting it out of my system?
Was I being a selfish bastard?

In Berlin, the dwarf said, "Only the broken heart is truly open."
What are these two hearts opening to?
What comes next?
I see myself reflected in her eyes.
Ugly.
And cruel.

Eek! Spooky ketchup face!

Devil's Night

wind and scary sound effects. Four follow spots shaft me, swirl through the girls. The crowd goes insane. No one expected I'd enter through the rear. Ghouls, ghosts, goblins, skeletons, vampires, pirates, bikers, witches, Barbies, sluts, devils, and people in costume paw at me. A year and seven months ago I introduced AC/DC here; tonight, Angus introduces Mancow to this sold-out crowd of 35,000 screaming hellion fans. *Mancow's Hell-o-ween Spectacular* begins.

I hear the roar of the greasepaint.

I suck the smell of the crowd.

The Impotent Sea Snakes, the ultimate hell-night band, play "Sympathy for the Devil."

The audience chants: Man-Cow! Man-Cow!

We work our way 100 yards across the back of the house that Michael Jordan built, the United Center, and down 200 yards to the stage while the Impotent Sea Snakes' naked Cadaver Woman charms the one-eyed man from the pants of the guy on stilts. Didn't expect that. My mom's sitting in row eight?

As I walk through the gate at the side of the stage, Jimmy the Fixer and Bob Zmuda (Andy Kaufman's writer and sidekick) high-five me. The dwarf slaps my knee.

I walk onstage.

I claim it.

The audience goes nuts.

I kiss Morticia's naked breast.

The crowd goes insane.

I look out at the crowd. Tonight, I'm P. T. Barnum.

I scream, "This is hell night! Where all the rules are off! Where we get down and party while we still can! Police State Amerika may never let a night like this take place again, but we're gonna do it tonight!"

A maniac priest runs onstage. "You're all going to hell! You're all going to hell!"

"Listen, Suit! Your idea of heaven IS hell to me! Tonight, we ALL take a giant step away from your mind-control tricks! Tonight, we treat ourselves to a little unbridled fun!" I look to the audience. "Are you with me? Trick? Or . . ."

Thirty-five thousand people shout for treats.

This is going to be fun.

"You're all going to hell!"

"I'm ready for hell tonight! And I'm not going alone! I'm taking all of you with me!" Huge cheers.

As my *Mancow's Morning Madhouse* crew comes onstage, the audience chant begins. "Turd! Turd! Turd!" Well, give the people what they want! Black thong lost in fat, the jumbo, naked, Day-Glo orange-greasepainted Great Turd Pumpkin enters.

"Where's da girls from Crazy Horse?!" Turd chortles and jiggles. He drools like every man in the audience, hoping he'll be chosen for the World's Largest Lap Dance. While the Crazy Horse girls come onstage and my crew collects lucky men, I grab Bob Zmuda's telephonino and scam Lou Mallnati's Pizza until all the lucky lap-dance listeners come onstage. When I order 35,000 pizzas delivered to the United Center, Lou finally hangs up.

Evening gowns are coming off and falling to the floor.

"Why do women worry about wearing matching underwear, dwarf? I don't care if they match. When they're in her hand and coming off, white cotton panties can be the sexiest thing in the world." The dwarf nods, drooling as a naked girl pushes her panties in his face. Sitting on lucky listeners' laps, *all* the girls are out of their bras, and most of them are out of their panties.

The crowd is creaming, "Take your *Mancow Halloween Spectacular* ticket stubs to the Crazy Horse tonight and get in free! Isn't that better than pizza?"

Trick? Or treat?

Seven beefy men carry the thirty-five-foot Gargantua onstage. This snake is huge! Ears through his red straw hat, Danny, the world's smallest donkey, resists so hard it takes three men to pull him onstage.

"We live on a death *machine*! I eat you until you eat me until something bigger eats us both! Animal Control people said they'd shut this show down if my snake eats this donkey. Let's do it!" Beefy men pull Danny and Gargantua together. Men root for the snake. Women root for the ass. The women lose. It's a bloodbath! Snake eats Donkey! Bones crunch loudly. Four rows get splattered with donkey hair and blood.

(At least that's what *Mancow's Morning Madhouse* listeners will think tomorrow when we talk about this show. Fiction can be stranger than fact. I could never kill an animal. This time my giant snake didn't get a little ass.)

T2 comes out blowing smoke rings through his eye hole. He puts a flashlight in his mouth to become the official *Mancow Hell-o-ween Spectacular* jack-o'-lantern.

I introduce an act I've wanted to see since peeing two streams of Farts in Berlin.

"I followed blue flames to England to find this man. The godfather of flatulence, the John Phillip Sousa of butt shunder, the wizard of wind, the master of metabolic mellifluousness, the emperor of anal emissions—Mr. Methane!"

Mr. Methane's chartreuse crotchless super-hero tights are specially designed to let him blow songs out his ass! As this asshole plays three songs, I throw toilet paper like party streamers for anyone who wants to sing along. While Mr. Methane pumps out the song, we surprise Phone Girl with a birthday cake. With one mighty gust, Mr. Methane blows out the candles—with his ass.

Trick? Or treat?

A huge dungeon wall rolls onstage for another hell-night band, GWAR. A seven-foot foam rubber dragon stomps on rhythm guitar. A guy in ten-inch platform knee-high boots stomps out wearing a huge foam rubber clown mask. A twenty-inch leather dick hangs between his hairy naked thighs. He plays lead guitar. Two more mutants stomp on other instruments. When GWAR's music takes off, I know what it feels like to stand inside a 747 engine. A six-foot toilet dances onstage. With its giant toilet-seat teeth it tries to bite off Twenty-Inch Dick while GWAR rocks out "AIDS What a Bummer." A fat old Elvis dances onstage. The tip of a fast riffin' guitar slices him down the belly. Six miles of the King's intestines spill across the stage. Red blood pumps forty rows of audience.

Mom already moved to higher ground.

A GWAR mutant dances a Princess Di doll around stage. Another monster beheads her. Blue blood pumps on the audience. That's very funny.

I hit trouble when Di died. A dwarf fax from Italy reported what his ex-Commie friends were saying. I read it on the air. "Here's a woman from one of the richest families in England who married into *the* richest family in Europe becoming daughter-in-law to the richest woman in the world! Where did all that money come from? Off the working man's back! Di became a propaganda stunt for a royal family who, unlike everyone else in Great Britain, pays no taxes on their lands. By their very existence royal families preserve the illusion that some people are better than others. Why should anyone but that family feel sorry that she's dead?"

"What about her two children?" callers demanded.

"What about the thousands of American children whose Revolutionary soldier dads died trying to free us from that whole royalty thing?" I shot back. "Her brother's an Earl in the House of Lords. Who needs Lords in their lives except the one Lord that is God that is Love? But we are also still talking about a private citizen here, who may be dead for not wearing a seatbelt and getting in a car with a driver people claim was drunk."

"She was running from paparazzi!"

"And for this people clamor to slam a lid on free press!"

Twenty-Inch Dick starts fucking Di in the neck. Whoa! That's waaay over the line even for me.

Intermission.

The dwarf slaps a bottle of water in my hand and peels off my blue-blood and sweat-drenched outfit that no laundry in the world will ever get clean again.

"Most outrageous fucking thing I've ever seen, Mancow!" It's Billy Corgan and Smashing Pumpkins. "You *are* P. T. Barnum!"

"Greatest showman in America!"

"Billy! Introduce the mystery band?"

"Well, I . . ."

"Please."

"He came to enjoy the show, not get onstage. Let him be anonymous tonight if he wants, Cow. You'll want the same someday."

"I like this dwarf!" Billy Corgan says.

"We're fourteen minutes over," Zmuda yells. "That puts us into Golden." Fuck! "We can't run over!"

"Because it's you, Mancow, we might get ten minutes before the unions start clocking. They won't go fifteen."

Jesus! "Ten would be a Godsend, Jimmy." Can Mr. Fix-It do that? "Okay! Cut Bobbing for Breast Implants and run the *Morning Madhouse-Reservoir Dogs* video as people come back with beers."

"The casket's ready," says Bob Zmuda. "Tom's backstage. He's really nervous, but I think he'll be okay. The coroner's here."

"Places!" someone calls waaaaay too soon.

I head for the stage. Billy Corgan passes me and intros the band.

"Why are they getting booed?"

"The way you hyped the mystery band, Mancow, they expected Kiss or Smashing Pumpkins," Freak says. "Not these guys. Not Ratt."

(Okay! Tomorrow my radio audience learns that the mystery band was Metallica! Barnum's painted finger rests on painted lips . . . "Shhh!")

Trick? Or treat?

I send a giant rat to dance onstage. Ratt hates it. Audience loves it. They'll love it even more when the rat takes off his head. Never happens. The rat dances close to the edge of the stage. A rat bastard guitarist gives the one-hip. Turd falls between audience members. Whack! His head hits a chair. Fuck! Turd's up! He's standing! Security hustles him sidestage. Jesus! Something in that rat head cut him bad. He's bleeding a ton.

"Who are you?"

"I'm Turd."

Thank God! "How many fingers?"

"One. And fuck you too, Mancow. I'm okay."

Turd gets stretchered backstage.

I blow off the mystery band midsong.

There's eight minutes saved.

Cowboy Ray! The first time this man called the *Madhouse* I listened dumbfounded for twenty-five minutes. Forty years old and sex-obsessed, his thirteen-year-old brain can only think about getting laid. He needs to get laid bad. I pleaded with my listeners, "Find someone for Cowboy Ray!" Tonight, Cowboy Ray meets Crazy Mary, whose mind stopped at twelve, so she seems a whole lot more mature than Cowboy Ray. Their Mancow Date with Destiny comes tomorrow night. Ray hopes she'll go all the way. Mary thinks she might. If Cowboy Ray is nice. And pays attention.

"Time for the costume contest! Vixxxen! Come on out here!"

"Can I go out with Vixxxen?"

"That's not very nice to ask in front of Crazy Mary, Cowboy Ray. Vixxxen, come on over. Cowboy Ray wants to drool." I turn to the audience. "Most places the prizes aren't worth shit are they? Not here! Tonight, one of these lucky costume contestants wins a free ride in Vixxxen, the anal populist porno star."

The *Hellraiser* pinhead gets good Applause-o-Meter response. The guy with a bloody hatchet in his head might get head from Vixxxen. Limp reaction to the walking condom. The walking tree might do better if he didn't seem so wooden. Sucky response for Vampire lady. Then, the Applause-o-Meter breaks its scale for what everybody in the house wants to wrap their lips around (and Vixxxen will suck on later): the Nine-Foot Walking Bong with the glowing bowl.

• • •

"Most of you have heard Tom, or heard about him, these last two months on *Mancow's Morning Madhouse.* Immigrants from Cuba, Nicaragua, El Salvador, Chile, Iran, China, and other left- or right-wing fascist states have called to tell their stories of husbands, fathers, and sons vanishing, never to be heard from again. Recent news reports claim that the CIA helped form and train at least some of the goon squads taking these people away. Tom's brother 'disappeared' in Guatemala. Anyone out there tonight who helped us track Tom's brother's coffin and bring it to Chicago for reburial, anyone who reported the rumor that the body in this casket might not be Tom's brother, thank you. Now we get the answer. Are you ready, Tom?"

"No, Mancow. No one could be ready for this. This is hard. But I really do want to know."

As we roll the news clip of the exhumation from a Chicago cemetery, the walnut casket rolls centerstage.

Wearing a white coat, mask, and surgical gloves, it takes the coroner's assistant some time to open the casket.

What rests inside is grotesque. The body looks inhuman, like my dad did at the end. Decaying face slashed, hands tied, legs broken, I don't need the coroner to tell me this decaying corpse of a tortured ten-year-old Guatemalan Indian boy is not Tom's brother.

I have to leave the stage. I vomit. I cry.

In my mind, coffins, death, bodies, and Halloween all went together. But . . . what have I done? This was wrong. I regret it.

• • •

But the show must go on!

Freak runs a *Jerry Springer Show* clip that no one's ever seen because it's not Jerry's guests who beat each other up this time—it's Jerry Springer losing it and beating the crap out of me! "Take care of yourself—and each other."

A trick? Or treat?

More film clips. Restlessness in the audience. We're going down in flames.

Tony Clifton's intro tape rolls. Finally! Merv Griffin, Dick Cavett, Johnny Carson, Frank Sinatra—everybody—sing Tony Clifton's praises while I blow lunch. Still fat and jowly, Tony Clifton sings like a dumptruck pouring nails across Mrs. Guttman's chalkboard. By Tony's second song the audience is throwing things. Maybe the show's okay after all. Tony snarls. Baits them. Dares them. Tony wants to take on all 35,000 hellion fans. The audience doesn't realize that Tony Clifton's a fake, a character Andy Kaufman created and played. When Bob Zmuda did gigs as Clifton, people thought it was Andy from *Taxi*. It wasn't.

Trick? Or treat?

Next onstage, Anthrax kills.

Direct from the Tom Cruise movie *Cocktail,* Dr. Dirty plays amazingly XXX songs while Anthrax, GWAR, the Impotent Sea Snakes, Mr. Methane, Vixxxen, and the rest all come onstage. The balls of the Impotent Sea Snakes guys are hanging out. All the girls are naked. Sex of every description is happening in front of 35,000 enthusiastic fans—and my mom—as I reach the stage.

Screaming Tony Clifton fights his way onstage before me to ear-splitting booing. As he hits centerstage, I throw my hands at Tony's head and rip at his face until pieces come off in my hands. I must expose who this guy really is! ME! The audience gasps.

"Good night everybody!"

Life is always a trick.
Or treat.

* * *

"Did you enjoy the show, Mom?"

" 'Enjoy' isn't the first word that springs to mind. Your fans certainly loved it. And I love you. I thought you were great."

"Really?"

"Really. Amazing! I feel like I just attended a stag party in hell."

"I understand, Mom."

"Great fucking show, Mancow!" a Missouri buddy yells. I'm surprised my mom doesn't whack him with a wooden spoon for swearing.

"Really great show, buddy," Green Bay quarterback Lynn Dickey says, shaking my hand and pulling me in for a hug. Twenty-five other guys and my brothers arrive at the party.

"I have a present for you. . . . Isn't that funny! I don't know whether to call you Erich or Mancow or son. Anyway, I've given the same thing to each of your brothers, so no arguments."

Inside the envelope is an airline ticket to New Orleans.

"You know your father wanted to take you when you turned twenty-one."

He couldn't. My twenty-first year of June twenty-firsts, Dad told me he was strapped. I was in the real world. I understood. All those years of planning faded in the face of the cute bulldog puppy he gave me. Then, Dad died. And Maxine died. Something started telling me I had to go to New Orleans. I couldn't. Not without my dad.

"Thanks to the birthday present you and Johnny and Mark gave me, I'm not paying a mortgage every month anymore am I, Elvis? Your dad would have been happy here tonight. Really happy. Not about the content—he would have preferred Big Band music over your stuff—but you made people smile."

I'm about to cry when I hear a loon. Can't be. But it is. Baby B the midget dances naked on the coffee table, his face buried in porno tits as Vixxxen does bird calls.

"Jesus is coming back and he is pissed at New Orleans!" my dad used to joke. New Orleans was one of his favorite spots. Combining what my dad told me with stories from others who have been there, New Orleans may be as close to the Amsterdam spirit as America gets.

· · ·

Two weeks later, I fly to L.A. for meetings with people I've been told can change my life. I love the 20th Century Fox lot. Here all the world *is* a stage. And everybody knows it. Lunching in the Fox dining room, I see one of the most powerful media magnates on earth, Rupert Murdoch. He runs Fox. He's looking through a *Star Wars Phantom Menace* script when I walk up.

"Mr. Murdoch, you don't know me, but I just want to say thank you for the Fox Network. Thanks for the reality in television."

"Manco'. Si'down. Join us for a spot a'lunch."

I blow off the HBO producer who brung me, and si'down. Everyone freaks! Who do I think I am?

Rupert loved me.

• • •

New Orleans is spiritual. But it's muggy. All the corpses are buried above ground because the city's built on a swamp. I wonder if I've just passed a toilet until I realize the smell's everywhere. This is the land of Anne Rice vampire novels, a dangerous city, where cops fear tourists will turn down a dead-end street and end up dead. This is not Amsterdam. Lots of people hate New Orleans. I don't. I could never live here though. I'd get really, really, really fat. Breakfast at Brennens, gumbo at Felix's, beignets (donuts) at Café Du Monde—the food is to die for. And the pralines!

Mark couldn't come. It's okay. Johnny came here lots of times with our dad. We stay in the French Quarter. We drink in every bar. Tourist gimmick that it is, I even drink a Pat O'Brien's Hurricane. I'm overserved and love it. Beads-for-boobs is a New Orleans rule. I wear really nice strings of ceramic and glass beads around my neck. All the women, from young pert Memphis college girls to 'gator-loving grannies with knee-hanging nipples, flash me boobs to get my beads. Johnny's hepped me up. The nice beads stay around my neck while I slip flashers cheap black plastic beads from my pockets. Gimme a break! It's not like they're selling me Manhattan. We see some nice sets. Sometimes women don't want to be judged by their minds at all.

After chicory coffee we pay six bucks to stumble over mouse-sized cock-a-roaches into Preservation Hall. It's small. A dive. But inside

Preservation Hall I feel the power. The place is packed with people hungry for Dixieland jazz. Johnny heads for the stage. The crowd parts like he's Charlton Heston and they're the red Jell-O sea. We're right up front on a rickety bench when the Preservation Hall jazz band kicks into "Basin Street."

That's when Dad joins us. His spirit is there. I can't see him, but every cell of my body, every fiber of my soul, knows he's here. I feel him. Powerful. Familiar. So real. I reach for Johnny as he grabs me. We hug each other.

"He's here."

"I know. I feel him too."

We hold each other and cry.

Thoughts race through my head, but they're not my thoughts, they're my dad's. "Glad you came. Glad you're together. It means a lot. My dad came here before me, and your kids and grandkids may come here too." My dad's voice is present in my head. Clear. Happy. Johnny lets go as I do. I'm glad we're up front. I'm glad the music's loud. I'm crying harder than I have ever cried in my life.

We all die. But we are *all* part of a bigger network. One we almost never tune in to. One we can never understand. I feel my dad embrace me. I feel his spirit pulsing through me. My tears fall like a horde of angels passing messages between us. I feel alive. At peace.

When we leave Preservation Hall, Johnny and I walk in silence through New Orleans' French Quarter streets. My big blue shirt dries white from the salt of my tears.

• • •

The next day Johnny and I try to talk. Try to put otherworldly love into earthbound phrases. We find no words.

We stumble through New Orleans trying to scratch Johnny's itch to find the town's best gumbo. Soon my head turns to follow a beautiful Creole woman as she passes. Can't take my eyes off her. My body turns to follow her as Johnny keeps walking.

She turns. Looking five miles through the windows of my soul, she touches something I have never felt before.

"Johnny, you're eating alone," I say, not turning. If I let this woman out of my sight she'll disappear. Our eye lock never breaks.

When I reach her she smiles. Starts walking. I walk beside.

She slips her arm through mine.

Over a wrought-iron railing three stories up on a French Quarter porch in New Orleans, I learn the meaning of "the Big Easy."

Mom and Dad—
impossibly young and
in love.

Bringin' It All Back
Home

"Wake up, America! Mancow's Morning *Madhouse* is coming at you live from the freest city in the world! Welcome to Amsterdam!"

Massive applause and cheering from the crew and the live crowd around us.

"We're in Amsterdam, where women in lingerie beckon you into their boudoirs. We're in Amsterdam, where getting stoned is legal! We're in

Amsterdam, where you can buy fresh mushrooms. We're in Amsterdam, where everybody smiles! We're in Amsterdam, where Police State Amerika isn't breathing down our necks to keep us away from freedom! We're in Amsterdam, where a human being can feel like a human being! Today we're where everybody is happy! Today, we're in Amsterdam!!"

Massive applause and cheering.

"Yesterday, we brought our luggage to the show because as soon as *Mancow's Morning Madhouse* ended we went straight to O'Hare for our KLM flight to freedom! Most of you prob'ly had some sleep since yesterday. I haven't shut my eyes since I talked to you last. Doesn't matter. I feel great! I feel like we've come from the BAD *Enterprise* to the GOOD *Enterprise* in a topsy-turvy *Star Trek* world, and for the next two days we will do everything we can to bring a taste of Amsterdam freedom to you live through the radio! Most of you have prob'ly changed your clothes since you heard us yesterday, but I haven't. We landed at Amsterdam Schiphol Airport, caught the train into town, checked into the Renaissance Hotel, and came straight here to Café Dante to broadcast back to you in America. Freak?"

"Same clothes I got up in yesterday, Mancow."

"Luv Cheez?"

"Same clothes, Mancow."

"Bob Fukuda, our engineer?"

"Same clothes, Mancow."

"Turd, I know from the smell that those are the same clothes you had on yesterday."

"And the day before."

"I hope you brought something to change into, Turd, or we're going to have to throw you in a canal!"

Cheers and whistles from the live audience around us.

"Irma, did you change?"

"Of course, Mancow."

"Phone Girl?"

"Yep."

"How do they do that? In the short time we've been here, Turd, what have you seen that you like best?"

"It was incredible, Mancow! Right there on the street as we were walking here to work, behind this big picture window, this woman was motioning at me to come inside! I liked that!"

"Why was she there, Turd?"

"I don't know, but I wanted to go in! She liked me."

"I thought she was a little heavy, Turd."

"Just the way I like 'em, Mancow!" Turd chortles until the room shakes.

"Turd, that woman welcomes every man like that," I tell him.

"She does? Wow! She must like to . . . you know."

"Did you see a red light anywhere, Turd?"

"I was just looking at the woman!"

"I . . . uh . . . I saw a red light, Mancow!"

"DJ Luv Cheez, do you know what the red light means?"

"She was a hooker?" Turd deadpans.

"Yes, she was. And folks, we weren't even in the Red Light District. We walked along a normal Amsterdam street on our way here to Café—"

"I like the girls on bicycles."

"DJ Luv Cheez is right, but you have to be careful here, folks. Bikes have their own lane where they have the right-of-way. Hear a bike bell and don't skedaddle, you'll be roadkill for a steel-thighed Nordic beauty. Freak, you're jumping up and down."

"I want to go to a coffee shop."

"We're going later, Freak."

"Did you see the police car?" Irma asks. "Did you see what was written on the side?"

"It said Polite!" Turd answers.

"Turd, the letters were P-O-L-I-T-I-E."

"Like I said! Polite!"

"And do you know why?" I ask. "Because we're in Amsterdam! Where the police *are* polite. Because we're in Amsterdam, where the police

don't have to wonder if I'm smoking marijuana because smoking marijuana is legal. Where the police don't have to worry about stopping prostitution because prostitution is legal. Where the police don't have to
worry about smack addicts stealing or killing because addicts here get
heroine prescriptions for fifteen bucks a fix instead of $1,500. Why is
all of this true? Because *Mancow's Morning Madhouse* is broadcasting
to you today live from Amsterdam!"

I move to an older dude in the cheering crowd.

"Sir, you look happy."

"I *am* happy. Welcome to Amsterdam, Mancow."

"Thanks, man. You got here last night, right?"

"I did."

"Did you go to the Red Light District?"

"Oh yeah!"

"Tell us about it. What's it like?"

"Well, it's streets and streets full of women in lingerie standing in
picture windows."

"Where all the view is on your side. How much do they cost?"

"Fifty guilders."

"Fifty fairy-tale guilders. How much is that in real American money?"

"$22.75."

"Less than the last time I was here! Okay! Did you pop for fifty
guilders last night?"

"Several times, Mancow. And they take more time. It's the off-
season."

"Okay! You've picked your girl. Now what?"

"When you go to the door, she opens it. You go inside. You give her
fifty guilders. You undress. She undresses. She gets you . . ."

"Hard."

"Usually that's already happened. She gets you ready."

"How?"

"By rolling on a condom."

"I've had them do that with their mouth. Did you like it?"

"It was wonderful. Amsterdam is a wonderful place."

"Whatever time it is, wherever you are on the Free Speech Radio Network, 5:40, 6:40, 7:40, it's twenty minutes to one in the afternoon here in Amsterdam and a lot of this crowd is drinking. Everyone listening can be here with us today. Live! Call us up from anywhere in America, 1-888-2MANCOW! Let's hear it for Amsterdam!"

Back in Chicago Prison Bitch pushes in "Rockin' in the Free World." My headphones come off for the first time.

"How do we sound?"

"Perfect on every station."

I thank the president of Amstel for bringing all of us here.

"You go on like this three hours every day?"

"Four and a half. Could I interview you on the air?"

"Yah. Fine."

"I want to ask you about Amstel and Heineken being the same company."

"Ask whatever you like. It's a free country."

"Man! Yes it is."

"Places!" Phone Girl cries.

"Can I interview you twice? Once as yourself, and then as a guy who responds to everything I ask in Dutch?"

"They'll know it's the same voice."

God! I love Amsterdam!

I put on my headphones. I pick up my mike. "I love the sight of a female ass on a bicycle seat! Don't you? But there's not any seat on this bicycle, and unless you've been to the Freedom City of this worldwide carnival we live in, you have never seen anything like this folks. I'm standing with the owner of the Amsterdam Sex Museum, and—what is going on there, exactly?"

"Every time the pedals turn, the woman's v . . ."

"You can say 'vagina.' "

"The woman's vagina descends onto a dildo, which rises up to meet her through the tube, which would normally hold a seat."

"She's wooden, but she looks like she's enjoying it, folks. What period does this piece of—art—date from?"

"It depicts a very famous Dutch woman who lived in Amsterdam in 1880s."

"And it's full-sized, folks. We're here just off the sidewalk of the Dam looking at some pretty amazing stuff, actually . . . that anyone can see for free just dropping by the entrance to the Amsterdam Sex Museum. How much does it cost to push inside?"

"Six guilders."

"Buck and half. Let's go. Give me a tour."

As the owner sits across the table from me at Café Dante, I point at pictures in his Sex Museum brochure.

"What's this?"

"Here we have pornography from pyramid times in Egypt."

"Wow! Pretty graphic. Is fellatio as old as sex?"

"They certainly had it in Egypt."

"Wow! Yes they did! Is sex changing?"

"A thousand years ago in India everything was much freer."

"Freer than in Amsterdam today?!!"

"Much freer."

"Whoa . . . that's uh. . . . What did they call it there? Nirvana?"

• • •

Down the street Irma interviews the people at Chocolata, makers of space cakes and passion drops and marijuana elixirs hiding in a tasty chocolate shell.

I finally have time to pee.

• • •

"I am inside a huge stainless-steel vat. How's the echo?"

"You're coming through fine, Mancow."

"This is full of Amstel sometimes?"

"155,000 gallons."

"Almost enough for Turd. I see all this advertising everywhere—

Amstel against Heineken, Heineken vs. Amstel—but they're the same company. Isn't that cheating?"

We talk together on air as we tour the brewery.

"This is our master brewer, Mancow. I must leave you with him. I have another engagement."

"Thank you, Mr. President. Hello, sir, my name is Mancow Muller."

Dutch.

"How long have you been the master brewer here at Amstel?"

Dutch.

"Is it true that you met your wife in the Red Light District?"

Dutch. Happy Dutch. Sweet. Full of life.

This guy's president of a huge company?

"Okay! I am back at Café Dante in Amsterdam—with a beautiful woman. Isn't she pretty? This is Heidi. But not the Heidi I met my first trip to Amsterdam. We're a big story over here, folks, and *this* Heidi is interviewing me for Holland's biggest newspaper. What's your first question?"

"What were you like as a child?"

"I was the kind of child who . . . well . . . I should have grown up in Amsterdam. Did you grow up here?"

"Yes. It was very happy for me."

"Why?"

"Well, I didn't know until I went to other places, but in Amsterdam there are fewer rules."

"I swear! I have never spoken to this woman before in my life."

"I would not like to grow up with people always telling me no. Everything you hide, children want. I like that nothing is hidden from children here."

"Heidi, we think alike. Human beings are meant to explore. But the Borg are winning. Have heaven now! Buy, buy, buy! Don't tickle your kid. Don't talk to your child. Buy them a talking Elmo vibrator doll. Teach them to love a machine! In *Terminator 2* John sees boys pointing sticks at one another like guns. 'We haven't got a chance, do we?' John asks. 'No,' the Terminator replies. But in Amsterdam the windows of the soul sparkle, they twinkle like there's a happy god in there carving his initials with Independence Day sparklers."

I find the president of Amstel to thank him again. He's outside on his portable phone hustling up technicians and equipment to take tomorrow's show worldwide, with cameras, on the Web. Yes!

"Someone just handed me a beautiful joint that I can't smoke right now, because you wouldn't want to hear this show if I did, but I can sure tell all you listeners about it. If only in America. How much did this beautiful cone-shaped bomber cost you, sir?"

"Six guilders."

"Another buck and a half."

"$2.77, Mancow," the dwarf corrects.

"I've been coming to Amsterdam for two years now. When I first came, my dad had just died of cancer. He ranted against marijuana every day of my life, and I knew he'd disapprove of everything I was seeing and doing here. But I'm not so sure anymore. Last month, in New Orleans, I learned that my dad asked my brothers to buy him some marijuana because no pills he took could cut his cancer pain and he didn't want to go morphine-tripping yet. For two weeks before I got to Kansas City my dad smoked marijuana—and got relief. My brothers risked their jobs, their careers, risked going to jail to buy our dad marijuana. But in Amsterdam, they have menus for it! I'm looking at two of those menus now—one for marijuana, one for hashish. How far did you have to go to get these?"

"Around the corner."

"White Widow Bio: outside grown, a nice high, eight guilders a gram. K2 Hydro: higher than the mountain, fifteen guilders. Snow White: smoke it and see the seven dwarfs, twelve-and-a-half fairy-tale guilders a gram. How much is—"

"Under six bucks, Mancow."

"I know my brothers paid a lot more than that for the pot they bought for our dad. No wonder giant drug corporations don't want this stuff around! It grows more places than cock-a-roaches—*and,* for it to really be any fun, you have to smoke it with a friend. Over and over again, scientific studies prove that *the* most effective medicine for overcoming depression, drug addiction, and a host of other diseases is having friends! Wake up, America!"

• • •

Fox News in Chicago had its highest ever ratings on Hell-o-ween night when it showed the Mancow interview, so Fox hired a stringer crew to capture Mancow in Amsterdam. Dutchman Rick arrives to film the last forty minutes of the show. The little red eye on Rick's camera clicks on. Rick pans a swirling circle up and down through the cheering crowd. Never seen a camera used like that—completely un-American. And free.

Thirty-nine minutes later, I say, "Amsterdam *is* the feeling of freedom. I will live here someday. I love the light in the eyes. I love the joy on the faces. I love that adults still play here. This trip, more than anything, I love that all of you could come here with us live in the freest city in the world . . ."

"Amsterdam!" everyone shouts as the Free Speech Radio Network shuts down for the day, and Rick's red eye blinks off.

• • •

Out in the Amsterdam night, in Mancow logo jackets, my crew looks like a tour group from Adventures on the Other Side.

I walk backward to see their faces as they feel that Amsterdam feeling for the first time.

I watch the fears come off.

I remember.

You can't feel what Amsterdam's like until you get there. Most Americans walk around inside an envelope of fear. To be in Amsterdam is to find yourself in a place where no punishing parent or big brother

Bringin' It All Back Home

waits to scold you. In Amsterdam I never hear demon preachers in my head making my soul afraid of burning in the lake of fire if I get it wrong. The fear melts. The paranoia dissipates, gets wrung out of your body like water from a washcloth. It's a revelation. Amsterdam is the red pill that awakens you from the matrix that is America today.

I delight in the change happening in my crew. It's in their eyes. It's in the way they hold their bodies. I see the padlocks open and the chains fall away.

I remember.

In the Red Light District, after a block of women in their windows, Turd stops to drool.

"She's a great looker, Turd. You got the money?"

"The missus gimme the money I brought. If I . . . uh . . . that'd be like cheatin' on the missus."

"She's twenty-five dollars, Turd." I open her door. I float fifty fairy-tale guilders down the canyon between her breasts. "She's waiting."

After thirty-seven seconds of Turd's tortured indecision, the dwarf squeaks through the open door and slams it shut.

"People! You have to be alert for the show tomorrow. All of you! No excuses! We'll meet in the lobby at 10 A.M." I leave my friends to explore the Red Light on their own a little while.

Do It Again!

"We're here in the City of Freedom! Again! And today, we're worldwide at www.mancow.com. This broadcast is history-making. *A first.* It's not like being on the moon . . . except . . . well . . . I *do* feel that far away from the U.S. police state here. One small step for Mancow, one giant leap for mankind. Join us here! Make a free call to Amsterdam from anywhere in America at 1–888–2MANCOW. Internet cameras are running and we've got some honeys here you want to see live in Amsterdam. Phone Girl, will you flash your tits for the world?"

"I don't think so."

"Yesterday I went to the Anne Frank house. I stood in that little room thinking how much freedom there is here in Amsterdam. There was a light fog outside. The little church bell chimed. I could see Anne Frank making love to her only lover. Then, outside, I heard the stomp of Nazi boots. They were here sixty years ago. But they're not here now. We have to spread the spirit of freedom I feel here in Amsterdam today! We can't let oppression win!"

Pete was a *Madhouse* listener until he came to Amsterdam to study art. Right! He's been telling the Free Speech Radio Network what it's like for one American boy to move to Amsterdam.

"Can you see that on the Web? Hold that bomber up to the camera, Pete. Take a toke."

Pete used to call his mom every other week. Collect. I'll pay this time.

"Okay, Pete, it's ringing. What time is it in Illinois? Do you know? Are we waking your mother up? She doesn't know he smokes the evil weed, folks. Pete prob'ly hasn't told her about the hookers he's had either. Doris? Is this Doris? I'm Mancow and—Mancow. I do a radio show in Chicago, but today *Mancow's Morning Madhouse* is broadcasting from Amsterdam and we ran into your boy, Pete, who said he hadn't talked to you in two months, and I thought you should talk. Doris, do you have any idea what Pete's doing here in Amsterdam? Besides studying art. Well, I think your son may be falling into some bad habits, Doris."

The sudden stoned terror invading Pete's eyes is exquisite.

"Well, for one thing, Doris, right now, Pete's standing in front of me with a . . . what *is* that Pete?"

Pete's reaching for the phone kind of desperately.

"With an Amstel in his hand. That's a beer, Doris. What do you mean that's all right, it's barely noon! Uh-huh. Well, like lots of other things, but I think Pete should tell you about the rest himself—the nude studies, the smoking. Have you ever been to Amsterdam, Doris? I didn't think so. Let me just put Pete on."

Doris is great. She could be my mom. I like her. Why does Pete hide from her? Too bad.

Next live call.

"Folks, we got the number for this escort service from a sign hanging on a lamppost in front of our hotel. It's ringing."

"Good afternoon. How may we serve your pleasure?"

"Little lady, I was wondering if you could provide me with some companionship for tonight?"

"Would you like a man or a woman?"

"Pshe-ew! You got *men?*"

"You'd like a lady."

"Well, yeah! Of course! Do you get many requests for . . ."

"At which hotel are you staying?"

"I'm, uh, over here at the Renaissance."

"An excellent choice. Room number?"

"Listen, little lady, how much is this gonna cost me?"

"Two hundred fifty guilders for an all-inclusive hour at your hotel. You can have as many hours as you like. Three hours is seven hundred guilders."

"Uh . . . how much is that in real money?"

"Today, that would be three hundred fifty dollars."

"For three hours? Uh. My room's 646."

"The Ambassador suite! My! Welcome to Amsterdam, Mr. . . ."

"Swaggert. J. J. Swaggert. What's your name, little lady?"

"Merika."

"How much would two girls cost?"

"The prices would double."

"Can my wife watch?"

"If that's all she wishes to do."

"Uh . . . can I . . . can I have a man at the same price?"

"Of course."

"For my wife!"

"Whatever your pleasure."

"Merika, what about a dog?"

Turd starts barking.

"One with a really long tongue?"

Merika hangs up.

• • •

We pay a Red Light whore to open up for Irma. Freak holds the "appliance" during their "intercourse." I play the tape.

"How much do you make?"

"Without working hard I can earn two thousand guilders a day. That's an eight-hour day. When I really enjoy myself I can make much more."

"What do you do with the money?"

"Mostly, I use the money to travel."

"Do you have a . . . pimp?"

"I work for myself. The room is one hundred twenty-five guilders. Everything more is mine. I take the room two days a week."

"Do your parents know?"

"Yes."

"Cause any problems?"

"My mother says every person uses their body to work. She says it's forgetting the body that's dangerous. Then we become machines."

"Tell us what you do."

As the happy hooker elaborates, back at the Top of the Cock in Chicago, Sergeant Hairclub—the boss—wanders the halls like the walking wounded muttering, "He can't do this. Oh my God, she does that with her tongue?"

• • •

"Complete freedom. Think you have it? You don't!

"We're brainwashed to believe we're free, but Police State Amerika has laws against everything! Want to smoke pot in Amsterdam? Your choice. Why should Uncle Sam throw you in prison if you want to smoke some weed?

"When I first came to Amsterdam, going to the Grasshopper, the Grey Area, and Excalibur was like getting out of jail to this American boy, but to people in Amsterdam it's no big thing because people in Amsterdam are *free.*

"What government has the right to say, 'No drinking, smoking, or looking at sexy things?' Yes, some will end up drunks, die of cancer, and become porno addicts, but the choice should *still* belong to the individual. If some guy's stupid enough to ride a motorcycle without a helmet—let him die! Who wants to live in a cage?

"Humans have to decide for themselves when enough is enough. God gives each of us free choice for that reason. We can't allow governments to regulate our choices. People need to escape from what is mostly a life of hard work. But maybe we should stop escaping.

"Think about it! Maybe we should stop escaping and push down the prison!

"They've done it here in Amsterdam.

"Let's bring the freedom back!"

My second, and final, Amsterdam broadcast ends.

Time to party!

• • •

At Café Dante the president of Amstel/Heineken turns me on to a fresh cherry beer you can only get in Holland in November. My crew eats Chocolata space cakes and chocolates made with marijuana extract. We smoke the Grey Area's Bubble Gum—last year's Marijuana Cup winner.

We float from Café Dante not knowing where we're headed, and not really caring because in fact we're already there.

• • •

After we eat my first ever twenty-one course Indonesian rijsttafel meal at Sama Sebo, I waddle down Amsterdam streets with my crew.

Suddenly, the most dangerous sound in Amsterdam!

Everyone scatters, but no mounted Amsterdam fox whizzes past with breeze in her bush. Hell, we're not even on the bike path!

Ring-ring!

Luv Cheez grins like a little kid. Ring-ring!

"Cheez, you're brilliant!"

We hustle up behind a group on the sidewalk.

Ring-ring!

The group scatters, then looks around, confused to find no sidewalk-ruling bike in sight.

Ring-ring!

We do it twice to every group. Then Luv Cheez opens his fist to reveal the bike bell hanging from his thumb.

Ninety-two percent of the people smile, giggle, or laugh out loud when they see the joke. The rest are German tourists.

* * *

"Everywhere we've gone tonight we've seen that black rag doll in the window with Santa," I say to two drugstore clerks while Cheez runs tape.

"St. Nicholas and Schwartza Pete."

"Who is Schwartza Pete?"

"Schwartza Pete is only in Holland. He delivers the presents for St. Nicholas. That's why he's black. From going down the chimneys."

"Do you leave out cookies and stuff?"

"No! Children leave a carrot for St. Nicholas' horse."

"Nothing for Nick?"

"St. Nicholas' horse does the work. He needs the food."

"Do good children get good stuff and get lumps of coal if they're bad?"

"In Holland it's important to be brave. Brave children receive presents. Schwartza Pete takes cowards away to Spain."

"Wait a minute." I'm laughing. "Spain?"

"The Spanish enslaved Holland for three hundred years. Often people disappeared to Spain."

"So people had to be brave."

"Yes."

"Why does Schwartza Pete look so happy?"

"Because Dutch children are brave."

"Children here don't have to be good?"

"To be brave . . . is more important."

People are the most magnificent curiosities. I love this freak show all of us create. That Hitler Youth, college fraternity idea of belonging has never worked for me. My ego has never needed or wanted yes men. Why would anyone choose to be surrounded by mirror images? What a boring world that makes! How dull the world would be if every flower in it were a daisy! The carnival of color makes a meadow exciting.

Chocolate-and-hallucinogenic mushroom-packed philosopher stones look like little black walnuts. The two that Stoner Pete brought me are kicking in, dropping me even deeper into the Amsterdam experience.

"What would marijuana honey taste like?" I ask as I toke down a lungful of the Grey Area's Bubble Gum.

"It would come from happy bees," laughs the dwarf. "If they could find their way to the hive."

What we remember most about anyone is exactly what makes them different from everybody else. We remember their uniqueness, how they broke the mold of expectation, how they escaped standardization's cage.

"I've never seen this statue," I exclaim as we wander down Amsterdam's streets.

"That general died in his bed. All four horse hooves are on the ground," observes the dwarf. "If one horse's leg is raised the rider died of battle injuries. A man on a rearing mount died in battle."

"When I was a kid in Missouri we lived near a stable. A few miles from the stables there was a lake. I was out walking in the still, lifeless winter. The icy cold day made my skin ache. As I neared the lake I saw something sticking out of it. I walked closer. It was the neck and head of a horse in water deep enough to cover its back. The horse wasn't swimming. It was standing still. Gray-haired, with a mane moving to silver, it was an Arabian. As I went closer, I saw the light of the sun dancing in its huge, dark eyes. My approach didn't disturb him. He just stood there. When I got to the edge of the lake I could see his body clearly. He stood on three legs, left foreleg raised like statue mounts of cavalry generals who die from injuries suffered in battle. I stood looking a long time at this magnificent Arabian stallion. I wondered how he could stand so still. Slowly I realized that, unable to climb the bank, the chill of the lake had sucked his heat from him. All that gave him life had left his perfect body. The moisture from his nostrils had created an icy lump that looked like breath rising up from hell. Three hooves in the mud. One leg raised. A flawless illusion of life in motion frozen in a lake of ice as crystalline as glass."

"How fitting! The Ambassador suite." A coughed chuckle empties from the dwarf's throat as I sit in one of the very comfortable overstuffed chairs.

"If God created the *universe* and made man in his image, every human must possess boundless creativity. Why are so many people frightened of it?"

"Remember what Nelson Mandela said?"

"After all those years in prison, he comes out saying man's deepest fear isn't being inadequate but powerful beyond measure. That it's our light, not our darkness, that frightens us most. That we were born to make manifest the glory of God that's within us. Not just in some of us, in all of us."

The dwarf hurtles from his easy chair like he's springing from middle earth. Gnomish fingers leaf through the Bible from the nightstand.

"Matthew 5:14, 'Ye are the light of the world. A city that is set on a hill cannot be hid.' "

"Exactly!"

"Matthew 5:15. 'Neither do men light a candle, and put it under a bushel, but on a candlestick; and it giveth light unto all that are in the house.' "

"So many people hide who they are, build a cage around themselves, their creativity, their emotions. Why? Because they only feel safe if they don't feel. That's not safety, it's prison."

"Horse in the ice, Mancow."

"Jesus!"

"What?"

"I'm seven years old. I'm riding with my dad. His horse shies. Rears to stomp a copperhead snake. Throws my dad. Bolts away. I laugh at my dad lying on the ground pretending he can't move. Okay, that's enough. You can get up now, Dad. Dad! You're scaring me. I skuddle off Shoe-shoe. I go to my dad. His eyes are closed. Dad! Dad! His eyes open, trying to focus. So quietly the wind almost steals his words, 'Get help.' Come on, Dad! Get up. Stop playing. 'Erich, get help! Fast as you can!' I race to my pony, but Shoe-shoe shies as I grab for the reins. Dashes away. 'Run, Erich. Run, son.' I run through tall summer grass. Briars, thistles, dragon's claws rip at my skin, try to slow me down. I run. I reach the stable. I scream for help. With the last breath in my body, I pant, 'My dad!' and point. Mr. Hoffman picks me up. Races to his jeep. Throws me in. Tears away. I grip with my life. Terrifying bounces try to throw me out. What's happened to my dad? We reach him. He hasn't moved. 'Your ribs are broken, John.' I grip the back wall of the jeep with my hands. Arms straight, feet out. A ramp. Mr. Hoffman drags my dad over me. Hurtles into the jeep. Drives slow, eyes scanning the earth. Finds the smoothest route. My dad's a week in the hospital. Without me there, without someone there, he would have died. Alone. Like the Arabian in the lake. Jesus! The stallion in the lake was the horse that threw my dad."

Live music from a club somewhere drifts to my ears through a crisp Amsterdam night.

A different kind of being in the world, a new kind of life, a whole new level of exploration began with my dad's funeral.

Every boy becomes a man the day of his father's death.
Doesn't matter if you're seven or twenty-seven
you have no choice.
You're on your own.
The grieving is horrific.
The missing is an endless chasm.
But there is a kind of freedom in it.
Freedom in having to stand on your own.
Then, a day arrives when you realize you carry them in you,
giving their mortality a second act.

You can't change people.
You can only show them possibilities.
Open a door.
They walk through it if they choose.

A flicker,
a flash,
an escaping vapor,
is our life.

This is not a dress rehearsal.
Tomorrow is never promised.
Don't wait!

I look out across the expanse of freedom—for the first time—again.
I laugh silently.

A calm descends.
I feel a touch on my shoulder.
I don't have to look.
I know who's there.
I'm glad he's come to my town.
It's my dad.
He's smiling.
We are both finally free.

My dad out of his earth suit,
me still in mine,
we roller-coaster forward,
dancing down
freedom road.

Permissions